RHCSA™/RHCE® Red Hat® Linux Certification Practice Exams with Virtual Machines

(Exams EX200 & EX300)

Michael Jang

New York   Chicago   San Francisco   Lisbon   London   Madrid
Mexico City   Milan   New Delhi   San Juan   Seoul   Singapore   Sydney   Toronto

Cataloging-in-Publication Data is on file with the Library of Congress.

McGraw-Hill books are available at special quantity discounts to use as premiums and sales promotions, or for use in corporate training programs. To contact a representative, please e-mail us at bulksales@mcgraw-hill.com.

RHCSA™/RHCE® Red Hat® Linux Certification Practice Exams with Virtual Machines (Exams EX200 & EX300)

234567890 DOC/DOC 109876543

ISBN: Book p/n 978-0-07-180157-7 and DVD p/n 978-0-07-180158-4
of set 978-0-07-180160-7

MHID: Book p/n 0-07-180157-X and DVD p/n 0-07-180158-8
of set 0-07-180160-X

Sponsoring Editor Meghan Riley Manfre	**Technical Editor** Elizabeth Zinkann	**Production Supervisor** Jim Kussow
Editorial Supervisor Jody McKenzie	**Copy Editor** LeeAnn Pickrell	**Composition** Peter Hancik - Eurodesign
Project Editor LeeAnn Pickrell	**Proofreader** Paul Tyler	**Illustration** Peter Hancik - Eurodesign
Acquisitions Coordinator Stephanie Evans	**Indexer** Rebecca Plunkett	**Art Director, Cover** Jeff Weeks

For the young widows and widowers,
may they find the courage to face their fears,
to navigate their way through the pain,
and to find hope for a brighter future.

ABOUT THE CONTRIBUTORS

Author

Michael Jang (RHCE, LPIC-2, UCP, LCP, Linux+, MCP) is currently a full-time writer, specializing in operating systems and networks. His experience with computers goes back to the days of jumbled punch cards. He has written other books on Linux certification, including this book's companion Study Guide, *RHCSA™/ RHCE® Red Hat® Linux Certification Study Guide, Sixth Edition*, and *LPIC-1 in Depth, Mike Meyers' Linux+ Certification Passport*, and *Sair GNU/Linux Installation and Configuration Exam Cram*. His other Linux books include *Linux Annoyances for Geeks, Linux Patch Management*, and *Mastering Fedora Core Linux 5*. He has also written or contributed to books on other operating systems, including *Oracle Solaris 11 System Administration: The Complete Reference™*, *MCSE Guide to Microsoft Windows 98*, and *Mastering Windows XP Professional, Second Edition*.

Technical Editor

Elizabeth Zinkann is a logical Linux catalyst, a freelance technical editor, and an independent computer consultant. She was a contributing editor and review columnist for *Sys Admin Magazine* for ten years. As an editor, some of her projects have included *RHCSA™/RHCE® Red Hat® Linux Certification Study Guide, Sixth Edition, Mastering Fedora Core Linux 5, LPIC-1 in Depth, Linux Patch Management*, and *Linux All-in-One Desk Reference for Dummies, Fourth Edition*. In a former life, she also programmed communications features, including ISDN at AT&T Network Systems.

CONTENTS AT A GLANCE

CONTENTS

ACKNOWLEDGMENTS

I personally would like to thank the following people:

- My wife Donna: With hope and love, you make my life worth living. With your love and support, my life is now better than ever.
- The technical editor, Elizabeth Zinkann: You've shown incredible patience while editing so many of my books. I value your friendship highly.
- My agent, Carole Jelen: Your ability to keep me gainfully busy in the midst of multiple economic cycles is remarkable.
- All the incredibly hard-working folks at McGraw-Hill: Meghan Riley Manfre, Stephanie Evans, LeeAnn Pickrell, Paul Tyler, and Rebecca Plunkett for their help in launching a great series and being solid team players.

In This Book

This book is designed as a companion to the *RHCSA™/RHCE® Red Hat® Linux Certification Study Guide (Exams EX200 & EX300), Sixth Edition*, but both books are discrete and complete test prep guides. (Hereafter, I refer to the *RHCSA™/RHCE® Red Hat® Linux Certification Study Guide* as the *Study Guide*.) All chapters include a short summary of each relevant objective, along with supplemental fill-in-the-blank questions.

Chapter 1 includes detailed instructions on decompressing and installing the virtual machines (VMs) included on the book's DVD into Red Hat's native virtualization solution, the Kernel-based Virtual Machine (KVM). Some of the key components of this book can be found only within the compressed VMs that you can load from the DVD. Starting with the fourth lab of Chapter 1, the lab questions can be found on the first VM, in the /home/testuser/Desktop/ChapterLabs directory in text format. You can find the lab answers at the end of each chapter.

The RHCSA and the RHCE are separate exams. If you're studying for both exams, this book can help you remember the differences. For example, you'll find coverage of the RHCSA objectives on the Secure Shell (SSH) as a client in Chapter 2. In contrast, the RHCE objectives related to SSH as a server are covered in Chapter 11.

While this book is organized to serve as an in-depth review for the RHCSA and RHCE exams for both experienced Linux and Unix professionals, it is not intended as a substitute for Red Hat courses or, more importantly, real-world experience. Nevertheless, each chapter covers a major aspect of the exam, with an emphasis on the "why" as well as the "how to" of working with and supporting RHEL as a systems administrator or engineer.

---

exam

ⓦatch *As the actual RHCSA and RHCE objectives (www.redhat.com/ certification/rhcsa/objectives and www .redhat.com/certification /rhce/objectives)* *change with every release of RHEL (and even sometimes between releases), refer to the noted URL for the latest information.*

Red Hat says it's important to have real-world experience to pass their exams, and they're right! However, for the RHCSA and RHCE exams, they do focus on a specific set of Linux administrative skills, as depicted in the respective objectives. This book is intended to help you take advantage of the skills you already have—and more to the point, brush up in those areas where you may have a bit less experience.

Although a risky production practice, it is fastest to administer RHEL during the exam by logging in to the root user account. The command prompt and **PATH** assume use of that account. When logged in to the root account, you see a command line prompt similar to

```
[root@gamma root]#
```

As the length of this prompt would lead to a number of broken and wrapped code lines throughout this book, I've normally abbreviated the root account prompt as

```
#
```

Be careful. The hash mark (#) is also used as a comment character in Linux scripts and programs; for example, here is an excerpt from /etc/inittab:

```
# Default runlevel. The runlevels used are:
```

When logged in as a regular user, you see a slightly different prompt; for user testuser, it typically looks like the following:

```
[testuser@gamma testuser]$
```

In a similar fashion, I've abbreviated this as

```
$
```

There are a number of command lines and blocks of code interspersed throughout the chapters. Commands embedded within regular text, such as **ls -l**, are shown in bold. User entries, and some variables in regular text, are also shown in bold.

Sometimes, commands exceed the available length of a line. Take this example:

```
# virt-install -n other.example.org -r 768 --disk path=/var/lib/
libvirt/images/other.example.org.img -l ftp://192.168.122.1/pub/
inst -x "ks=ftp://192.168.122.1/pub/ks1.cfg"
```

Unless this command is carefully formatted, line breaks might appear in unfortunate places, such as between the two dashes in front of the --disk switch. One way to address this is with the backslash (\), which "escapes" the meaning of the carriage return that follows. (The backslash can also "escape" the meaning of a space, making it easier to work with multiple-word filenames.) So while the following command appears as if it is on four different lines, the backslashes mean that Linux reads it as one single command:

```
# virt-install -n other.example.org -r 768 --disk \
path=/var/lib/libvirt/images/other.example.org.img \
-l ftp://192.168.122.1/pub/inst \
-x "ks=ftp://192.168.122.1/pub/ks1.cfg"
```

Just be aware that the backslash doesn't work with every command.

Sometimes, the differences are subtle. Sometimes, you need to actually type in a command or a response to a question at a command line. In that case, you'll see an instruction such as type **y**. Alternatively, some menus require a key press; for instance, you may be asked to press P to access a password prompt. In that case, the letter *p* is not added to the screen when you press that letter. In addition, the A, despite its appearances, is in lowercase. In contrast, A is the uppercase version of that letter.

One area where some publishers have trouble is with the double-dash. Some publishing programs change the double-dash to an "em dash." But that can be a problem. The double-dash is common in many Linux commands. For example, the following command lists all packages currently installed on the local system:

```
# rpm --query --all
```

When I ran this command on my RHEL 6 system, it listed 1300 packages.

In contrast, the following command lists all files in all packages on the local system:

```
# rpm --query -all
```

When I ran this command on my RHEL 6 system, it listed 133,000 files, a rather different result. So pay attention to the dashes, and rest assured that the team who produced this book took care to make sure that double-dashes are shown as is!

Exam Readiness Checklist

At the end of the introduction, you will find an Exam Readiness Checklist. This checklist has been constructed to allow you to cross-reference the official exam objectives with the objectives as they are covered in this book. The checklist also allows you to gauge your level of expertise on each objective at the outset of your studies. This should allow you to check your progress and make sure you spend the time you need on more difficult or unfamiliar sections. References have been provided for the objective exactly as the vendor presents it; the chapter of this book that covers that objective, along with a page reference, is also listed.

In Every Chapter

For this series, I've created a set of chapter components that call your attention to important items, reinforce important points, and provide helpful exam-taking hints. Take a look at what you'll find in every chapter:

- Every chapter begins with the **Exam Objectives**—the skills you need to master in order to pass the section on the exam associated with the chapter topic. The Exam Objective headings identify the objectives within the chapter, so you'll always know an objective when you see it.

exam Watch

- **Exam Watch** notes call attention to information about, and potential pitfalls in, the exam.

on the Job

- **On the Job** notes describe the issues that come up most often in real-world settings. They provide a valuable perspective on certification- and product-related topics. They point out common mistakes and address questions that have arisen from on-the-job discussions and experience.

- The **Certification Summary** is a succinct review of the chapter and a restatement of salient skills regarding the exams.

Q&A

- The **Self Test** offers fill-in-the-blank questions designed to help test your practical knowledge associated with the exams. The answers to these questions, as well as explanations of the answers, can be found at the end of each chapter. By taking the Self Test after completing each chapter, you'll reinforce what you've learned from that chapter. This book does not include multiple-choice questions, as Red Hat does not include any such questions on their exams.

- The **Lab Questions** at the end of the Self Test section offer a unique and challenging question format that requires you to understand multiple chapter concepts to answer correctly. Starting with Chapter 1, Lab 4, all lab questions are available only on the first VM, available from the DVD. That is consistent with the electronic format associated with the Red Hat exams. Remember, the Red Hat exams contain *only* lab-type questions. If you can answer these questions, you have proven that you know the subject!

Additional Resources

Some readers will want to go further. Of course, the first "additional resource" that I recommend is the companion *Study Guide*.

If you want to go even further, Red Hat has excellent documentation on RHEL 6. Much of what I learned about RHEL 6 comes from the documents available at http://docs.redhat.com/docs/en-US/Red_Hat_Enterprise_Linux/. For our purposes, perhaps these are the most important of these guides:

■ **Installation Guide**   As the Red Hat exams are given on preconfigured systems, the *Installation Guide* is somewhat less important, but it includes key information on Kickstart.

■ **Deployment Guide**   The *Deployment Guide* is perhaps the most important with respect to Red Hat recommendations on how services can be configured for basic operation.

■ **Security-Enhanced Linux**   The *Security Enhanced Linux Guide* details the options that can help further secure your systems.

Some Pointers

Once you've finished reading this book, set aside some time to do a thorough review. You might want to return to the book several times and make use of all the methods it offers for reviewing the material:

■ *Retake the Self Tests.* Focus on the labs, as there are no multiple-choice (or even fill-in-the-blank) questions on the Red Hat exams. I've included fill-in-the-blank questions just to test your mastery of the practical material in each chapter.

■ *Solve the Labs again.* Lab questions provide the essence of a hands-on exam. Furthermore, if you know how to solve practical lab problems, you'll be ahead of the competition in a job search. While getting certified as an RHCSA and RHCE is great, the objective for most of you is to get a better job.

The Red Hat Exam Challenge

This introduction covers the reasons for pursuing industry-recognized certification, explains the importance of your RHCSA or RHCE certification, and prepares you for taking the actual examinations. It gives you a few pointers on how to prepare, what to expect, and what to do on exam day.

This book covers every published exam objective at the time of this writing. For the latest objectives, see www.redhat.com/training/courses/ex200/examobjective and www.redhat.com/training/courses/ex300/examobjective. Red Hat has also published a syllabus for its prep courses for these exams, described shortly. While the published exam objectives are accurate, the prep course syllabi provide additional information. Each Red Hat prep course provides an excellent grounding in systems administration, network administration, security, and more. To that end, this book also includes coverage based on the public syllabi of Red Hat courses RH124, RH134/RH135, and RH254/RH255, described later.

Nevertheless, this book is not intended to be a substitute for any Red Hat course.

Leaping Ahead of the Competition!

Red Hat's RHCSA and RHCE certification exams are hands-on exams. As such, they are respected throughout the industry as a sign of genuine practical knowledge. If you pass, you will be head and shoulders above the candidate who has passed only a "standard" multiple-choice certification exam.

Red Hat has offered its hands-on exams since 1999. They've evolved over the years. As detailed in Chapter 1, the RHCSA is a 2.5-hour exam, and the RHCE is now a 2.0-hour exam. The requirements are detailed in the Exam Readiness Checklist later in this introduction. While the passing score for these exams is not currently published, it was at one time 70 percent for the relevant Red Hat exams on RHEL 5. Published third-party reports suggest that passing score has not changed.

Why a Hands-On Exam?

Most certifications today are based on multiple-choice exams. These types of exams are relatively inexpensive to set up and easy to proctor. Unfortunately, many people without real-world skills are good at taking multiple-choice exams. In some cases, the answers to these multiple-choice exams are already available online. This results in problems on the job with "certified" engineers, who have an image as "paper tigers" and do not have any real-world skills.

In response, Red Hat wanted to develop a certification program that matters. In my opinion, they have succeeded with the RHCSA, the RHCE, and their other advanced certifications.

Linux administrators sometimes have to install Linux on a computer or virtual machine. In fact, the RHCSA includes several objectives on this subject. Depending on the configuration, they may need to install Linux from a central source through a network. Installing Linux is not enough to make it useful. Administrators need to know how to configure Linux: add users, install and configure services, create firewalls, and more.

---

e x a m

ⓦ a t c h

The RHCSA and RHCE exams are Red Hat exams. Knowledge of Unix or a Linux distribution such as Ubuntu is certainly helpful, as well as experience with services like Apache, SMB, NFS, DNS, iptables, and SSH. But it is important to know how to set up, configure, install, and debug these services under Red Hat Enterprise Linux (or rebuild distributions that use the same source code, such as Scientific Linux, CentOS, or Oracle Linux). Do not use Fedora or Ubuntu Linux to study for the Red Hat exams.

Prepare for the RHCSA and RHCE Exams

With the release of RHEL 6, Red Hat has introduced the RHCSA as a replacement for the RHCT. The topics associated with the RHCSA are now independent of the RHCE. Yes, there is some overlap. For example, SELinux is covered on both exams. But the coverage is different. The RHCSA and RHCE certifications are based on separate exams.

The RHCSA is now the entry-level Red Hat certification. While you can take the RHCE exam first, Red Hat won't award you an RHCE unless you've also passed the RHCSA exam. Some candidates take both exams on the same day. As discussed in Chapter 1, Red Hat has also publicly stated that their exams are now "presented electronically." This book includes (most) labs and sample exams in electronic format on the first VM, available in compressed format, on the DVD that accompanies this book.

Work with Red Hat Enterprise Linux. Install it on a computer that you don't need for any other purpose. Configure the services described in this book. Find different ways to secure each of these services. Test the results from systems both inside and outside a network.

As you read this book, you have the opportunity to practice configuring RHEL in a number of different ways. With three different VMs available on the DVD, you get to test these options with different network services. Then you can work with the different network services. Testing your work becomes especially important when verifying the security features that are required on an exam, or in a production network.

Red Hat Certification Program

Red Hat offers several courses that can help you prepare for the RHCSA and RHCE. Most of these courses are four or five days long. In some cases, the courses are offered electronically.

These aren't the only Red Hat courses available; there are a number of others related to the Red Hat Certified Architect (RHCA), Red Hat Certified Virtualization Administrator (RHCVA), Red Hat Certified Datacenter Specialist (RHCDS), and Red Hat Certified Security Specialist (RHCSS) certifications. But study this first; the RHCSA and RHCE are prerequisites for all Red Hat certifications but the RHCVA.

Should You Take an RHCSA/RHCE Course?

This book is *not* intended as a substitute for any particular Red Hat RHCSA or RHCE prep course. However, the topics in this book are based in part on the topics listed in the course outlines provided at www.redhat.com/courses. By design, these topics may help Linux users qualify as real-world administrators and can also be used as such. Just remember, Red Hat can change these topics and course outlines at any time, so monitor www.redhat.com for the latest updates. Table 1 describes those courses associated with the RHCSA and RHCE exams.

The courses given by Red Hat are excellent. The Red Hat instructors who teach these courses are highly skilled. If you have the skills, it is the best way to prepare for the RHCSA and RHCE exams. If you feel the need for classroom instruction, read this book, and then take the appropriate course.

If you're not sure you're ready for the course or book, navigate to www .mhprofessional.com/product.php?cat=39&isbn=007180160X and take the pre-assessment test. It's different from the Red Hat pre-assessment, as it includes

| TABLE I | Red Hat RHCSA/RHCE-Related Courses |

Course	Description
RH124	System Administration I: Core system administration skills
RH134	System Administration II: Command-line skills for Linux administrators (RH135 without the RHCSA exam)
RH135	System Administration II with the RHCSA exam
RH199	RHCSA rapid-track course for experienced administrators
RH200	RH199 + RHCSA exam
EX200	Just the RHCSA exam
RH254	System Administration III: Advanced security and server skills
RH255	System Administration III with the RHCE exam
RH299	Red Hat rapid-track course for experienced administrators
RH300	RH299 + RHCSA and RHCE exams
EX300	The RHCE exam

fill-in-the-blank questions. As such, you'll have to read over the answers and judge your own readiness for the exam.

If you're new to Linux or Unix, this book may not be enough to you. For detail more suited to newer users, you may need to refer to more elementary books on Linux or Unix. Just be sure those books are focused on the command-line interface.

Signing Up for the RHCSA/RHCE Course and/or Exam

Red Hat provides convenient web-based registration systems for the courses and test. To sign up for any of the Red Hat courses or exams, navigate to www.redhat.com/training/courses, and select the desired course or exam. As shown in Table 1, exams may be taken as their own independent course. For example, the RHCSA and RHCE exams are associated with courses EX200 and EX300, respectively. Exams may also be taken as part of an online or instructor-led course. Alternatively, contact Red Hat Enrollment Central at training@redhat.com or (866) 626-2994.

Discounts may be available for candidates who have been previously certified as an RHCT or RHCE. Current discounts are shown at https://listman.redhat.com/training/specials/. Remember to present any "offer code" before paying for the desired exam.

Before signing up, read current Red Hat policies, available at www.redhat.com/training/policy/. Be aware: Red Hat has sometimes canceled exams for low attendance.

In a limited number of locations, Red Hat supports "Individual Exam Sessions" on a more flexible schedule. For more information, see www.redhat.com/training/certifications/exam-kiosk.html.

Final Preparations

The Red Hat exams are grueling. Once you have the skills, the most important thing that you can take to the exam is a clear head. If you're tired or frantic, you may miss the easy solutions that are often available. Get the sleep you need the night before the exam. Eat a good breakfast. Bring snacks that can keep your mind in top condition.

The RHCSA exam is two-and-a-half hours long. The RHCE exam is two hours long. In many cases, Red Hat makes it possible for candidates to take both exams in the same day. Although a terrific convenience for those who have to travel to Red Hat exam facilities (in over 40 cities just in North America), taking the two exams in the same day is like running two world-class marathons.

RHCSA and RHCE Exam Readiness Checklists

The following Exam Readiness Checklists list each official objective on the RHCSA and RHCE exams, and specify the corresponding chapters where the objectives are covered. The checklists in this book differ from Exam Readiness Checklists in the *Study Guide* in two respects. First, the section titles in each chapter of this book match the wording of each official exam objective as closely as possible, as opposed to the *Study Guide* where the section titles in each chapter are unique to that book alone. Second, the following checklists reflect some minor changes made to the Red Hat objectives since the *Study Guide* was released. (For example, NTP is now solely covered in the RHCE exam.)

exam watch

As the actual RHCSA and RHCE objectives (www.redhat.com/certification/rhcsa/objectives and www.redhat.com/certification/rhce/objectives) change with every release of RHEL (and even sometimes between releases), refer to the noted URL for the latest information.

The RHCSA Exam

TABLE 2	RHCSA Objective Exam Readiness Checklist

RHCSA Exam Readiness Checklist

Certification Objective	Ch #	Pg #
Category: Understand and Use Essential Tools		
Access a shell prompt and issue commands with correct syntax	3	62
Use input/output redirection	3	63
Use **grep** and regular expressions to analyze text	3	64
Access remote systems using SSH	2	51
Access remote systems using VNC	9	152
Log in and switch users in multiuser runlevels	8	138
Archive, compress, unpack, and uncompress files using **tar**, **star**, **gzip**, and **bzip2**	9	**152**
Create and edit text files	3	66
Create, delete, copy, and move files and directories	3	63
Create hard and soft links	3	64
List, set, and change standard ugo/rwx permissions	4	78
Locate, read, and use system documentation including **man**, **info**, and files in /usr/share/doc	3	65
Category: Operate Running Systems		
Boot, reboot, and shut down a system normally	5	96
Boot systems into different runlevels manually	5	97
Use single-user mode to gain access to a system	5	98
Identify CPU/memory intensive processes, adjust process priority with **renice**, and **kill** processes	9	153
Locate and interpret system log files	9	155
Access a virtual machine's console	2	51
Start and stop virtual machines	2	48
Start, stop, and check the status of network services	3	67
Category: Configure Local Storage		
List, create, delete, and set partition type for primary, extended, and logical partitions	6	111

RHCSA Exam Readiness Checklist

Certification Objective	Ch #	Pg #
Create and remove physical volumes, assign physical volumes to volume groups, and create and delete logical volumes	6	112
Create and configure LUKS-encrypted partitions and logical volumes to prompt for password and mount a decrypted file system at boot	6	116
Configure systems to mount file systems at boot by Universally Unique ID (UUID) or label	6	115
Add new partitions and logical volumes, and swap to a system non-destructively	6	111
Category: Create and Configure File Systems		
Create, mount, unmount, and use ext2, ext3, and ext4 file systems	6	114
Mount, unmount, and use LUKS-encrypted file systems	6	117
Mount and unmount CIFS and NFS network file systems	6	115
Configure systems to mount ext4, LUKS-encrypted and network file systems automatically	6	118
Extend existing unencrypted ext4-formatted logical volumes	6	113
Configure and set-GID directories for collaboration	8	141
Create and manage Access Control Lists (ACLs)	4	80
Diagnose and correct file permission problems	4	79
Category: Deploy, Configure, and Maintain Systems		
Configure networking and hostname resolution statically or dynamically	3	67
Schedule tasks using cron	9	154
Configure systems to boot into a specific runlevel automatically	5	99
Install Red Hat Enterprise Linux automatically using Kickstart	2	52
Configure a physical machine to host virtual guests	1	34
Install Red Hat Enterprise Linux systems as virtual guests	2	51
Configure systems to launch virtual machines at boot	2	49
Configure network services to start automatically at boot	5	100
Configure a system to run a default configuration HTTP server	1	36
Configure a system to run a default configuration FTP server	1	35
Install and update software packages from Red Hat Network, a remote repository, or from the local file system	7	130
Update the kernel package appropriately to ensure a bootable system	7	131

RHCSA Exam Readiness Checklist

Certification Objective	Ch #	Pg #
Modify the system bootloader	5	108
Category: Manage Users and Groups		
Create, delete, and modify local user accounts	8	139
Change passwords and adjust password aging for local user accounts	8	139
Create, delete, and modify local groups and group memberships	8	140
Configure a system to use an existing LDAP directory service for user and group information	8	142
Category: Manage Security		
Configure firewall settings using system-config-firewall or iptables	4	80
Set enforcing and permissive modes for SELinux	4	81
List and identify SELinux file and process context	4	82
Restore default file contexts	4	83
Use boolean settings to modify system SELinux settings	4	84
Diagnose and address routine SELinux policy violations	4	84

TABLE 3   RHCE Exam Readiness Objective Checklist

RHCE Exam Readiness Checklist

Certification Objective	Ch #	Pg #
Category: System Configuration and Management		
Route IP traffic and create static routes	12	196
Use iptables to implement packet filtering and configure network address translation (NAT)	10	164
Use /proc/sys and sysctl to modify and set kernel runtime parameters	12	191
Configure system to authenticate using Kerberos	12	195
Build a simple RPM that packages a single file	12	192
Configure a system as an iSCSI initiator that persistently mounts an iSCSI target	12	194

RHCE Exam Readiness Checklist

Certification Objective	Ch #	Pg #
Produce and deliver reports on utilization (processor, memory, disk, and network)	17	268
Use shell scripting to automate system maintenance tasks	12	190
Configure a system to log to a remote system	17	269
Configure a system to accept logging from a remote system	17	270
Category: Network Services (The following five objectives apply to all network services)		
Install the packages need to provide the service	11-17	176, 206, 220, 240, 254, 271
Configure SELinux to support the service	11-17	178, 207, 221, 240, 254, 271
Configure the service to start when the system is booted	11-17	177, 207, 223, 242, 255, 272
Configure the service for basic operation	11-17	208, 223, 242, 256, 272
Configure host-based and user-based security for the service	10-17	165, 208, 224, 243, 256, 273
Subcategory: HTTP/HTTPS		
Configure a virtual host	14	225
Configure private directories	14	226
Deploy a basic CGI application	14	227
Configure group-managed content	14	227
Subcategory: DNS (Candidates are not expected to configure master or slave name servers)		
Configure a caching-only name server	17	273
Configure a caching-only name server to forward DNS queries	17	274
Subcategory: FTP		
Configure anonymous-only download	16	257
Subcategory: NFS		
Provide network shares to specific clients	16	258
Provide network shares suitable to group collaboration	16	259

RHCE Exam Readiness Checklist

Certification Objective	Ch #	Pg #
Subcategory: SMB		
Provide network shares to specific clients	15	244
Provide network shares suitable to group collaboration	15	245
Subcategory: SMTP		
Configure a mail transfer agent (MTA) to accept inbound email from other systems	13	209
Configure an MTA to forward (relay) email through a smart host	13	211
Subcategory: SSH		
Configure key-based authentication	11	179
Configure additional options described in documentation	11	180
Subcategory: NTP		
Synchronize time using other NTP peers	17	275

For Instructors and More

I encourage everyone to read this section for instructors. This book is organized to help you prepare coursework for, or study for, one exam at a time.

Perhaps the biggest change in this book is designed to help the instructor. Since the RHCSA and RHCE are two entirely separate exams, I've reorganized this book to reflect those changes. If you're studying just for the RHCSA, read Chapters 1 through 9. If you're studying just for the RHCE, read Chapter 1 for instructions on loading VMs from the DVD, and then read Chapters 10 through 17. The same changes will help you as a certification candidate as well, so you know what skills to gain for each exam.

Many, perhaps most, candidates have trouble finishing the tasks associated with the RHCSA and RHCE exams in the time allotted. One way to save time during these exams is to keep things simple. While it's important to read over the questions carefully, it's also important not to overdo things. For example, there's no need to configure virtual Apache servers for the RHCSA exam. As suggested by one RHCE-related objective, it's normally sufficient to "configure the service for basic operation."

Every chapter includes 5 to 10 fill-in-the-blank questions. Although there are no multiple-choice or file-in-the-blank questions on Red Hat exams, such questions can still help measure student mastery of chapter material. And the fill-in-the-blank format puts a premium on the practical experience required on the exam.

In the same fashion, for the RHCE exam, unless directed to do otherwise, keep everything as simple as possible. Don't include that production list of suspect IP addresses in your firewall for the exam. Configure a firewall that allows access to just the services specified. Simple firewalls are faster to set up, and many security experts suggest that simple firewalls are safer.

As several services are covered in both the RHCSA and RHCE objectives, several services are covered in multiple chapters. For example, the RHCSA objective on the HTTP and FTP services are covered in Chapter 1. The RHCE objectives related to the same services are addressed in Chapters 14 and 16, respectively.

1
Prepare for Red Hat Hands-on Certifications

T he format of this book and chapter is different from other *Practice Exams* book in the McGraw-Hill series. Each chapter will include a brief overview of several different objectives on the Red Hat Certified System Administrator (RHCSA) and Red Hat Certified Engineer (RHCE) exams. This chapter starts with a description of the exams. It continues with an overview of the 64-bit hardware required to set up the virtual machine (VM) software covered by the RHCSA exam. It also includes instructions for how to load the preconfigured VMs compressed on the DVD.

The Red Hat exams are an advanced challenge. While this book provides labs and sample tests to help you prepare for the RHCSA and RHCE exams, it provides minimal explanation of exam objectives. If you want additional information, I encourage you to start with the *RHCSA/RHCE Red Hat Linux Certification Study Guide (Exams EX200 & EX300), 6th Edition*. In addition, Red Hat offers several courses to help prepare for these exams, as described in the front matter.

ex**a m**

ⓦ**atch**   *Hereafter, I refer to*
the **RHCSA/RHCE Red Hat Linux**
Certification Study Guide (Exams
EX200 & EX300), 6th Edition *as the*
Study Guide.

To prepare for the Red Hat exams, you need a physical 64-bit system that can support hardware-based virtualization. The objectives for the Red Hat exams specify virtualization. Red Hat's default virtual machine (VM) solution is the Kernel-based Virtual Machine (KVM). Red Hat offers KVM software that can host VMs only on its 64-bit releases. (As options that support "nested" virtualization are not free, they have not been tested for this book.)

In this chapter, you'll set up RHEL 6 on such a 64-bit system, with KVM in place. (Yes, based on a related RHCSA objective, there will be a lab where you'll demonstrate how to install KVM-based software after installation is complete.) You'll then use the compressed virtual machines available on the DVD. As they're based on the same source code used for RHEL 6, "rebuild" distributions such as the Community Enterprise Operating System (CentOS) and Scientific Linux (SL) should work in the same fashion. In general, most tasks can be performed on the VMs. But there are at least two exceptions when it's better to run a task on the physical system: when you create an installation HTTP/FTP server later in this chapter and when you set up a Virtual Network Computing (VNC) client in Chapter 9. Other labs may also use the physical host system.

exam

ⓦatch *From this point forward, when I refer to RHEL 6, you may assume that the same actions work for rebuild distributions such as Scientific Linux 6 and CentOS 6. The exceptions generally relate to references to the Red Hat Network (RHN) and related references to rebuild-only software repositories configured in the /etc/yum.repos.d directory.*

For the purpose of this book, I'll run most commands as the Linux administrative user, root. Logging in as the root user is normally discouraged unless you're administering a computer.

on the

ⓙob *Root logins at the GUI are especially discouraged. If you log in SL6.2 as root, you see the following message: "You are currently trying to run as the root super user. The super user is a specialized account that is not designed to run a normal user session. Various programs will not function properly, and actions performed under this account can cause unrecoverable damage to the operating system."*

However, because the RHCSA and RHCE exams test your administrative skills, it's appropriate to run commands in this book as the root user. But you also need to know how to set up regular users with partial or full administrative privileges.

As with the rest of the book, no guarantees are provided for the VMs compressed on the DVD.

All chapters in this book include a brief discussion of relevant exam objectives. Every objective on both the RHCSA and RHCE exams is covered in one or more of the 17 chapters in this book. Three RHCSA objectives are covered in this chapter. Just be aware, Red Hat has been known to modify objectives from time to time, so be sure to review them as you go through this book. As of this writing, the objectives were just moved to the following URLs: www.redhat.com/training/courses/ex200/ examobjective and www.redhat.com/training/courses/ex300/examobjective.

The RHCSA and RHCE Exams

The first Red Hat exams were given in 1999. And they've evolved since then. Until 2003, there was actually a multiple-choice component to the RHCE exam. At that time, the three-part exam was 6.5 hours long.

In 2009, Red Hat removed the requirement to install RHEL on a bare-metal system. They've since refocused the requirement for installation on a VM. In addition, there is no longer a separate troubleshooting section on either exam.

The RHCSA was introduced with the release of RHEL 6, as a replacement for the Red Hat Certified Technician (RHCT) exam. The RHCT was a complete subset of the RHCE. The RHCSA is different. Although the topics are closely related, they are separate from those now listed for the RHCE.

Red Hat provides "pre-assessment" tests for Red Hat RHCSA and RHCE Exam Prep courses. They correspond to the RH134 and RH254 courses, respectively. These tests are available through the Red Hat web pages for each course. Red Hat requires contact information before providing those pre-assessment tests. In addition, you can take the pre-assessment tests provided at http://www.mhprofessional.com/product.php?cat=39&isbn=007180160X.

The Exam Experience

Red Hat's certification tests are hands-on exams. As such, they are respected throughout the industry as a sign of genuine practical knowledge. When you pass a Red Hat exam, you will stand head and shoulders above the candidate who has passed only a "standard" multiple-choice certification exam.

When time starts, you'll be faced with a live system. You'll be given actual configuration problems associated with the items listed in the exam objectives for each certification. Naturally, this book is dedicated to helping you master the skills associated with those objectives.

While you won't have Internet access during the exam, you will have access to online documentation such as man and info pages as well as documentation in the /usr/share/doc/ directories, assuming appropriate packages are installed.

In addition, Red Hat provides the exam in electronic format. While the basic instructions may be in a local language such as English, the RHCSA and RHCE exams are available in 12 different languages: English, Simplified Chinese, Traditional Chinese, Dutch, French, Italian, Japanese, Korean, Portuguese, Russian, Spanish, and Turkish. (If you're unsure, contact Red Hat training at US 1-866-626-2994, or via www.redhat.com/training/.)

e**x**a**m**

ⓦatch

This book's coverage of the items listed in the RHCSA and RHCE exam objectives can be found on the first few pages of this book, in Table 2, page xxviii.

Red Hat also has prep courses for both exams. The outlines for those courses are available from www.redhat.com. While this book is not intended as a substitute for such courses, it is consistent with the outline of those courses. This book covers the objectives associated with each of these exams.

The RHCSA Exam

The RHCSA exam allows you to demonstrate your ability to configure live physical and virtual systems for networking, security, custom file systems, package updates, user management, and more. In essence, the RHCSA exam covers skills required to configure and administer a Linux workstation in the enterprise.

You have two and a half hours to complete the tasks given on the RHCSA exam. You complete the tasks by configuring a live RHEL system. Any changes that are made must survive a reboot. When you've completed the given tasks, the person grading the exam will see if the system is configured to meet the requirements. For example, if you're told to "create, delete, and modify local user accounts," it doesn't matter if the associated configuration file has been modified with the vi editor or the graphical User Manager tool. As long as you don't cheat, it's the results that matter.

Chapters 1 through 9 focus on coverage of the RHCSA exam.

The RHCE Exam

The RHCE exam tests your ability to configure live physical and virtual servers to configure network services such as Apache, vsFTP, the Network File System (NFS), Samba, remote logging, and more. It also tests your ability to handle complex configuration options associated with Security Enhanced Linux (SELinux), firewalls, networking, and more. In essence, if you pass the RHCE exam, hiring managers will know that you're qualified to help manage their enterprises of Linux systems.

The RHCE exam lasts two hours. When you sit down to take the exam, you are given tasks to perform on a live RHEL system. As with the RHCSA, any changes that are made must survive a reboot. In any case, it doesn't matter if you've configured the associated configuration file with the nano editor or a GUI tool. As long as you don't cheat, it's the results that matter.

The topics in the Red Hat preparation courses in a few areas go beyond those listed in the Red Hat Exam Preparation Guide. While such topics are not currently part of the exam, they may be included in future versions of the Red Hat exams.

Although the objectives for the RHCE exam are covered in Chapters 10 through 17, you should also read this chapter to install the VMs from the DVD for the test network.

Evolving Requirements

The requirements for the Red Hat exams are subject to change. You can see that in the differences between the RHCT and the RHCSA. You can see that in the changes to the exam format, where bare-metal installations are no longer required. In fact, that change happened over two years into the life of RHEL 5. Changes also occurred in the first month after RHEL 6 was released. So when you're preparing for the RHCSA and/or RHCE exams, watch the associated exam objectives carefully. In addition, Red Hat announced its most recent format changes through the WordPress blog publishing site, at http://redhatcertification.wordpress.com/.

Basic Hardware Requirements

Now it's time to explore in detail the hardware that Red Hat Enterprise Linux can handle. While some manufacturers now include their own Linux hardware drivers, most Linux hardware support comes from third parties, starting with the work of volunteers. Fortunately, there is a vast community of Linux users, many of whom produce drivers for Linux and distribute them freely on the Internet. If a certain piece of hardware is popular, you can be certain that Linux support for that piece of hardware will pop up somewhere on the Internet and will be incorporated into various Linux distributions, including Red Hat Enterprise Linux.

Hardware Compatibility

If you only have 32-bit systems available, be prepared to spend some money. KVM is the default VM solution for RHEL 6. Red Hat has built KVM server packages only for 64-bit systems. Fortunately, most PCs and servers sold today meet this requirement. Even the lowly Intel i3 CPU can handle 64-bit operating systems. There are even 64-bit versions of the Intel Atom CPU common on netbook systems. Similar comparisons can be made for CPUs from Advanced Micro Devices. If you're planning to configure VMs on RHEL 6, be sure to choose an architecture that supports hardware-assisted virtualization, along with Basic Input/Output System (BIOS) or Universal Extensible Firmware Interface (UEFI) menu options that allow you to activate that feature. Such a configuration, when active, will have either the **vmx** (Intel) or **svm** (AMD) flag in the /proc/cpuinfo file.

on the **job**

If you're about to purchase a new system, see if you can try it out at the "store" with one of the "Live CD" distributions. Both CentOS and Scientific Linux have one available based on RHEL 6 source code. If allowed by store personnel, review the BIOS or UEFI menus, and enable hardware-assisted virtualization. Boot the system from that Live CD (or DVD). Once booted, you should be able to access the /proc/cpuinfo file from the command line. A system configured to support hardware-assisted virtualization has the vmx or svm flag in that file.

In any case, you shouldn't assume Linux will install or run flawlessly on *any* computer, especially if the system in question is a state-of-the-art laptop computer. (And you do need a 64-bit system to prepare for the Red Hat exams.) Laptops are often designed with proprietary configurations that work with Linux only after some reverse engineering. For example, when I installed RHEL 6 on a brand-name business laptop built in 2010, I had to do a bit of extra work to make the wireless adapter work with RHEL 6. (These issues were addressed by the time I installed CentOS-6 on my laptop in early 2012.)

Even when a manufacturer creates a device for a CPU platform, it may not work with Linux. Therefore, it's important to know the basic architecture of a computer. But strictly speaking, if you want hardware compatible with and supported by Red Hat, consult the hardware compatibility list at http://hardware.redhat.com/hcl/.

RAM Requirements

This chapter assumes that you'll install RHEL 6 four times on the same system: once on the physical host, and once each on the three virtual machines. Although 4GB is a reasonable minimum for such a configuration, I've written this book on a laptop with 8GB of RAM.

But the RAM requirements for individual systems aren't that great. While it's possible to run RHEL 6 on less, the RAM memory requirements are driven by the needs of the Red Hat installer. For basic Intel/AMD-based 32- and 64-bit architectures, Red Hat officially requires 512MB of RAM and recommends at least 1GB of RAM per system. But don't forget to add it all together. Take the RAM for the three VMs, and then add the RAM required for the physical system.

Hard Drive Options

Before a computer can start Linux, the BIOS or UEFI has to recognize the hard drives that are connected to the system. It should also be able to read the Master Boot Record (MBR), the first 512 bytes on that drive. When Linux is installed, the MBR on one of the first two hard drives should include a pointer to the bootloader. The BIOS or UEFI can then set up and initialize that hard drive, read the MBR, and then read the GRUB bootloader. The system can read the contents of GRUB and then load Linux boot files as specified in the associated configuration file.

Get Red Hat Enterprise Linux

The RHCSA and RHCE exams are based on your knowledge of RHEL. Some of the requirements are based on RHEL software that has been built only for "standard" 64-bit computers. To get RHEL 6, you can go in one of two basic directions. You can get an official copy of RHEL 6, or you can download an option known as a "rebuild" distribution.

To get an official copy of RHEL, you need a subscription. That costs money. But the benefit is that you get a copy of the operating system that's actually used for the Red Hat exams. While trial subscriptions and academic discounts are available, those options may take more effort than the alternative.

The Point Releases Don't Matter

Red Hat releases "point" updates to all of its enterprise Linux versions. There is no significant difference among these releases. All RHEL 6 releases include kernel version 2.6.32. All commands, tools, and utilities have the same intended functionality throughout the RHEL 6 lifecycle. While third-party software such as the Firefox web browser may change, that has no effect on the Red Hat exam objectives.

So if you can't get the latest point release of RHEL 6 or a rebuild distribution, don't worry about it.

on the **Job**

Yes, version 2.6.32 sounds "old" compared to current "stable" releases in the 3.2 and later series. Rest assured, Red Hat maintains the RHEL 6 kernel in different ways. And the stability of the "older" kernel promotes reliability on mission-critical systems.

The Choices

If you don't need the same "look and feel" as RHEL to prepare for an exam, third-party rebuilds such as CentOS and Scientific Linux are available. As such, "rebuilds" use the same source code as RHEL, and they are functionally almost identical to RHEL. They've been built from the source code released by Red Hat under open source licenses. They're different in three basic ways:

- No Red Hat trademarks. It does mean that a rebuild distribution has a different "look" than RHEL.
- No RHN. That's not a problem, as the associated administrative commands work in essentially the same way for rebuild distributions without access to the RHN.
- Additional files in the /etc/yum.repos.d directory to configure connections to remote repositories.

With those limits in mind, rebuild distributions such as CentOS 6 and Scientific Linux 6 work in the same way as RHEL 6. They have the same file structure as RHEL 6. They include the same tools, which function identically to how they function in a genuine copy of RHEL 6.

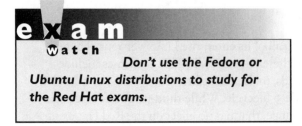

Don't use the Fedora or Ubuntu Linux distributions to study for the Red Hat exams.

While it's true that Fedora is a testbed for RHEL, the software as built for RHEL 6 has a different look, a different feel, and, in many cases, a different functionality. Students who use Fedora to study for Red Hat exams may be confused (and more) if they see genuine RHEL 6 systems for the first time on an exam.

Purchase an RHEL 6 Subscription

Different subscriptions are available for desktops, workstations, and servers. While the RHCSA is focused on workstations, it also requires the configuration of HTTP and FTP servers. Of course, the RHCE also requires the configuration of a variety of server services. So most readers need a server subscription.

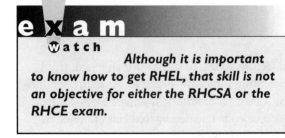

Watch *Although it is important to know how to get RHEL, that skill is not an objective for either the RHCSA or the RHCE exam.*

A variety of server subscriptions are available, depending on the number of CPU sockets and virtual guests. A system associated with a regular RHEL Server subscription is limited to two CPU sockets and one virtual guest. Each socket can have a multicore CPU. Significant discounts for academic users are available. In contrast, Desktop and Workstation subscriptions do not include support for virtual guests.

Get an Evaluation Copy

Red Hat currently offers a 30-day unsupported evaluation option for RHEL. Red Hat requires some personal information from such users. Once approved by Red Hat, you'll get instructions on how to download the distribution. For more information, see www.redhat.com/rhel/details/eval. The 30-day limit is simply a limit on access between your system and the RHN. The operating system continues to work, but without updates. No support is given.

Putting RHEL 6 to Work

Once you purchase a subscription or get approved for an evaluation copy, you'll be able to download RHEL 6 from the RHN at https://rhn.redhat.com/. Downloads are available for the operating system in a format appropriate for a DVD. There's also a download available for a network boot CD. These downloads are in ISO format, with an .iso extension. Such files can be burned to appropriate media, using standard tools such as Brasero in the GNOME desktop, a variation on the **cdrecord** command, or even corresponding tools on Microsoft systems. Alternatively, you can set up a VM where the virtual CD/DVD drive hardware points directly to the ISO file. Unless you purchase an actual boxed subscription, the burning or other use of these ISO files is your responsibility.

on the
()ob

An ISO file is an image file that can be burned to CD/DVD media. The actual acronym is irrelevant, as it is based on a political compromise.

Third-Party Rebuilds

You don't have to pay for operating system support to prepare for Red Hat exams. You don't have to live with a limited test subscription. To comply with the General Public License (GPL) and other applicable open source licenses, Red Hat releases the source code for just about every RHEL package at ftp.redhat.com. However, the GPL only requires that Red Hat release the source code. Red Hat interprets these licenses in a way that means they don't have to release the binary packages compiled from that source code.

on the
()ob

The description of the GPL and trademark law in this book is not a legal opinion and is not intended as legal advice.

Under trademark law, Red Hat can prevent others from releasing software with its trademarks, such as its red Fedora symbol. Nevertheless, the GPL, as an "open source" license, gives anyone the right to compile that source code. If they make changes, all they need to do is release their changes under the same license. And that's how third parties such as CentOS and Scientific Linux take the source code, remove the trademarks, and build the software into their own rebuild distributions.

The source code is released in Source RPM package format, which means the RPM packages can be built using various **rpm** (and **rpmbuild**) commands. However, the build process for a distribution, even from source code, is a tricky process. But once complete, the rebuild has the same functionality as RHEL. Red Hat releases its source code when it releases updates. And the developers behind rebuild distributions follow these releases to keep their repositories up to date. Here's a bit more about two of the major options for rebuild distributions:

■ **Community Enterprise Operating System (CentOS)** The rebuild known as CentOS includes a number of experienced developers who have been working with RHEL source code since the release of RHEL 3 back in 2002. For more information, see www.centos.org.

■ **Scientific Linux** This distribution is developed and unofficially supported by the U.S. government's Fermilab and the CERN (European Organization for Nuclear Research). The people associated with these labs are among the smartest scientists around. For more information, see www.scientificlinux.org.

on the *Job*

A number of the figures in this book are based on "snapshots" from both rebuild distributions that uses RHEL 6 source code—CentOS and Scientific Linux. While CentOS is a community project, Scientific Linux is backed by scientists from the international research institutions known as Fermilab and CERN.

To help with your studies, McGraw-Hill has created a mirror of Scientific Linux release 6.2, the same version used to create the VMs used for this book.

Installation Requirements

According to the Red Hat certification blog, Red Hat now provides "pre-installed systems" for their exams. So on an exam you won't start from scratch for the host physical system. But to set up a practice environment, you have to start with a 64-bit physical system. On a preinstalled system, the other requirements suggest that you need to know how to set up RHEL 6 installations on KVM-based VMs. But just in case, predefined VMs are available on the DVD. You'll set those up in a test network later in this chapter.

To create a physical host for test VMs, make sure to have enough room available for the host physical system and the guest VMs. This section suggests you make sure there's room for at least three test VMs. Since three VMs are available in a compressed format on the DVD, no backups are needed. For this purpose, 80GB of free space on a physical system should be more than sufficient. The suggested configuration, including basic information on the uncompressed VMs from the DVD, is shown in Figure 1-1.

Just keep in mind that the noted IP addresses assume an active eth0 network device on a specific Media Access Control (MAC) address. Those MAC addresses are listed in Table 1-2 later in this chapter. When you unpack the VMs from the DVD, KVM assigns a different MAC address, by default, leading to an eth1 network device and a dynamically assigned IP address.

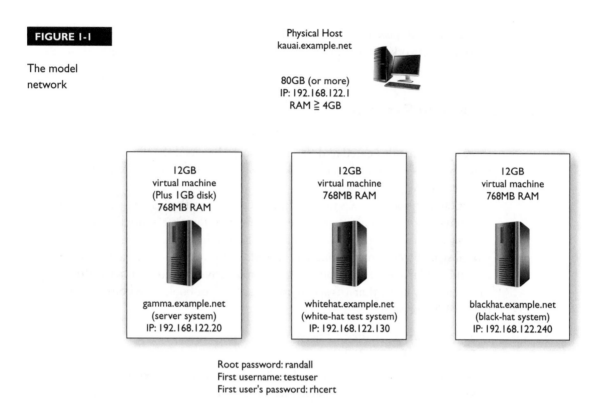

FIGURE 1-1

The model network

Physical Host
kauai.example.net

80GB (or more)
IP: 192.168.122.1
RAM ≧ 4GB

| 12GB virtual machine (Plus 1GB disk) 768MB RAM | 12GB virtual machine 768MB RAM | 12GB virtual machine 768MB RAM |

gamma.example.net
(server system)
IP: 192.168.122.20

whitehat.example.net
(white-hat test system)
IP: 192.168.122.130

blackhat.example.net
(black-hat system)
IP: 192.168.122.240

Root password: randall
First username: testuser
First user's password: rhcert

Until you address the network card issue in Chapter 3, you may need to run the **dhclient eth1** command each time you boot one or more of the VMs to make sure it can communicate on a network.

Red Hat and Virtual Machines

The objectives associated with the RHCSA suggest that you need to know how to "configure a physical machine to host virtual guests." They also suggest you need to know how to perform a number of tasks with VMs, some of which are covered in the labs in Chapter 2.

One of the advantages of a VM is how it supports the use of an ISO file on a virtual CD/DVD drive. Files accessed from that virtual drive are not slowed by the mechanical speed of physical CD/DVD media. And as such access may not be slowed by network traffic, virtual CD/DVD drives may be as fast as network access from a host system.

Virtual and Physical Systems

It's possible to install a substantial number of VMs on a single physical system. If those systems are dedicated to different services, they load the physical system at different times. Such loads makes it possible to "overbook" the RAM and other resources of the physical system.

For our purposes, there is no real difference whether the installation is performed on a physical or a virtual system. The software functions in essentially the same way. As long as IP forwarding is enabled on the physical host system, networking on the virtual system works in the same way as well. To make sure, open the /etc/sysctl. conf file, and make sure the following option is active, by setting it to 1. Most geeks should already know that 1 is synonymous for "on" for boolean directives such as **net.ipv4.ip_forward**.

```
# Controls IP packet forwarding
net.ipv4.ip_forward = 1
```

This directive makes sure IP forwarding is implemented the next time the system is booted, in the following dynamic file: /proc/sys/net/ipv4/ip_forward. The corresponding directive for IPv6 networking is **net.ipv6.conf.all.forwarding**. One way to implement these changes without a reboot is with the following command:

```
# echo "1" > /proc/sys/net/ipv4/ip_forward
```

Unless IP forwarding is configured on the physical host system, the VMs are unable to access outside networks.

In addition, you'll need to set up the virtual network adapter as a trusted interface in the firewall. You'll do so shortly, after installing KVM.

Installation Options

Even most beginning Linux users can install RHEL 6 from a CD/DVD. While this section addresses some of the options associated with installation, it is focused on the creation of that baseline system that can be used to set up other custom RHEL 6 systems, including the installation of KVM.

The steps described in this section assume installation on a physical system from a DVD, and that you know how to boot a system from that media. In addition, these steps assume that you understand the basics of Linux device files, at least as they relate to partitions. For example, you should already know that the /dev/sda1 drive represents the first partition on the first regular drive on a system.

The steps described in this chapter are modestly different if you're installing RHEL 6 over a network from an FTP or HTTP server. The steps associated with a network installation, as well as an explanation of Linux device files for partitions, are described in the *Study Guide*.

As the VMs depicted in Figure 1-1 are already available on the DVD, this book does not describe the installation process within a KVM-based VM. However, there will be a lab on the topic in Chapter 2.

Boot Media

When installing RHEL 6, the simplest option is to boot it from the RHEL 6 DVD. Rebuild distributions such as CentOS and Scientific Linux include extra packages and, therefore, supply two DVDs. As RHEL does not offer a live media option at this time, you should ignore the corresponding live media options (Live CD, DVD, or USB) available for rebuild distributions. Other options such as network boot CDs support installation over a network from an FTP or HTTP server.

Booting the RHEL 6 Installation

Now you can boot a target system from the installation DVD. After a few files are opened and decompressed, an RHEL installation screen should appear with at least the following four options:

- Install or upgrade an existing system
- Install system with basic video driver
- Rescue installed system
- Boot from local drive

The first option should work for most users. If there is trouble with the graphics after the first option, try rebooting the system and work with the second option, which specifies a standard Video Electronics Standard Association (VESA) adapter associated with older Super Video Graphics Association (SVGA) monitors.

For simplicity, I'll focus on a graphical installation on a physical host system. To start that installation, select the Install Or Upgrade An Existing System option.

Basic Installation Steps

The basic RHEL installation is straightforward and should already be well understood by any Red Hat certification candidate. Most of the steps are described here for reference. You can find a more detailed illustration of the installation process in the *Study Guide*. For this section, I make the following assumptions:

- Installation from the first DVD from a rebuild distribution such as CentOS or Scientific Linux (The installation procedure for RHEL 6 works in essentially the same way.)
- At least 4GB of RAM to accommodate multiple VMs
- RHEL 6 as the only operating system on the local computer

Dual-boot situations are acceptable, however. In fact, I've written this book on a Intel I7 laptop system in a triple-boot configuration where CentOS 6 coexists with Windows 7 and RHEL 6. If you're installing the system on a dedicated physical computer or a VM, the basic steps are the same. As a physical host is required for VMs, I assume you are installing RHEL 6 on a physical system.

on the *Job*

Before installing Linux, I make sure to have a drive with free, preferably unpartitioned space. If I'm overwriting partitions on an existing drive, I print out the current partition map, and then mark it up with partitions for the /boot and top-level root (/) directories, along with swap space. Of course, I test a backup first, but life is easier when you don't have to restore anything from a backup.

I focus on an installation from a DVD on a physical system. If you're the kind of reader who does not follow instructions, these details may not be for you.

1. Boot your computer from the RHEL or rebuild DVD. Select the Install Or Upgrade An Existing System option shown in Figure 1-2. If there's trouble with the graphics during the installation, restart the system and try the second option listed.

2. The system responds with a Disc Found screen. The first steps of the network installation process start in *text mode* (which is actually a low-resolution graphical mode), even if sufficient RAM is available. Choices are not "clickable." In this mode, use the TAB key to switch between options, and the SPACE or ENTER key to select or deselect an option. You can use the options to test

The installation
boot screen

```
                  Welcome to Scientific Linux 6.2!

        Install or upgrade an existing system
        Install system with basic video driver
        Rescue installed system
        Boot from local drive
        Memory test




                    Press [Tab] to edit options
```

the integrity of the media. For now, I assume the DVD is good and select Skip
to continue. Just be aware, if you do run the test, it "ejects" the media after
the test is complete.

3. Assuming sufficient RAM is available, you should now see a graphical installation screen. In most cases, the only instruction is a Next button in the
   lower-right corner of the screen. Click that button.

4. In the following two screens, you are prompted to select a language and
   keyboard. Several dozen options are available for each setting. These instructions assume that you select English (English) as a language, US English as a
   keyboard. Make the appropriate selections and click Next.

5. The next screen relates to local or specialized storage devices. Yes, you can install RHEL 6 on network-based storage. These instructions assume that you're
   installing RHEL 6 on one or more "regular" local hard drives (SATA, PATA,
   or a virtual hard drive on a KVM system). In that case, select Basic Storage
   Devices, and click Next.

6. If there's an existing Linux installation on the local system, you'll be prompted to select Fresh Installation or Upgrade An Existing Installation. If you're
   upgrading a previous installation of Linux, you may want to choose that. For
   simplicity, if you see these options, select Fresh Installation and click Next to

continue. (Of course, if there's existing data of any importance on the current system, back it up!)

7. You're now asked to provide a hostname for the local system. My system is shown in this book as kauai.example.net. While you're free to choose your own hostname for the local system, just be aware that my references to kauai.example.net represent my physical host system.

8. Click Configure Network to open the Network Connections tool, shown in Figure 1-3. The default includes dynamically assigned IPv4 addresses and no IPv6 addresses for detected wired and wireless network cards. These are the external addresses of the host system, different from the 192.168.122.1 address shown for the physical host (kauai) in Figure 1-1, earlier in this chapter. Select the desired network card, make any needed changes, click Close to return to the hostname screen, and click Next to continue.

9. Now you'll see a world map, where you can select the time zone of the local system. The System Clock Uses UTC option is a reference to the local hardware clock and the atomic realization of Greenwich Mean Time. (UTC is a non–English language acronym based on a political compromise.) While incompatible with Microsoft Windows, the UTC option supports changes for daylight saving time. Make appropriate changes and click Next to continue.

10. The next step is to enter the password for the root administrative user, twice. Do so and click Next to continue.

FIGURE 1-3

Network Connections tool during installation

11. The next step, shown in Figure 1-4, determines how space on configured hard disks, local and remote, is used. The options are fairly well explained in the figure. For the purpose of this installation, select Create Custom Layout. Note how that blanks out the deselection of the Encrypt System and the selection of the Review And Modify Partitioning Layout options. Click Next to continue.

12. Now you'll see the Please Select A Device screen, shown in Figure 1-5. This is the Red Hat Disk Druid screen, the RHEL graphical tool used to configure partitions, logical volumes, and RAID arrays.

13. For just about all RHEL systems, it can be helpful to configure one partition for the /boot directory. The Red Hat standard for this partition is 500MB. You'll also want to allocate room for swap space as well as the top-level root directory.

FIGURE 1-4	Partition layout options

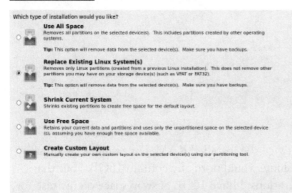

FIGURE 1-5 Disk Druid for configuring volumes

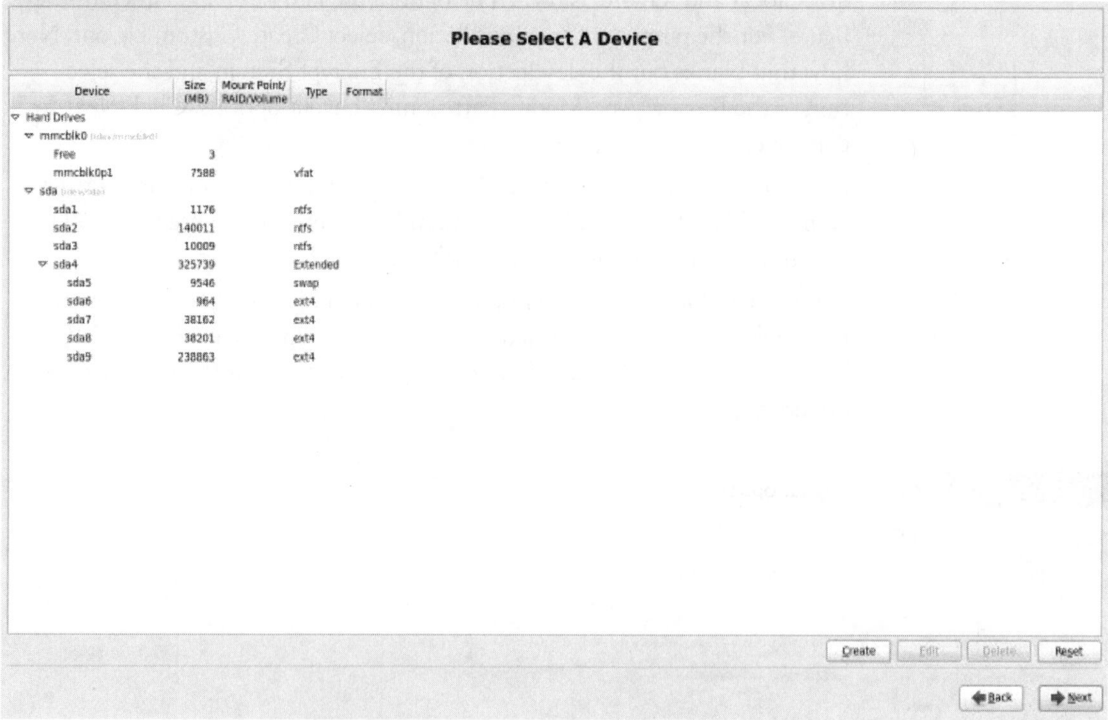

The standard for swap space is twice the installed RAM. For example, if a system has 8GB of RAM, a swap space volume would normally contain 16GB. (But that's more than plenty for most configurations; I have 10GB of swap space on my test system with 8GB of RAM. Very little of that swap space actually gets used.) If you have significantly more than 80GB available for the installation, you may choose to set up logical volumes or RAID arrays. One possible configuration is shown in Table 1-1. If you have more space available for the physical host, you may want to set up separate volumes for directories such as /home and even /var/lib/libvirt/images (which contains the KVM virtual disks).

As you're loading nearly 40GB of files (from compressed archives) from the DVD, you may want more space for the volume associated with the top-level root directory.

14. To configure a volume (partition, logical volume, or RAID array), click Create. It opens the Create Storage window, shown in Figure 1-6, which includes options for each of these types of volumes.

TABLE 1-1	Directory	Volume Size
Sample Volume Configuration for a KVM Host	/boot	500MB
	/	70GB (or more)
	Swap	10GB (the standard is twice the amount of RAM)

15. Once configuration is complete, click Next. If you've made any changes that require formatting, you'll see a warning to that effect. If and when you're satisfied with the volume configuration, click Write Changes To Disk to continue.

16. Next, you review the basic configuration for GRUB, the GRand Unified Bootloader. Be aware, RHEL 6 uses a slightly older version of GRUB, version 0.97. The settings shown in Figure 1-7 are reasonable defaults for a dual-boot configuration. In most cases, you can leave the options as is and click Next to continue.

on the **Ö**ob

The terms boot loader and bootloader are interchangeable. Both are frequently found in Red Hat documentation.

17. After configuring the GRUB bootloader, you'll see the options shown in Figure 1-8, which allow you to configure the local system to a desired functionality. For

FIGURE 1-6

Create Storage options

Create Storage

Create Partition
◉ Standard Partition
  General purpose partition creation

Create Software RAID   Information
○ RAID Partition
  Create a RAID formated partition
○ RAID Device
  Requires at least 2 free RAID formated partitions

Create LVM   Information
○ LVM Volume Group
  Requires at least 1 free LVM formated partition
○ LVM Logical Volume
  Create a logical volume on selected volume group
○ LVM Physical Volume
  Create an LVM formated partition

[Cancel]   [Create]

Configure the
bootloader

the physical system, select Virtual Host. It installs the KVM-related packages
needed to host VMs available from the DVD. Also select Customize Now, and
then click Next.

on the
Job

*If you're installing RHEL 6 on most VMs, don't try including Virtual Host
packages. The installation will stop with an error, as it should, as RHEL 6 inside
a VM can't itself host other VMs. (The VM systems I created for this book are
based on a modified Minimal Desktop.)*

18. In the next installation screen that appears, select Desktops in the left-hand
    pane. Select General Purpose Desktop and X Window System in the right-
    hand pane, as shown in Figure 1-9 to ensure the appropriate GUI packages
    are included with the Virtual Machine Manager. Make any additional desired
    selections.

19. Click Next to start the installation process.

FIGURE 1-8   Select system functionality

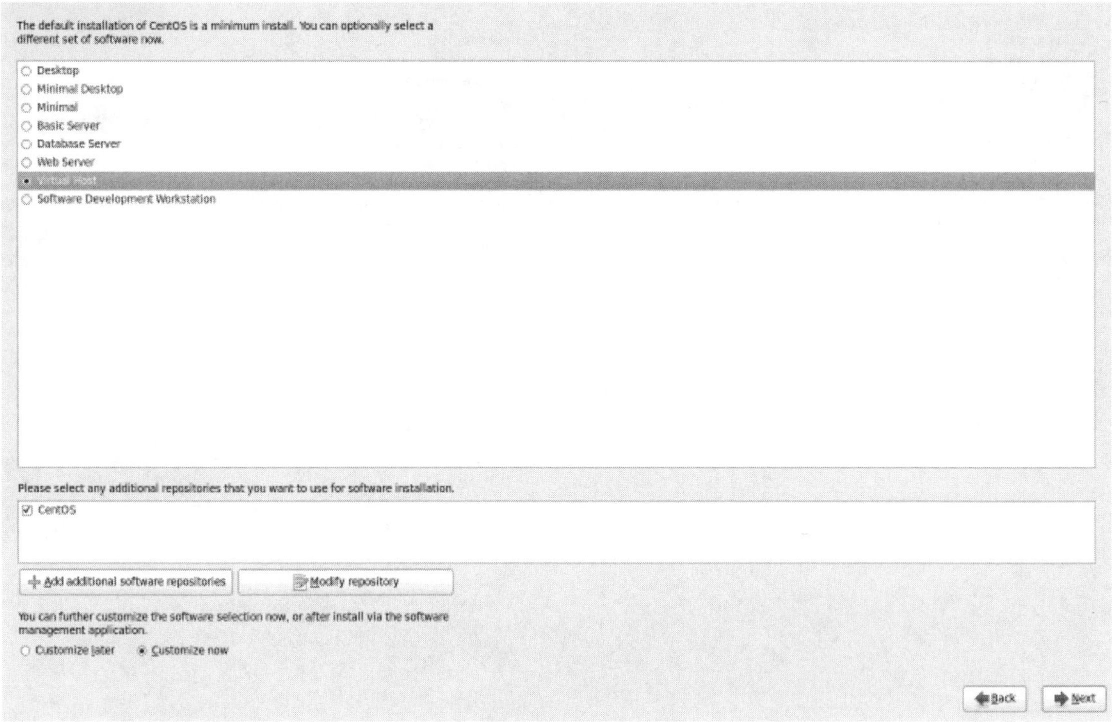

The default installation of CentOS is a minimum install. You can optionally select a
different set of software now.

○ Desktop
○ Minimal Desktop
○ Minimal
○ Basic Server
○ Database Server
○ Web Server
● Virtual Host
○ Software Development Workstation

Please select any additional repositories that you want to use for software installation.

☑ CentOS

[✚ _A_dd additional software repositories] [⬚ _M_odify repository]

You can further customize the software selection now, or after install via the software
management application.

○ Customize _l_ater   ● _C_ustomize now

[⬅ _B_ack] [➡ _N_ext]

20. When installation is complete, you'll see a final message to that effect, with
an option to reboot the system. From this physical system, don't forget to
eject or remove the installation DVD.

21. But installation isn't quite complete. The first time RHEL 6 boots in the GUI
on a freshly installed system, you go through a one-time process known as *First
Boot*. While there's a similar text-mode version, these steps are based on a
graphical First Boot. It starts with a welcome screen. Click Forward to continue.

22. The First Boot process continues with a license agreement, which varies
depending on whether this is RHEL 6 or a rebuild distribution. (There's no
requirement for a rebuild distribution to include any license at this stage.) If
you refuse the license agreement, you're prompted to shut down and remove
the operating system from the local computer. If you can accept this agreement, select Yes and click Forward to continue. If you're working from a
rebuild distribution, skip to step 24.

FIGURE 1-9 Functional installation options

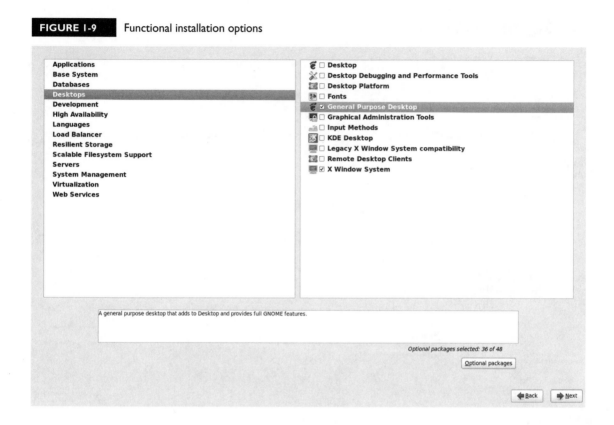

23. On an actual RHEL 6 system, you're prompted to connect the system to the RHN. To register, you need an RHN account, with an available subscription. As that is not required for the RHCSA/RHCE exams, proceed through the prompts to bypass registering this system.

24. The next step allows you to create a regular user. Although you can also connect to a remote database of users, a regular local user is required in this step. Create a regular user of your choice.

25. Now you can set up a date and time for the local system. The date and time that appears reflects that configured in the local hardware during the installation process. Make desired changes and click Forward to continue.

26. Unless your system has a lot of memory (more than 4GB), you are prompted with the following message: "Insufficient memory to configure kdump," which collects data associated with kernel crashes. Click OK or make appropriate changes, and click Finish. You should be taken to the graphical login screen.

Default Security Settings

When RHEL 6 is installed, there are default settings associated with SELinux and **iptables**-based firewalls. This section is just reference information for a default installation; for more information, see the *Study Guide*.

First, SELinux is enabled in enforcing mode by default. You can confirm the setting with the **sestatus** command, which should lead to the following output:

```
SELinux status:              enabled
SELinuxfs mount:             /selinux
Current mode:                enforcing
Mode from config file:       enforcing
Policy version:              24
Policy from config file:     targeted
```

If you want detailed information about the current **iptables** command, examine the /etc/sysconfig/iptables file. That file is used by the iptables service, courtesy of the /etc/init.d/iptables script. The following line from that file allows traffic sent through port 22 access from the outside.

```
-A INPUT -m state --state NEW -m tcp -p tcp --dport 22 -j ACCEPT
```

Port 22 is the default port for the Secure Shell (SSH) service, which supports remote administration of the local system. If there's a good network connection, you'll be able to connect remotely to this system. If the local IP address is 192.168.122.20, you can connect remotely to user testuser's account with the following command:

```
# ssh testuser@192.168.122.20
```

One advantage of the Firewall Configuration tool is in the configuration of the connection-tracking module used for FTP services. When you set up a local FTP server and allow access with the Firewall Configuration tool, it includes the following module in the iptables-config file in the /etc/sysconfig directory:

```
IPTABLES_MODULES="nf_conntrack_ftp"
```

If you edit the firewall configuration manually, you may need to add this module to the iptables-config file.

You also need to set up the firewall in a couple of special ways for the VMs. First, on the physical system, you should confirm the identity of the virtual network device. To do so, run the **ifconfig** command. Unless you've changed defaults, that device should be named virbr0, associated with IP address 192.168.122.1. Here"s how it looks on my system:

```
virbr0 Link encap:Ethernet  HWaddr 52:54:00:28:D3:D1
       inet addr:192.168.122.1  Bcast:192.168.122.255  Mask:255.255.255.0
       UP BROADCAST RUNNING MULTICAST  MTU:1500  Metric:1
       RX packets:20915 errors:0 dropped:0 overruns:0 frame:0
       TX packets:27765 errors:0 dropped:0 overruns:0 carrier:0
       collisions:0 txqueuelen:0
       RX bytes:3562198 (3.3 MiB)  TX bytes:17329384 (16.5 MiB
```

Now that you've confirmed virbr0 as the device for the virtual network adapter, you can make it a "Trusted Interface" in the Firewall Configuration tool. To open that tool in the GUI, click System | Administration | Firewall, or enter **system-config-firewall** at a GUI command line. Select Trusted Interfaces. Normally, the virbr0 device won't be on the list. You have to click Add to add it, as shown in Figure 1-10.

Once added to the Trusted Interface list, you have to select the interface to activate it, as shown in Figure 1-11.

Now you want to set up the physical network adapter to masquerade the IP addresses of the VMs. That adapter varies. You should be able to confirm the connected physical network adapter in the output to the **ifconfig** command. That

FIGURE 1-10

Add the virtual network adapter (virbr0) as a Trusted Interface

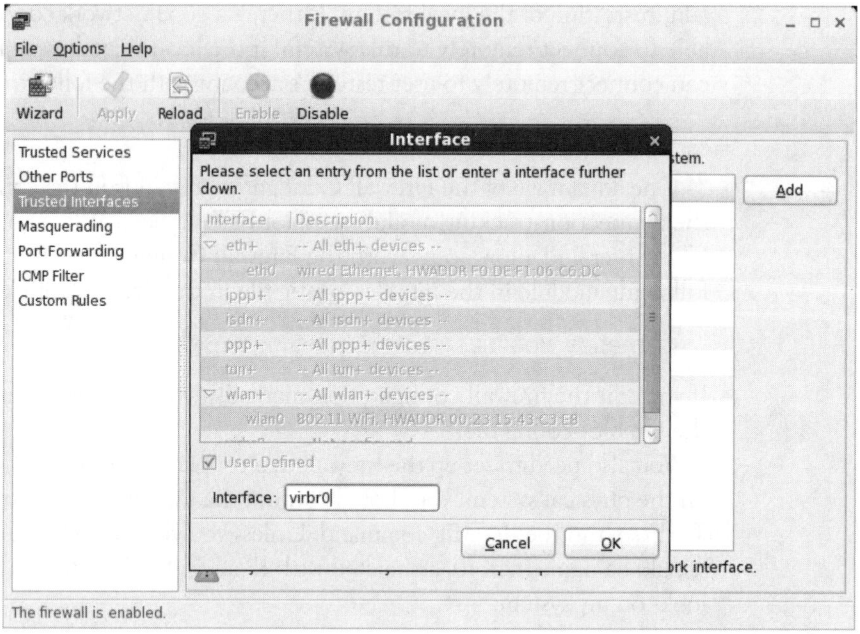

FIGURE 1-11

Activate the
virtual network
adapter as a
Trusted Interface

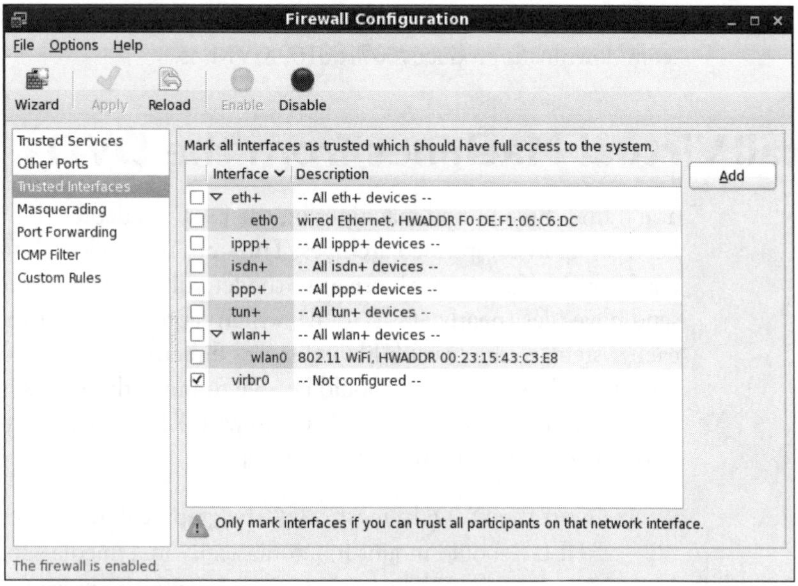

adapter can vary. Figure 1-12 shows two candidate device files on my laptop: eth0 and
wlan0. I normally use wlan0; selecting that adapter allows me to update my VMs from

FIGURE 1-12

Enable remote
access via
Masquerading

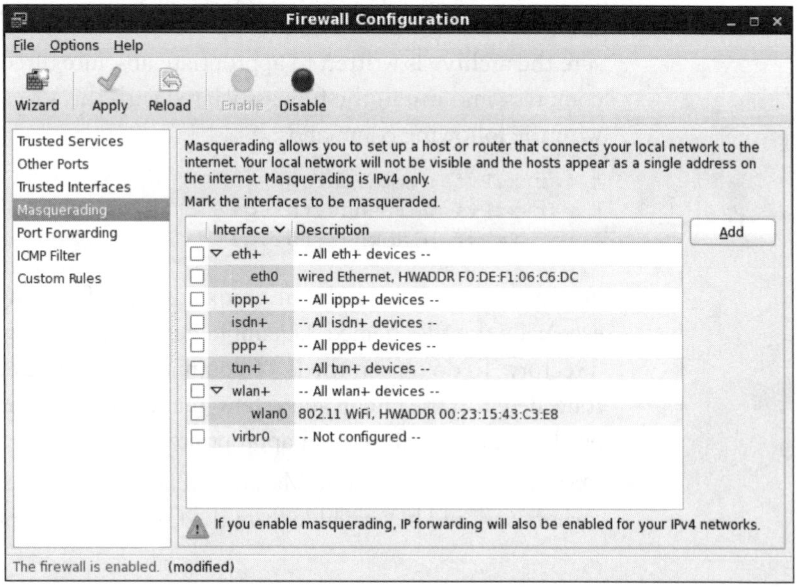

remote repositories, including the McGraw-Hill repository at www.mhprofessional
.com/downloads/products/007180160X/VM/os.

Install Virtual Machines from the DVD

You'll find three virtual machines on the DVD, as depicted in Figure 1-1. They've
been set up in compressed archives. The steps that follow should send the
configuration files in .xml format to the /etc/libvirt/qemu directory. They should also
send huge files (nearly 40GB total), which represent the virtual disks associated with
each system, to the /var/lib/libvirt/images directory. Slight errors may send files to
the wrong directories; you should be able to move those files if needed.

Once you've set up a physical system with KVM software, you can install these
virtual machines using the following steps:

1. Insert the DVD. In most cases, the graphical desktop environment within
   RHEL 6 should mount it automatically in a /media subdirectory. If it isn't
   already mounted, one way to do so is with the **mount /dev/cdrom /mnt**
   command.

2. Review the contents of the mounted directory; in this case, it's /mnt. It
   should include three files with .tar.gz extensions.

3. Unpack and uncompress the archive. The files are set up as a tar archive,
   compressed in a GZIP format. You'll want to include the **P** switch to make
   sure the archive is written to appropriate absolute directories. To unpack, uncompress, and install the files associated with the VMs, you can unpack them
   with the following commands:

   ```
   # tar xzPvf gamma.tar.gz
   # tar xzPvf whitehat.tar.gz
   # tar xzPvf blackhat.tar.gz
   ```

   You may want to check the SELinux context of the unpacked archives,
   especially the files named *.example.net*.img in the /var/lib/libvirt/images
   directory. To do so, run the **ls -Z** command in that directory as the root user.
   If needed, run the **chcon -u system_u** and **chcon -t virt_image_t** commands
   on the applicable files to set appropriate file contexts.

4. Open the Virtual Machine Manager. If you've installed RHEL 6 as described
   earlier, it should be available from the GUI. Click Applications | System

Tools | Virtual Machine Manager. It should open the window shown in Figure 1-13.

5. Just a reminder: as noted in Figure 1-1, the password for testuser is **rhcert**; the password for root is **randall**.

You need to make a connection to a QEMU hypervisor. (Officially, QEMU is not an acronym.) Double-click the regular hypervisor, and enter the root password when prompted. (Some systems include an extra usermode hypervisor.) The "Not Connected" note, if shown, should disappear.

6. Right-click the now connected hypervisor, and click New in the pop-up menu that appears. You'll see the New VM window, shown in Figure 1-14. Even though the caption suggests that you'll be creating a new virtual machine, you're actually importing a disk image. Here, I'm importing the gamma.example.net system from the associated disk image, unpacked and uncompressed from the DVD. Make appropriate entries on your system and click Forward to continue.

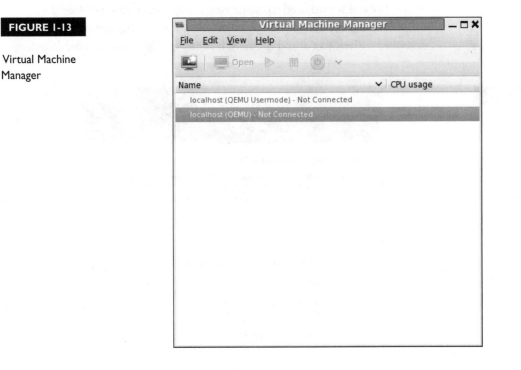

FIGURE 1-13

Virtual Machine
Manager

FIGURE I-14

Import a virtual
machine,
Step I of 4

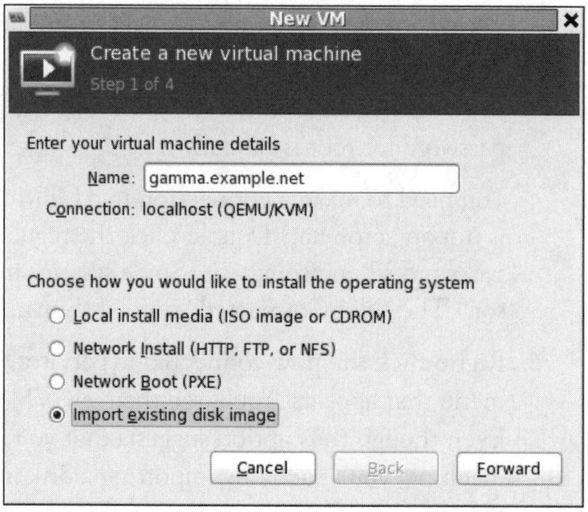

7. Now proceed to the next screen and Step 2, as shown in Figure 1-15. (This
is step 2 of the wizard used to create new virtual machines, not step 2 in
this numbered list.) If you've unpacked the archive using the instructions
described earlier, you'll find the hard disk image file, gamma.example.net.

FIGURE I-15

Import a virtual
machine,
Step 2 of 4

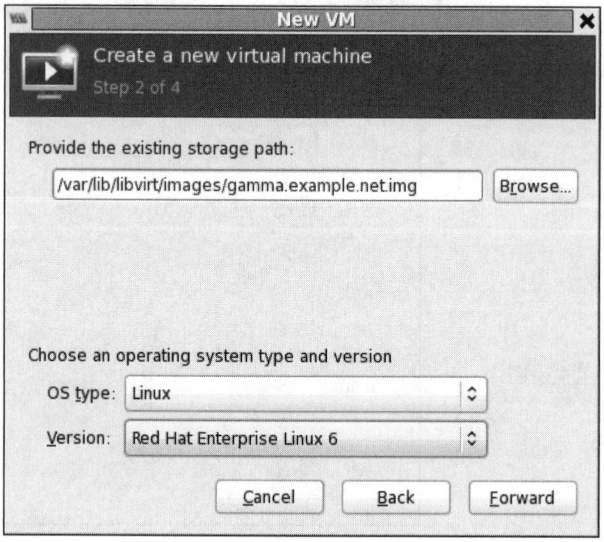

img, in the /var/lib/libvirt/images directory. Make sure to set the OS Type and Version appropriately, and then click Forward to continue.

8. In Step 3, as shown in Figure 1-16, you allocate RAM and numbers of CPUs for the system. You can allocate as many CPU cores as exists on the local physical system. The systems on the DVD are based on 768MB of RAM.

9. In Step 4, as shown in Figure 1-17, you can review the basic options that will be used for the VM. In general, no changes are required at this step, and you can click Finish to finish importing the VM.

   The Virtual Machine Manager normally assigns a random hardware address to the network card, and it's set up with a device name of eth1. If you want to see the original configuration as specified, click Advanced Options, and enter the associated MAC (Media Access Control) address. It's available in the XML files on the DVD and specified in Table 1-2.

10. When the process is complete, the VM should start automatically. You may briefly see flashes of a graphical screen during this process. You should be able to power off the system from within the VM window that appears.

In Lab 3, you repeat this process with the other two VMs, unpacked from the DVD.

FIGURE 1-16

Import a virtual machine,
Step 3 of 4

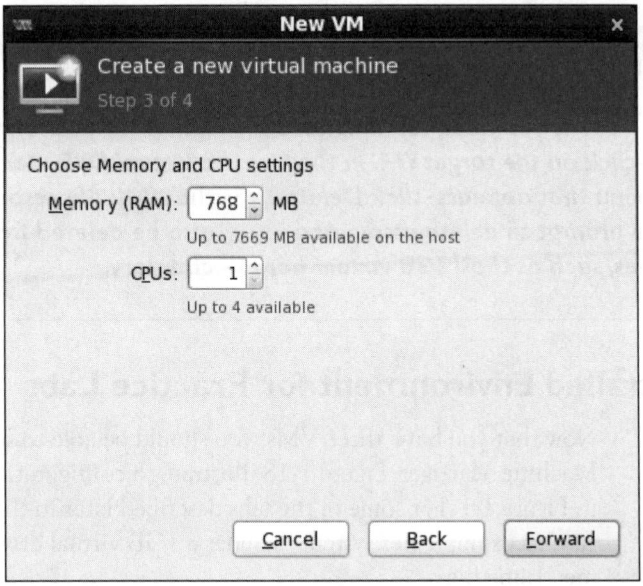

FIGURE 1-17

Import a virtual
machine,
Step 4 of 4

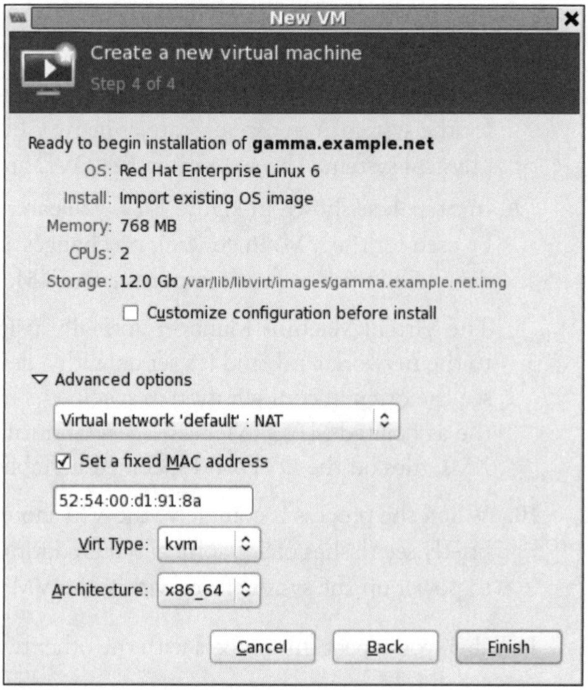

exam
watch

If you need to uninstall a VM, right-click on the target VM. In the pop-up menu that appears, click Delete. Follow the prompt to delete associated storage files, such as the 12GB virtual hard *disk from your system. Be careful; if you use a virtual DVD, don't delete it! If successful, the XML file associated with the VM will also be deleted from the /etc/libvirt/qemu directory.*

A Preinstalled Environment for Practice Labs

Now that you have three VMs, you should be able to start them from the Virtual Machine Manager. Figure 1-18 illustrates a configuration with the three VMs shown in Figure 1-1. For some of the labs described later in the book, the archive for the gamma.example.net system includes a 1GB virtual drive, in the gamma.example .net-1.img file.

TABLE 1-2	System	MAC Address
Original Ethernet MAC Addresses	gamma.example.net	52:54:00:b8:a7:ea
	whitehat.example.net	52:54:00:ec:81:11
	blackhat.example.net	52:54:00:9e:e2:28

System Roles

Ideally, you can set up several systems, each dedicated to different roles. A network with a dedicated DNS (Domain Name Service) server, a dedicated DHCP (Dynamic Host Configuration Protocol) server, a dedicated Samba file sharing server, and so on, is more secure. In that situation, a security breach in one system does not affect any other services.

However, that's not practical, especially during the Red Hat exams. Table 1-3 lists the roles appropriate for the physical and the three VM systems described in Figure 1-18.

on the **job**

Until you change the hardware address associated with the Ethernet adapter in Chapter 3, the noted VMs are unlikely to use the IP addresses shown in Table 1-3. In that chapter, you'll also set up the /etc/hosts file on each system to help them communicate with each other.

FIGURE 1-18

Virtual Machine Manager with three VMs

Virtual Machine Manager

File   Edit   View   Help

Open

Name   CPU usage

▽ localhost (QEMU)

  blackhat.example.net
  Running

  gamma.example.net
  Running

  whitehat.example.net
  Running

TABLE I-3	System	Roles
Roles for Test Systems	kauai.example.net	Physical host system on IP address 192.168.122.1
	gamma1.example.net	Server system on IP address 192.168.122.20
	whitehat.example.net	Friendly test system on IP address 192.168.122.130
	blackhat.example.net	Simulated compromised test system on IP address 192.168.122.240

The following excerpt from the **ifconfig** command on the physical host system displays the virbr0 adapter:

```
virbr0 Link encap:Ethernet  HWaddr 9E:56:D5:F3:75:51
       inet addr:192.168.122.1 Bcast:192.168.122.255 Mask:255.255.255.0
```

The address associated with this virbr0 adapter, 192.168.122.1, is the default given to the physical host.

The gamma.example.net system is the designated exam system, which will be used for exercises that address actual Red Hat exam requirements.

The whitehat.example.net system will be used to verify the configuration on the gamma1 system. For example, if you've configured two virtual websites with different names, you should be able to access both websites from the whitehat system. The Red Hat exams assume you may connect a system as a client to servers such as Samba and LDAP. They also assume that a DNS server is configured with appropriate hostnames and IP addresses. While the configuration of some servers such as Kerberos is beyond the scope of the RHCSA/RHCE exams, they may be used during the exams by the other systems as clients.

Finally, the blackhat.example.net system is essentially an insecure system on the same local network. While it's configured on the same network as the others, computer security should still work, even when any system on an internal network is compromised.

Configure a Physical Machine for Virtual Guests

Read the objective carefully. To quote, you need to know how to "configure a physical machine to host virtual guests." As the Kernel-based Virtual Machine (KVM) is the only VM solution supported by Red Hat on RHEL 6, it's safe to assume you'll have to learn to use KVM.

While it's simplest to install KVM during the installation process, Randy Russell, Red Hat's Director of Certification, has written that Red Hat exams are no longer given on "bare-metal" systems. In other words, you need to know how to install KVM on a live system.

Nevertheless, this chapter describes how you can install KVM during the installation process. In other words, if you have trouble with the labs, this chapter provides "fail-safe" instructions so you'll have VMs for the remainder of the book. This is necessary to allow you to run all other labs in this book. However, you get a chance to set up KVM on a preinstalled system during one of the labs. Here's a hint for you: the relevant package groups are Virtualization, Virtualization Client, and Virtualization Platform. In case you forget these names, you can list them with the following command:

```
# yum grouplist | grep Virtual
```

The output also shows the Virtualization Tools package group, which is not required. Of course, you can install these package groups with the help of the **yum groupinstall** command or with the Add/Remove Software tool in the GUI. While many other excellent VM solutions are available, don't use them when preparing for a Red Hat exam. Red Hat's one and only virtualization solution for RHEL 6 is KVM. Use it. Learn it. That knowledge of KVM will also serve you well in your career.

A Default Configuration FTP Server

The exact wording of the objective is to "Configure a system to run a default configuration FTP server." Let's break down that objective. First, "default configuration" suggests that no changes are required to the configuration file that's installed with the FTP server package. Second "configure a system" suggests changes may be required to the software around the FTP server.

When RHEL 6 was first released, the wording of the objective was subtly different: "deploy file sharing services." In other words, Red Hat believes it's important to know how to set up an FTP server to actually share files.

Red Hat includes one package for FTP services in RHEL 6, vsftpd. It is based on the very secure FTP daemon. By default, it serves files from the /var/ftp directory. It includes the /var/ftp/pub directory for publishing files. While the default configuration reads files from these directories, it can also read files from associated subdirectories.

When you configure a system to accommodate FTP, you may need to add directories, modify firewalls, and adjust the SELinux contexts associated with those files and directories. Firewalls are fairly straightforward, especially with the help of the firewall configuration tool. Since the objective specifies the default configuration, you don't have to be concerned about nonstandard ports for FTP, at least during the RHCSA exam. In other words, preconfigured options in the Firewall Configuration tool can enable access to that FTP server from external systems. Just be aware, as suggested earlier, the FTP option in the firewall configuration tool adds the nf_conntrack_ftp module to the **IPTABLES_MODULES** directive in the /etc/sysconfig/iptables-config file.

Finally, don't let SELinux scare you. As long as you know how to read the SELinux contexts of default files and directories, you can set up SELinux contexts of any files and subdirectories that you may add.

A Default Configuration HTTP Server

The wording and history of this objective is quite similar to the previous one for the FTP server. The earlier version of the directive, to deploy a file-sharing service, was relevant to both the FTP and HTTP services.

The only HTTP server included with RHEL 6 is the Apache Web Server. While some rebuild distributions may include alternatives, focus your studies on Apache.

Based on the "default configuration," for Apache, you won't have to make any changes to the httpd.conf file in the /etc/httpd/conf directory. You can use the same Firewall Configuration tool to enable external access to the HTTP web server. While the SELinux settings in the /var/www/html directory are slightly different, you can still use commands like **ls -Z** to identify the default SELinux contexts, and **chcon** to change the contexts in any configured subdirectory.

Of course, the Apache Web Server is an entirely different animal from any FTP server. The defaults mean when you navigate to the hostname or IP address of that server, it brings up the standard Apache HTTP Server Test Page, similar to that shown in Figure 1-19.

But to set up a system for *file sharing*, you have to go further. And you don't have to make any changes to the default configuration to do so. All you need to do is add a directory to the default, include files that you want to share, and let users know where to navigate. For example, if you set up a /var/www/html/os directory with files, users can navigate to it in their browsers at the http://*hostname*/os URL. If there are errors with this or the FTP service, check the SELinux contexts of the files that are being shared, as well as the provisions in the firewall.

The default
Apache Test Page
in the elinks
browser

```
                              Apache HTTP Server Test Page powered by CentOS (1/4)
                              Apache 2 Test Page
                              powered by CentOS
        This page is used to test the proper operation of the Apache HTTP server
        after it has been installed. If you can read this page it means that the
        Apache HTTP server installed at this site is working properly.


        _____


If you are a member of the general public:

        The fact that you are seeing this page indicates that the website you just
        visited is either experiencing problems or is undergoing routine
        maintenance.

        If you would like to let the administrators of this website know that
        you've seen this page instead of the page you expected, you should send
        them e-mail. In general, mail sent to the name "webmaster" and directed to
        the website's domain should reach the appropriate person.

OK                                                                     [······]
```

CERTIFICATION SUMMARY

The RHCSA and RHCE exams are not for beginners. This chapter helps you install a basic RHEL system on a physical host, with software that supports KVM. It also provides instructions on how to load the compressed VMs from the DVD.

Just remember, both the RHCSA and RHCE exams are practical, hands-on exercises. When you sit for either exam, you'll be faced with a live RHEL system with a series of problems to solve and systems to configure. The RHCSA covers core system administration skills. The Red Hat exams now implicitly assume the use of a 64-bit system. Red Hat configures the default VM system, KVM, only in the 64-bit build of RHEL 6.

With a subscription to the RHN, you can download RHEL installation ISO files from the associated account. Since RHEL source code is released under open source licenses, third parties have compiled and built that source code into rebuild distributions with essentially the same functionality as RHEL 6. You can also download installation ISO files from third parties such as CentOS and Scientific Linux. As they have essentially the same functionality as RHEL 6, you can also use these rebuild distributions to study for the RHCSA and RHCE exams.

Finally, this chapter describes what you need to do to unpack the compressed virtual machines and set them up within the KVM software configured for the 64-bit host system.

SELF TEST

The following fill-in-the-blank questions help you measure your understanding of the topics associated with this chapter. As there are no multiple-choice questions on the Red Hat exams, there are no multiple-choice questions in this book. If you have trouble with one or more of these questions, you may need to research associated topics further. However, there's almost always more than one way to solve a problem in Linux. Getting results, not memorizing trivia, is what counts on the Red Hat exams.

While there's content in Chapter 1, the answers to these questions may or may not be found in the body of the chapter.

The RHCSA and RHCE Exams

1. What will you see at an exam station when you sit down for the RHCSA or RHCE exams?

   _____

Basic Hardware Requirements

2. When testing hardware, what do you need to see in the /proc/cpuinfo file to confirm that a system supports hardware-assisted virtualization?

   _____

Get Red Hat Enterprise Linux

3. List a website where you can download Scientific Linux 6.

   _____

Installation Requirements

4. What do you need to set to enable communication between VMs and outside networks?

   _____

Installation Options

5. Name two of the installation options shown in the initial screen when you boot from the RHEL 6 DVD.

_____

_____

Install Virtual Machines from the DVD

6. In what directory can you find standard KVM files used for virtual hard drives?

_____

Configure a Physical Machine for Virtual Guests

7. What command in the GUI starts the Virtual Machine Manager?

_____

A Default Configuration FTP Server

8. What command installs the FTP server used for RHEL 6?

_____

A Default Configuration HTTP Server

9. What command starts the Apache Web Server?

_____

LAB QUESTIONS

The first lab requires the use of a physical 64-bit system, with hardware-assisted virtualization enabled in the BIOS or UEFI menus. The second lab builds on that system, allowing you to install KVM host software on that physical system. In the third lab, you'll have another chance to install the VMs from the DVD. The fourth and fifth labs, which can be found on the gamma.example.net system, relate to the "default" FTP and HTTP services.

If you've already installed RHEL 6 on a local system per the instructions in the body of the chapter, feel free to skip Lab 1. But to prepare for Lab 2, uninstall the following packages (and dependencies): qemu-kvm, python-virtinst, virt-manager, virt-viewer, libvirt, libvirt-client, and virt-who.

For several of these labs, having a high-speed Internet connection is helpful. Alternatively, you could set up a local repository based on the contents of the installation DVD, based on instructions available in Chapter 7 of the *Study Guide*.

Lab 1

As just suggested, the purpose of this lab is to install RHEL 6 on a physical 64-bit system. The steps in this lab assume you have a DVD of RHEL 6, or a rebuild distribution such as Scientific Linux or CentOS 6. While you can certainly install RHEL 6 over a network, or even from an ISO file on a known partition, the steps required for those methods vary.

Before you start the process, make sure there's sufficient room available on a local hard drive. Back up any data that exists on that system. If you've already installed RHEL 6 per the instructions in the chapter, this lab should be just a review. Make sure you prepare a physical host system without KVM software. You'll install KVM after installation is complete in Chapter 2.

When you get to the software installation screen, don't hesitate to include as much software as desired. (Just don't set up a virtual host, and don't install any virtualization software at this time.) While this system will function as a server, installing a desktop system as suggested does not overwrite any server functionality.

See the solution for signs of a successful installation.

Lab 2

This lab assumes you have a physical system with RHEL 6 installed without KVM, which corresponds to the system configured in Lab 1. The objective of this lab is to install the packages required to support KVM-based VMs on the local physical system. It is a prerequisite for Lab 3, where you import the VMs available in compressed format on the DVD. As suggested earlier, if you installed KVM while reading the chapter, you should uninstall associated packages first. Practice is important.

If you're truly comfortable with the objectives of this lab, you should be able to install the needed packages or package groups with either an appropriate variation to the **yum** command or the Add/Remove Software utility.

Lab 3

In this lab, you unpack and import the compressed files available from the DVD. If successful, you'll be able to open each of the three VMs from the local system, from tools such as the Virtual Machine

Manager shown previously in Figure 1-15. Do not assign any special MAC addresses, as suggested in the body of the chapter. It will lead to a configuration issue that you will solve in a later chapter.

Lab 4

You'll find this lab in the Chapter1Labs4and5.txt file on the gamma.example.net system. Once you've loaded it within KVM, log into the testuser account. As noted in Figure 1-1, the password is **rhcert**. The labs for all chapters are available in the GUI, in the ChapterLabs folder on the desktop. When you double-click on the file icon, it should open the lab in the gEdit text editor.

Lab 5

You'll find this lab in the Chapter1-Labs4and5.txt file on the gamma.example.net system. You can access this file as described in the description for Lab 4.

SELF TEST ANSWERS

The RHCSA and RHCE Exams

1. When you sit down for the RHCSA or RHCE exams, you sit down to a live installed RHEL system, with the exam available electronically.

Basic Hardware Requirements

2. When you boot any modern version of Linux, including the "live" versions of CentOS 6 and Scientific Linux 6, you should see the **vmx** or **svm** flag in the /proc/cpuinfo file. That confirms the CPU supports hardware-assisted virtualization, and the BIOS/UEFI settings have been changed if and as needed to support it.

Get Red Hat Enterprise Linux

3. There are many public websites and FTP servers from where you can download Scientific Linux 6. A list of worldwide public mirrors is available at www.scientificlinux.org/download/mirrors.

Installation Requirements

4. To enable communication between VMs and outside networks, you need to activate IP forwarding in the /proc/sys/net/ipv4/ip_forward file and make it permanent by activating the net.ipv4.ip_forward boolean in the /etc/sysctl.conf file.

Installation Options

5. The installation options shown in the initial screen when you boot from the RHEL 6 DVD are:
   - Install or upgrade an existing system.
   - Install system with basic video driver.

   For the purpose of this test, exact wording is not required, as long as the intent of the two installation options is understood.

Install Virtual Machines from the DVD

6. Normally, KVM files used for virtual hard drives are stored in the /var/lib/libvirt/images directory.

Configure a Physical Machine for Virtual Guests

7. The command that starts the Virtual Machine Manager in the GUI is **virt-manager**. It's also acceptable to suggest that the command is available from Applications | System Tools.

A Default Configuration FTP Server

8. The FTP server associated with RHEL 6 is the very secure FTP server daemon, also known by its package name, vsftpd. You can install it in one of three ways:

- Download the installation RPM and apply the **rpm -ivh** command to it. (The **rpm -i vsftpd-*** command, or a variant that installs vsftpd from a remote location, is also acceptable.)

- With an active connection to the RHN or an appropriate repository, run the **yum install vsftpd** command.

- Open the Add/Remove Software tool and select vsftpd from the Server category, FTP Server subcategory.

A Default Configuration HTTP Server

9. There are multiple commands that start the Apache Web Server, including **/etc/init.d/httpd start**, **service httpd start**, and **apachectl start**.

LAB ANSWERS

Lab 1

Success in this lab is straightforward. Once you get through the installation and first boot processes, RHEL 6 should proceed to the login screen shown in Figure 1-20. You should see the user created during the first boot process in place of the testuser user shown in the figure.

Once you log in, click Applications | System Tools. If you see the Virtual Machine Manager in the menu, you did not follow the instructions in this lab.

FIGURE I-20

GUI login screen

Lab 2

Successful completion of this lab means your system has all of the components needed to host the KVM-based virtual machines available on the DVD. There are three basic ways to make that happen:

- Run the **yum groupinstall Virtualization "Virtualization Client" "Virtualization Platform"** command.
- Install the associated packages individually with the **yum** or **rpm** commands.
- Open the Add/Remove Software tool, navigate to Virtualization in the left-hand pane, and pick appropriate packages from the three categories noted in the **yum groupinstall** command shown previously. This method is the least efficient, as it's difficult to identify the essential packages from this tool.

Lab 3

Success in this lab is straightforward. You can match success against Figure 1-15. You can also measure success with the **virsh list --all** command as the root user, which leads to the following output:

```
Id Name                    State
----------------------------------
 1 whitehat.example.net  running
 - blackhat.example.net  shut off
 - gamma.example.net     shut off
```

But given the conditions associated with the lab, you may note the network cards are all eth1, and the IP address varies from those defined in Figure 1-1. You'll address that issue in Chapter 3.

Lab 4

When implementing this lab, you may have noticed the lack of FTP clients on the VMs. That's deliberate. While you could use the Firefox web browser as an FTP client, you should install an FTP client like **lftp** for test purposes. (One way to do so is with the **yum install lftp** command.) If successful, you should be able to download the gammaftp-ks.cfg file from the whitehat.example.net system.

Of course, you're going to have to check several things:

- The IP address of the gamma.example.net system. Since the network card is eth1, it doesn't correspond to the IP address shown in Figure 1-1.
- Installation of the vsftpd server; you also need to make sure it's running. Of course, you also need to make sure it's running after the next reboot with a command like **chkconfig vsftpd on**.
- Permissions on the /var/ftp/pub/ks directory and the gammaftp-ks.cfg file therein. Make sure they support access by anonymous users.
- The SELinux contexts of the noted directory and file to the default context on the /var/ftp directory.
- An open port 21 in the firewall to support access.

Lab 5

Given the availability of Firefox on the whitehat.example.net system, this lab should be easier to handle. Of course, you have to check the same basic factors for the Apache Web Server as you did for Lab 4. The names, SELinux contexts, and port numbers are different. If successful, you'll be able to navigate to the IP address of gamma.example.net and download the gamma-install.log file from the whitehat system.

2

Virtual Machines and Automated Installations

I f you followed the instructions in Chapter 1, you should have a lab of three virtual machines (VMs) on a 64-bit system, based on KVM. Hardware-assisted virtualization should be enabled, as shown with either the **svm** or **vmx** flag in the /proc/cpuinfo file.

In this and the remaining chapters of this book, you'll first get a brief overview of each relevant objective from the RHCSA and RHCE exams. If needed, you'll be able to find a more in-depth explanation in the *Study Guide*. You'll then proceed directly to the fill-in-the-blank review questions, followed by the chapter labs. Just remember, you can find the chapter labs only on the gamma.example.net VM available from the DVD. Each lab is explained at the end of the relevant chapter.

Start and Stop Virtual Machines

There are two basic steps associated with starting a VM. First, you need to connect to the hypervisor, and second, you start the VM. You can take these actions from the command line or from the GUI.

Starting and Stopping VMs from the Command Line

From the command line, the following command starts the hypervisor and moves to the **virsh #** prompt:

```
# virsh --connect qemu:///system
```

The following command can then be used to start the noted system:

```
virsh # start whitehat.example.net
```

You can then connect to the system remotely with a protocol such as SSH. Two command-line options are available to shut down a system. The first command shuts down the noted whitehat.example.net system gracefully; the second is functionally equivalent to a power shutdown:

```
virsh # shutdown whitehat.example.net
virsh # destroy whitehat.example.net
```

Those of you who have followed RHEL 6 closely may realize that the shutdown option didn't work when RHEL 6 was first released. To exit from the **virsh #** prompt, run the **quit** command.

Starting and Stopping VMs from the GUI

Of course, starting and stopping VMs from the GUI is, for many, a more intuitive process. As noted in Chapter 1, you can open the Virtual Machine Manager (VMM) from the default RHEL 6 GUI from the Applications | System Tools menu. As a regular user, you're then prompted for the root password.

You can then right-click on the system of your choice to open a pop-up menu shown in Figure 2-1. You can then start it by clicking Run. In a similar fashion, when a system is running, you can stop a system with the Shut Down or the Destroy options.

Configure Systems to Start Virtual Machines at Boot

You can configure a system to start automatically during the boot process in two ways. From the command line, you can start a system automatically. The following command sets it up in one step, by adding a link to the gamma.example.net.xml file from the /etc/libvirt/qemu/autostart directory:

```
# virsh autostart gamma.example.net
```

FIGURE 2-1

Starting and stopping a VM in the GUI

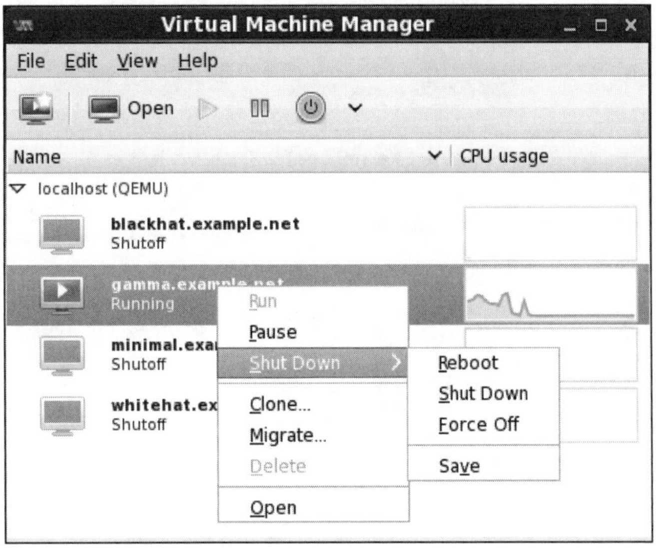

You can reverse the process with the following command:

```
# virsh autostart --disable gamma.example.net
```

In a similar fashion, you can configure the same system to start during the boot process from its GUI console. From a VMM for a specific system, click View | Details. In the screen that appears, click Boot Options to display Figure 2-2. If you select the Autostart Start Virtual Machine On Host Boot Up option, it also adds a link to the gamma.example.net.xml file from the /etc/libvirt/qemu/autostart directory.

These options depend on the operation of the **libvirtd** daemon. Make sure it's running in the appropriate runlevels the next time the system is booted.

FIGURE 2-2	Configuring Autostart in the GUI

Access a Virtual Machine's Console

There are two basic methods available to access a virtual machine's console. You can do so from the GUI, from the Virtual Network Computing (VNC) windows that open when you double-click a selected VM in the Virtual Machine Manager. You can also do so with the help of SSH, as noted in the following section.

Access Remote Systems Using SSH

If you're reading carefully, this is just half of the objective. The requirement is to "access remote systems using SSH and VNC." The VNC part of this objective is addressed in Chapter 9.

The Secure Shell (SSH) is important in Linux systems administration. It's installed by default even in minimal installations of RHEL 6. The default firewall configured for RHEL 6 includes a rule that allows access through port 22, which is the standard for SSH.

SSH includes several configuration files. For the system, you can find them in the /etc/ssh directory. As the RHCSA is more focused on the workstation, learn the options in the client configuration file, ssh_config.

For individual users, you can find SSH configuration files in individual home directories, in the hidden .ssh/ subdirectory. When administering my own systems, the related commands that I've found useful include:

- **ssh -X** Supports access to GUI tools from the command line
- **sftp** Accesses remote SSH systems with FTP-style commands and encryption
- **scp** Enables secure copying across an SSH connection

Install Red Hat Enterprise Linux Systems as Virtual Guests

The process for installing any system as a virtual guest is straightforward. If you're working from the command line, one way to do so is with the following command:

```
# virt-install --prompt
```

As suggested by the **--prompt** switch, this command prompts for required information, including the options listed in Table 2-1. It assumes the allocation of one virtual CPU core to the VM.

Alternatively, in the GUI VMM, you can right-click on the connected hypervisor. In the pop-up menu that appears, click New. You'll be taken through a five-step wizard that prompts for the information listed in Table 2-1, along with the number of virtual CPUs to allocate to the VM.

Install Red Hat Enterprise Linux Automatically Using Kickstart

A template Kickstart file is available in every RHEL 6 installation, in the root user's home directory (/root). It's shown in the anaconda-ks.cfg file. You can use that file as a template for an automated installation, or alternatively, you can set up a customized file with the help of the Kickstart Configurator in the GUI. Just be aware, that Kickstart template includes volume-related directives that are commented out by default.

Whether you work from the command line or the GUI, you have to customize the options within the Kickstart file. You have to activate the volume-related directives, change the hostname, any static IP addresses, along with any other information that should be unique to the target VM.

TABLE 2-1	Information Required by the **virt-install --prompt** Command

Required Information	Description
Virtual machine name	Specifies the name of the VM. Once created, you can list VMs on the local system with the **virsh list --all** command.
Allocated RAM	Assigns RAM to the running VM.
Path to virtual disk	Requests the full path to the virtual disk to be used. Normally should be set up in the /var/lib/libvirt/images directory, with the .img extension.
Size of the virtual disk	Specify in gigabytes.
Installation media	Specify the path to the ISO file or the URL of an installation FTP/HTTP server.

Once configured, you can set up the Kickstart file on a local or a network system. You can use the same basic options associated with the previous directive. For example, I used the following **virt-install** command to set up a minimal.example.net system from an Apache installation server on IP address 192.168.122.1, based on the minimal-ks.cfg Kickstart file, in the /var/www/html/os directory.

```
# virt-install -n minimal.example.net -r 768 --disk \
path=/var/lib/libvirt/images/minimal.example.net.img \
-l http://192.168.122.1/os/ \
-x "ks=http://192.168.122.1/os/minimal-ks.cfg"
```

Alternatively, you can use the aforementioned GUI installation tool from the VMM. If you select the Network Install option, you are prompted with a screen that supports installation from a Kickstart file, as shown in Figure 2-3.

FIGURE 2-3

Configuring a Kickstart installation in the GUI

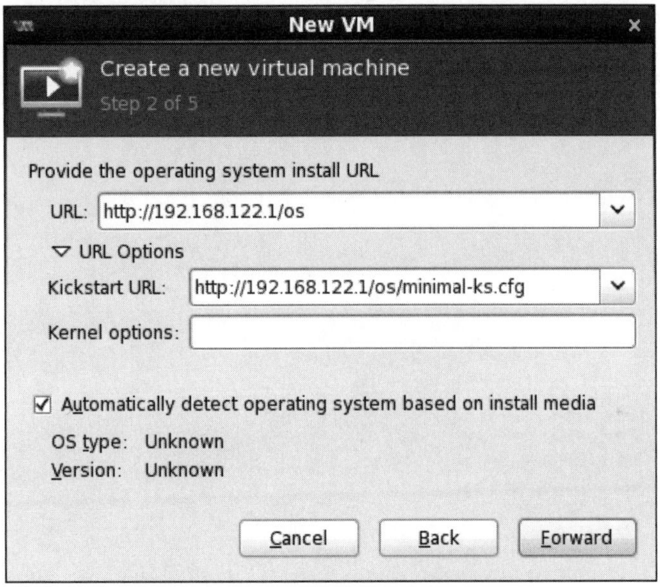

CERTIFICATION SUMMARY

The focus of this chapter is on the VM. Each relevant objective is listed as a section title. If you can work with the labs in this chapter, you should be able to work with KVM-based VMs. You'll be able to start and stop a VM. You'll be able to configure a VM to start automatically during the boot process. You'll know how to access the console of a VM. Sometimes, you'll access a VM using SSH in the same way you would access another remote system.

Of course, as this book covers the objectives of a Red Hat exam, you should know how to install RHEL 6 systems as a virtual guest. Although not limited to VMs, you should also know how to automate the process using Kickstart.

The explanation of each objective is brief. It does include hints. It is *not* intended as instruction to users who are unfamiliar with any of these objectives. For more information, see the *Study Guide*.

SELF TEST

The following fill-in-the-blank questions help you measure your understanding of the topics associated with this chapter. As there are no multiple-choice questions on the Red Hat exams, there are no multiple-choice questions in this book. If you have trouble with one or more of these questions, you may need to research associated topics further. However, there's almost always more than one way to solve a problem in Linux. Getting results, not memorizing trivia, is what counts on the Red Hat exams.

As this is a practice book, the answers to these questions may or may not be found in the body of the chapter. For more information, see the *Study Guide*.

Start and Stop Virtual Machines

1. What command would you run from the command-line to start the blackhat.example.net system?

   _____

Configure Systems to Start Virtual Machines on Boot

2. What command would you run from the command-line to make sure the blackhat.example.net KVM-based VM system starts automatically when you boot the physical host?

   _____

Access a Virtual Machine's Console

3. What types of connections can you use to access the console of a KVM-based VM?

   _____

Access Remote Systems Using SSH

4. What command would you use to connect to the testuser account on the system with IP address 192.168.122.20?

   _____

5. What command would you use to copy the abc.txt file to the testuser account, in that user's home directory on the system with IP address 192.168.122.20?

   _____

Install Red Hat Enterprise Linux Systems as Virtual Guests

6. What basic command (no switches) would you use to start the installation of a virtual guest from the command line?

_____

7. From the GUI, what command-line command starts the Virtual Machine Manager?

_____

Install Red Hat Enterprise Linux Automatically Using Kickstart

8. From the GUI command-line console, what command starts the Kickstart Configurator?

_____

LAB QUESTIONS

Red Hat presents its exams electronically. For that reason, the labs in this and future chapters are available from the gamma.example.net system, from the ChapterLabs/ folder that appears in the GUI desktop. See Chapter 1 for instructions on how to load the gamma.example.net system from the DVD, as a KVM-based VM.

SELF TEST ANSWERS

Start and Stop Virtual Machines

1. To start the blackhat.example.net system from the command line, you could run a command like **virsh start blackhat.example.net**. You can also run the **virsh** command to open the **virsh #** prompt, and then run the **start blackhat.example.net** command.

Configure Systems to Start Virtual Machines on Boot

2. To make sure the blackhat.example.net KVM-based VM system starts automatically when you boot the physical host, you can run the **virsh autostart blackhat.example.net** command. Alternatively, from the GUI, you can open the Virtual Machine Manager, open the console for the blackhat.example.net system, click View | Details, select Boot Options from the left-hand pane, and then activate the Start Virtual Machine On Host Boot Up option.

Access a Virtual Machine's Console

3. You can connect to the console of a KVM-based VM with the help of a VNC viewer. You can also access a command-line console remotely with an SSH connection.

Access Remote Systems Using SSH

4. Two options for commands that connect to the testuser account on the noted system with IP address 192.168.122.20 are

```
$ ssh testuser@192.168.122.20
$ ssh -l testuser 192.168.122.20
```

5. One command that can copy the noted file to the testuser account on the system is:

```
$ scp abc.txt testuser@192.168.122.20:
```

Several other options are available to copy the abc.txt file, including variations on the **rsync** command.

Install Red Hat Enterprise Linux Systems as Virtual Guests

6. The basic command that you use to start the installation of a virtual guest from the command line is **virt-install**.

7. From the GUI, the command-line command that starts the Virtual Machine Manager is **virt-manager**.

Install Red Hat Enterprise Linux Systems Automatically Using Kickstart

8. From the GUI, the command-line command that starts the Kickstart Configurator is **system-config-kickstart**.

LAB ANSWERS

Lab 1

One of the features of KVM is that it tries to save the current state of a VM. So if a system is running, it tries to make sure it runs again upon reboot. So while the Autostart feature ensures that a system starts on boot, you still have to shut down a system to make sure it's shut down the next time your system is booted.

Lab 2

One thing you demonstrate in this lab is the difference between the GUI and command-line tools for cloning a VM. Cloned hard drives from the VM are normally configured in the standard directory, /var/lib/libvirt/images.

When you clone a VM with the **virt-clone** command, you have to be especially careful. At the step where you specify a location for the cloned hard drive, you need to be really careful to specify the full path to the hard drive. Otherwise, that cloned hard drive will be created in the local directory, wherever that is.

If your system has limited space, delete the cloned system when you're finished with this lab. In fact, even if you have the extra space available, it may be simplest for your lab setup to limit the VMs to the three loaded from the DVD.

Lab 3

Lab 3 is like Lab 2 in some ways, as it allows you to compare the VM installation options associated with the command-line **virt-install** tool and the GUI Virtual Machine Manager. If you're not yet comfortable with the RHEL 6 installation process, this lab gives you an opportunity to practice. Twice.

Although having extra VMs available is wonderful, you may wish to delete the associated files when the process is complete. Just as with Lab 2, with the **virt-install** command, you need to specify the full path to the virtual hard drive. Otherwise, you'll find that drive file in the local directory. And you'll have to take care to keep track of that large file.

Lab 4

If you're not experienced with Kickstart configuration, some trial and error may be required. For example, if you get an error message related to a drive, check the Kickstart configuration file for directives such as **clearpart**. If the system tries to lead you through the First Boot process, it may be helpful to add options such as **firstboot --disabled** to the Kickstart configuration file.

In addition, if you mix a Kickstart file developed with one rebuild distribution such as Scientific Linux, it may include packages and/or package groups that aren't found in the package repository of a different distribution such as CentOS.

So if you encounter problems now, it's a good thing. It's best to learn what might happen here, instead of during a Red Hat exam or on the job. Of course, the ultimate objective is to set up a Kickstart configuration file that installs desired packages and creates needed settings on a system, with a minimum of human intervention.

The more you practice these scenarios, the more you'll be prepared for those surprises on the job—and yes, on the exam.

Lab 5

If you've recently run a Kickstart installation for the first time, this is your opportunity to practice, again. If you practice now, it means you'll be able to set up a Kickstart installation faster during an exam.

Here's one more scenario: use the **%post** directive, followed by a command to copy a file to the newly created VM. Just be sure to use the full path to appropriate commands.

Lab 6

This lab is designed to test your skills with the **ssh** command. With these skills in hand, you can test the gamma.example.net system from both other systems. Sure, you could access the whitehat .example.net and blackhat.example.net systems from the KVM console. But such consoles aren't always available on real networks.

Lab 7

While this lab isn't directly related to any Red Hat exam objective, it should increase your understanding of a useful tool, **nmap**. When used from outside a system, it displays ports that are open through any protective firewall. When used from inside a system, it displays the ports of active services. As suggested by their names, what you see with the **nmap** command should vary from the whitehat.example.net and blackhat.example.net systems.

Just be aware, the **nmap** developer website includes the following warning: "When used improperly, nmap can (in rare cases) get you sued, fired, expelled, jailed, or banned by your ISP."

3
Fundamental Command-Line Skills

The questions and lab exercises in this chapter are focused on basic skills. Many of these skills were actually listed as "prerequisites" in the Red Hat exam objectives for RHEL 5. While these objectives have been incorporated into the main body of the topics covered by the RHCSA, they are still skills associated with users who are newer to Linux. For that reason, these skills are also covered in little detail in the *Study Guide*.

Access a Shell Prompt and Issue Commands with Correct Syntax

As suggested by the title, you need to know how to access a shell prompt. You can run command-line commands from that prompt. Many experienced Linux users administer their systems from that prompt. Access to that prompt is trivial for these users.

The default shell for most of the major Linux distributions, including RHEL 6, is bash, short for the Bourne-Again Shell. You can access it directly by logging into the text console. You can also access it from the GUI by opening one of several available command-line screens, such as by clicking Applications | System Tools | Terminal. The default version of this terminal is associated with GNOME, known as gnome-terminal.

Normally, six consoles are available on RHEL 6 systems. You can switch between consoles by pressing CTRL-ALT plus the function key associated with the console. For example, the CTRL-ALT-F2 key combination moves to the second virtual console. When the GUI is installed, RHEL 6 assigns it to the first virtual console.

While the bash shell is the default, several other shells are available in RHEL 6, such as the ksh, dash, tcsh, and zsh shells. Commands described in this book assume the use of the bash shell. Users who run other shells may expect differences in syntax for many commands.

When you log into a shell, either from a command-line console or through a GUI option such as the gnome-terminal, it first checks with the /etc/passwd file. The default shell for your user account, as defined in that file, determines the default login shell.

Use Input/Output Redirection

With the quantity of data available, administrators often think of it as a stream that can be redirected. In fact, data is already segregated into different streams for regular output and errors. As a certified administrator, you should be able to redirect data from a file as input to another program. You should know how to redirect the output of a program to a file for later analysis and processing. To that end, standard input/output redirection operators are listed in Table 3-1.

Create, Delete, Copy, and Move Files and Directories

The objective noted is straightforward, as each action can be associated with specific commands. But first, you should already realize that everything in Linux is represented as a file. Directories are simply a version of a file that can contain other files. This summary is very brief; most of the commands listed include a significant number of switches and options.

If a file doesn't already exist, the **touch** *filename* command creates it. If a directory doesn't already exist, the **mkdir** *dirname* creates it.

The **rm** *file1* command deletes that file. The **rmdir dir1/** command deletes that directory, if it is empty. The **rm -r dir1/** command deletes that directory, with the files contained therein, *recursively*.

The **cp** *file1 file2* command takes an existing *file1* and copies the contents to *file2*. If that file already exists, it is overwritten. The **-r** switch also works recursively to help copy directories.

TABLE 3-1	Operator	Description
Redirection Operators	*command < file*	Takes the content from the file to the right of the arrow as input
	command > file	Sends standard output to the noted *file*; overwrites existing data
	command >> file	Appends standard output to the end of *file*
	command 2 > file	Sends standard error messages to the noted *file*; overwrites existing data
	command 2 >> file	Appends standard error to the end of the *file*
	*command1	command2*	Redirects the output from *command1* as standard input to *command2*

The **mv *file1 file2*** command takes an existing *file1*, copies the contents to *file2*, and then deletes *file1*. If *file2* already exists, the contents are overwritten.

While you can create files and directories at the GUI with the help of file browsers such as Nautilus, the options are all "front-ends" to the noted commands.

Create Hard and Soft Links

File links are useful in a number of ways. They can support access from different volumes. For example, RHEL 6 includes a soft link for the GRUB (Grand Unified Bootloader) configuration file, grub.conf. Although it's normally stored in the /boot/ grub directory, it's also available in the /etc directory, courtesy of a soft link. You can confirm that from the following output to the **ls -l /etc/grub.conf** command:

```
lrwxrwxrwx. 1 root root 22 Jan 20 05:30 /etc/grub.conf ->
../boot/grub/grub.conf
```

For examples of hard-linked files, look at the scripts in the /etc/init.d and the /etc/ rc.d/init.d directory. You may note that the files in each directory have the same names. If you apply the **ls -i** command to each identically named file, you'll find that each set of files has the same inode number. In other words, a hard-linked file points to the same location on a volume from two different directory locations.

The following command creates a hard link from the /etc/samba/smb.conf directory to the /tmp directory:

```
# ln /etc/samba/smb.conf /tmp/
```

In contrast, the following command creates a soft link from the /home/michael/ RHCEbook/Ch1.doc file to a file of the same name in the /home/elizabeth directory:

```
# ln -s /home/michael/RHCEbook/Ch1.doc  /home/elizabeth
```

Use grep and Regular Expressions to Analyze Text

As suggested by the title, **grep** is just one command that can be used to analyze the text in a file. Such commands can **sort** the contents of text files (yes, **sort** is a command), analyze the difference between two different files, count the amount of data in a file, substitute for common elements of text, and even manipulate text as if it were a database. The following is just a single example of each relevant command.

First, the following **grep** command identifies all users who are configured to log into the bash shell by default:

```
$ grep bash /etc/passwd
```

Some text files are long. If someone has made a change to a text file, you can use the **diff** command to compare it to a backup. The following command compares the hypothetical config.txt file from two different locations:

```
$ diff backup/config.txt /etc/config.txt
```

The **wc** command can identify word count statistics from a text file; the following command identifies the number of lines, words, and characters in the /etc/passwd file:

```
$ wc /etc/passwd
```

The **sed** command is a stream editor that supports the substitution of one set of text for another. The following command substitutes ksh for all instances of bash in the /etc/passwd file, and writes the output to the local testpass file:

```
$ sed 's/bash/ksh/g' /etc/passwd > testpass
```

Finally, the **awk** command is a type of database manipulation tool. Unlike the **grep** command, **awk** supports searches in a specific column. The following example looks through the first column for instances of *tp*, such as ftp and ntp:

```
$ awk '/tp/ {print $1}' /etc/passwd
```

Locate, Read, and Use System Documentation

Start by looking at the full objective: "Locate, read, and use system documentation using **man, info,** and files in /usr/share/doc." That's a pretty straightforward summary of system documentation available on an RHEL 6 system, if the right packages are installed. One of the first lessons for any Linux user is to read the **man** page for more information on a command. While the **info** pages for commands aren't as extensive, those that are available often have more information. The files in the /usr/share/doc directory include documentation for many installed packages. In many cases, this documentation includes licenses, author information, and basic "readme" information about the software.

But there's a second part of the objective that should give the careful reader pause: "Note: Red Hat may use applications during the exam that are not included in Red Hat Enterprise Linux for the purpose of evaluating candidate's abilities to meet this objective."

The first part of the note, "applications during the exam that are not included in Red Hat Enterprise Linux" suggests one or more packages that are not included in RHEL 6; the package could be in standard RPM format, or it could be in another format such as .tar.gz or .tar.bz2.

The second part of the note suggests that the additional package tests your understanding of man pages, info manuals, and files in the /usr/share/doc directory. To that end, make sure you know how to call man pages from different chapters, how to navigate through info manuals, and the variety of information that you might expect to find in an appropriate /usr/share/doc subdirectory.

Create and Edit Text Files

Even though it's available for RHEL 6, don't use the OpenOffice.org Writer to edit text configuration files. It's far too easy to save the file accidentally in binary format. If you make that mistake with a critical configuration file, you could render the system unbootable.

While there is no guarantee you'll have access to the GUI, it is notable that an earlier version of the RHCSA objectives included a reference to the gedit text editor, part of the GNOME desktop environment. If the default GNOME desktop environment is installed, you can install the gedit package, and then access the editor from the Applications | Accessories menu.

The use of the gedit text editor is trivial for Linux users with any experience. Just be prepared to run alternatives such as **vi** or **nano** if the GUI is not available. While you don't need to become an expert on either editor, you should know how to do at least three things with one of the editors:

- Quit without saving; if you make a mistake, that can help you start fresh.
- Go into and exit from edit mode.
- Save changes into the current or a different file.

Start, Stop, and Check the Status of Network Services

On the surface, starting, stopping, and checking the status of a network service is simple. Associated scripts in the /etc/init.d directory support these options, and sometimes more. The following commands perform each function on the network service:

```
# /etc/init.d/network start
# /etc/init.d/network stop
# /etc/init.d/network status
```

The **service** command supports the same functionality; for example, the following command displays the current status of the vsFTP server:

```
# service vsftpd status
```

But sometimes, you have to go a bit further. A network service may be running, yet still be inaccessible in some fashion. If a network service is stopped, then perhaps networking is not working for some other reason, such as a misconfigured firewall or SELinux boolean. To that end, you need to know how to use commands like **ifconfig**, **ping**, **route**, and **traceroute**. The actual configuration of a network is covered in the final objective in this chapter.

However, you should not forget the /etc/sysconfig/network file. The following option activates networking with the help of the /etc/init.d/network script.

```
NETWORKING=yes
```

Configure Networking and Hostname Resolution

As suggested by the title, this is two interrelated topics. Whereas network configuration is associated with the network addresses of a system and a network, hostnames are associated with the human-readable names of the system and network. The full objective states: "Configure networking and hostname resolution statically or dynamically." In other words, you need to know how to set up both IP addresses and hostnames to some constant (static), or to take IP addresses and hostnames from a remote server, normally a Dynamic Host Configuration Protocol (DHCP) server. This objective, as originally written for the RHCSA, was more detailed:

- Manage network devices: understand basic IP networking/routing, configure IP addresses/default route statically or dynamically.
- Manage name resolution: set local hostname, configure /etc/hosts, configure to use existing DNS server.

The first network configuration file is /etc/sysconfig/network. As stated earlier, that file allows you to activate networking with the **NETWORKING=yes** directive. It also includes the hostname for the system. Configuration files for individual network cards are stored in the /etc/sysconfig/network-scripts directory. The key files are associated with network card devices; for example, the ifcfg-eth0 file sets configuration options for the eth0 network device. It can be set to access information from a DHCP server, or it can include static IP address information. The format of the /etc/hosts file includes IP addresses with hostnames and fully qualified domain names; it's effectively a static database.

Hostname resolution, which determines how a system finds an IP address, is configured first in the /etc/nsswitch.conf file. The following directive means that the local system looks first in the /etc/hosts file and then looks for IP address information from a DNS server:

```
hosts:    files  dns
```

You can configure the DNS servers to be searched in the /etc/resolv.conf file. The following directive in that file points to the DNS server configured on the noted IP address:

```
nameserver 192.168.122.1
```

You can edit these files directly, or you can use the RHEL 6 network configuration tools. To start the console-based tool, run the **system-config-network** command. To start the GUI-based Network Connections tool, run the **nm-connection-editor** command.

CERTIFICATION SUMMARY

While this chapter covered a substantial number of objectives associated with the RHCSA exam, most of them relate to fundamental command-line skills. As the Red Hat exams tests your ability to configure a system, these skills are, in most cases, just configuration tools.

Anyone who can get to the command line knows how to access a shell prompt. Anyone who has even a little experience at the command line can issue commands with correct syntax. It takes a bit more skill to redirect a stream of data to a file or another command. Other fundamental skills involve the use of commands such as **touch**, **cp**, **rm**, **mv**, and **mkdir**. Hard and soft links that you create with the **ln** command can also be useful. Commands like **grep**, **awk**, and **wc** can help analyze the contents of a text file.

While the use of system documentation with the **man** and **info** commands should be trivial, the Red Hat warning in the objectives should make you focus on the details. When editing a text file, use a text editor such as **vi, nano,** or **gedit**. When you manage a network service, go beyond the start, stop, and status options. When you configure networking and hostname resolution, pay attention to the configuration files, as well as associated command-line and GUI tools.

SELF TEST

The following fill-in-the-blank questions help you measure your understanding of the topics associated with this chapter. As there are no multiple-choice questions on the Red Hat exams, there are no multiple-choice questions in this book. If you have trouble with one or more of these questions, you may need to research associated topics further. However, there's almost always more than one way to solve a problem in Linux. Getting results, not memorizing trivia, is what counts on the Red Hat exams.

As this is a practice book, the answers to these questions may or may not be found in the body of the chapter. For more information, see the *Study Guide*.

Access a Shell Prompt and Issue Commands with Correct Syntax

1. What file contains the default shell for each user?

   _____

Use Input/Output Redirection

2. If you want to append the output of the **who** command to the file named logins, what command would you run?

   _____

Create, Delete, Copy, and Move Files and Directories

3. What command renames the /home/testuser/test1 directory to /home/testuser/test2?

   _____

Create Hard and Soft Links

4. What command creates a soft link from the ifcfg-eth0 file in the /etc/sysconfig/network-scripts directory to the /home/testuser directory?

   _____

Use grep and Regular Expressions to Analyze Text

5. What command identifies lines with the letters EE (which is associated with errors) in the /var/log/Xorg.0.log file?

_____

Locate, Read, and Use System Documentation

6. What packages are associated with man pages? (Note: although the solution isn't in the _Study Guide_, the answers can help you if man pages are missing from an RHEL 6 installation.)

_____

Create and Edit Text Files

7. Name a command that opens a console text editor from the command-line interface.

_____

Start, Stop, and Check the Status of Network Services

8. What command verifies the status of the Samba service? Hint: it's controlled by the smb script in the /etc/init.d directory.

_____

Configure Networking and Hostname Resolution

9. What is the full path to the configuration file that includes the IP address for the local DNS server?

_____

LAB QUESTIONS

Red Hat presents its exams electronically. For that reason, the labs in this and future chapters are available from the gamma.example.net system, from the ChapterLabs/ folder that appears in the GUI desktop. If you're running in a command-line console, you can find the labs in the /home/testuser/ Desktop/ChapterLabs directory.

SELF TEST ANSWERS

Access a Shell Prompt and Issue Commands with Correct Syntax

1. The file that contains the default shell for each user is /etc/passwd.

Use Input/Output Redirection

2. To append the output of the **who** command to the file named logins, you run the **who >> logins** command.

Create, Delete, Copy, and Move Files and Directories

3. One command is **mv /home/testuser/test1 /home/testuser/test2**; you could also first run the **cd /home/testuser** command before running **mv test1 test2**.

Create Hard and Soft Links

4. One command is **ln -s /etc/sysconfig/network-scripts/ifcfg-eth0 /home/testuser**. Just be aware, if /etc and /home are configured on different volumes, hard links won't work.

Use grep and Regular Expressions to Analyze Text

5. If you ever have a problem with starting the GUI, commands like **grep EE /var/log/Xorg.0.log** can help you identify any problems that appear with the X server.

Locate, Read, and Use System Documentation

6. Two such packages are man and man pages. If you don't see a man page that you expect on a system, don't hesitate to try installing these packages. Other man pages are included in functional packages; for example, Samba-related man pages are installed with the Samba package.

Create and Edit Text Files

7. Several answers are acceptable. The **vi** and **nano** commands start console text editors of the same name. Other acceptable commands include **emacs**, **joe**, and **pico**. Just remember, your favorite text editor may not be installed by default on RHEL 6.

Start, Stop, and Check the Status of Network Services

8. Two acceptable answers are **/etc/init.d/smb status** and **service smb status**.

Configure Networking and Hostname Resolution

9. The configuration file that includes the IP address for the local DNS server is /etc/resolv.conf.

LAB ANSWERS

Lab 1

If successful, you'll have already found the Chapter3a-labs.txt file on the gamma.example.net system, in the /usr/share/doc/book-1.0.0 directory. Remember the relevant objective: "Locate, read, and use system documentation including man, info, and files in /usr/share/doc," along with the warning "Note: Red Hat may use applications during the exam that are not included in Red Hat Enterprise Linux for the purpose of evaluating candidate's abilities to meet this objective."

Lab 2

This lab is an exercise in network configuration. It lets you examine the situation on the gamma. example.net system as loaded from the DVD. Unless you changed the MAC address of the network card to the original as defined for the eth0 device, your gamma.example.net system should be configured with an eth1 device. It should also show up in the GUI configuration tool as an auto eth1 wired device.

When you use the GUI configuration to modify the auto eth1 device, that configuration should be added to a file in the /etc/sysconfig/network-scripts directory. (The filename depends on the changes that you make with the GUI tool.) In addition, you should also see the device configured in the console-based tool, which you can access with the **system-config-network** command.

Make sure to shut down the gamma.example.net system, remove the current virtual network card, and replace it with a new network card. As suggested in the lab, the easiest way to do so is with the Virtual Machine Manager. In the gamma.example.net system window, click View | Details. As shown in Figure 3-1, you can highlight the Network Interface Card (NIC), and then click Remove. When you click Add Hardware, you can then add a new NIC, with the MAC hardware address defined in Chapter 1.

The address of the gamma.example.net system is 52:54:00:b8:a7:ea. The next time you boot that system, it should reflect the configuration described in Chapter 1, with a static IP address of 192.168.122.20.

FIGURE 3-1   Hardware on the gamma.example.net system

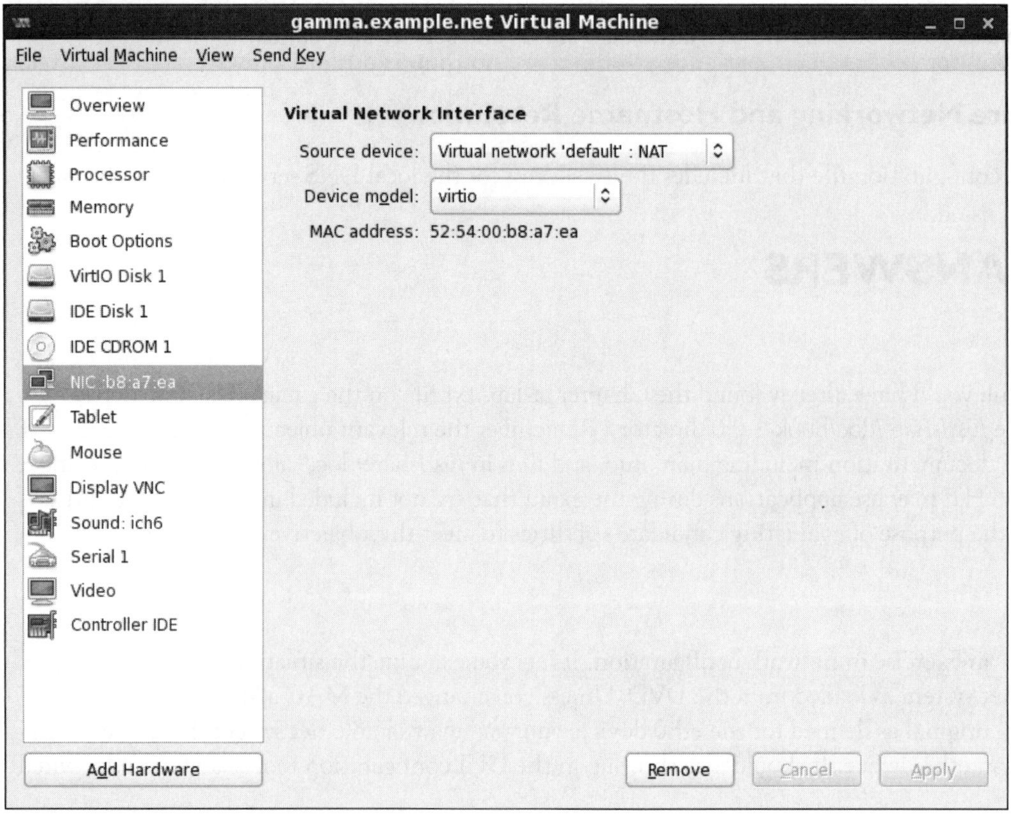

One more task for you: review the ifcfg-eth0 file in the /etc/sysconfig/network-scripts directory for the HWADDR parameter. Compare that to the hardware address shown in the output to the **ifconfig eth0** command.

Lab 3

In this lab, you should have taken the same basic steps for the whitehat.example.net system. Of course, the MAC hardware and IP addresses should vary from the gamma.example.net system. To measure success, boot the system, and confirm that the eth0 network card is active, with a hardware address of 52:54:00:ec:81:11, and an IP address of 192.168.122.130.

Lab 4

Once this lab is complete, you should have three VMs, loaded from the DVD, each configured with an active eth0 network card. You should be able to confirm the information shown in Table 3-2.

Lab 5

If successful, you'll see something similar to the following information in the /etc/hosts file on all three VMs listed in Table 3-2:

```
127.0.0.1    localhost localhost.localdomain localhost4 localhost4.localdomain4
::1          localhost localhost.localdomain localhost6 localhost6.localdomain6
192.168.122.20 gamma gamma.example.net
192.168.122.130 whitehat whitehat.example.net
192.168.122.240 blackhat blackhat.example.net
```

In addition, you should be able to verify the results with appropriate commands such as **ping**. For example, you should be able to run the **ping gamma** or the **ping gamma.example.net** commands from any of the three systems.

Lab 6

Here are the lessons you should learn from this lab:

■ The /etc/resolv.conf file includes the **nameserver** directive, which points to the DNS server(s) used for the local system.

■ The IP address for the KVM physical host can function as a caching DNS server, forwarding new requests to the DNS server configured on the host's /etc/resolv.conf file.

Remember to restore the **nameserver 192.168.122.1** directive to the /etc/resolv.conf file on the gamma.example.net system.

TABLE 3-2	Hardware and IP Addresses for Configured KVM-based VMs	
System	**MAC Address**	**IP Address**
gamma.example.net	52:54:00:b8:a7:ea	192.168.122.20
whitehat.example.net	52:54:00:ec:81:11	192.168.122.130
blackhat.example.net	52:54:00:9e:e2:28	192.168.122.240

Lab 7

While IP forwarding is not required to enable communication between VMs, it can be a terrific convenience. You then have access to either the Red Hat Network, or repositories associated with Scientific Linux or CentOS for installing new packages or updates. You never have to worry about loading the installation DVD.

But as Internet access would defeat the security associated with the Red Hat exams, you may want to disable IP forwarding on the physical host to isolate the network of VMs. Of course, that would require the configuration of a local network installation server, as described in Chapters 1 and 7 of the *Study Guide*.

4

RHCSA-Level Security Options

Τ he objectives at the heart of this chapter are focused on security. They start with the basic read, write, and execute permissions on a file, as they relate to user and group owners. They include features such as Access Control Lists (ACLs), and go on to fundamental skills associated with Security Enhanced Linux (SELinux). If you're comfortable with the objectives and labs in this chapter, you should be confident in your knowledge of Red Hat objectives as they relate to basic security.

List, Set, and Change Standard ugo/rwx Permissions

The basic ownership and permissions associated with Linux files are known as *discretionary access controls*. The discretion is in the permissions, where *ugo* represents the three groups of owners associated with a file: *users, groups,* and *others*. In contrast, the *rwx* represents the three basic permissions associated with a file: *read, write,* and *execute*.

Each group of owners may be assigned a different set of rwx permissions. For example, the following output suggests the user account that owns the config file has read, write, and execute permissions on that file. In contrast, users who are members of the proctors group have read and execute permissions. All other users have just read permissions on that file named config. Here is an example output from the **ls -l** *config* command:

```
-rwxr-xr--. 1 michael proctors  1754132 Jan 14  2011 config
```

You should be aware of what you might see in the output for the **ls -l** command, as it relates to different types of files, different user and group owners, as well as special super user and super group ID (SUID and SGID) permissions.

Finally, you should understand that the default set of permissions on a file and/or a directory are determined by the value of **umask**, which is normally set to different values for regular users and the root administrative user. Other key commands associated with this objective are **chmod**, **chown**, and **chgrp**. You may also appreciate the specialized file attributes that are shown with the **lsattr** command, which can be changed with the **chattr** command.

Diagnose and Correct File Permission Problems

With the commands described in the previous section, you should know how to diagnose and correct any problems that may exist with file permissions and, by implication, file ownership.

Some file permission problems are straightforward. For example, if you want to edit a file that is already owned by your user account, write permissions are required on that file. You can set such permissions as needed with the **chmod** command. To correct such problems, you need to know the formats that can be used with the **chmod** command, such as octal format or by user. For example, while the following command sets read permissions for all users on the local file named config:

```
$ chmod 444 config
```

this next command adds read permissions for all users on that same file, without overriding any other write or execute permissions that might already exist on that file:

```
$ chmod a+r config
```

If you see the following error message when trying to delete a file, the first issue that you should check is permissions and then ownership of that file.

```
rm: cannot remove `local.conf': Operation not permitted
```

However, that file can also be protected by the "immutable" bit, which prevents even the root administrative user from directly deleting that file. Of course, that root user can unset the immutable bit with the help of the **chattr** command. But that forces the root user to see what attribute bits are set on a file with the **lsattr** command.

If you want to transfer ownership of files to another user, the **chown** command can be helpful. The **chgrp** command performs the same function for the group owner of a file. The **chown** command can be used to change the user and group owners of a file simultaneously.

Create and Manage Access Control Lists (ACLs)

With ACLs, you can set up custom permissions on a file. But ACLs work only on filesystems mounted with the **acl** option. Once active, you can read the ACLs of a file with the **getfacl** command. You may note that the baseline ACLs for a file match its read, write, and execute permissions.

To make ACLs work, you need to set them on a directory and target files. Review the switches for the **setfacl** command in Table 4-1.

To make sure you understand ACLs, try configuring a file in a home directory for one user. Set up access for a second user. Try limiting access to files in the /etc directory to that same user. Once you've confirmed success, make sure you know how to restore the original ACL settings for the target files and directories.

Configure Firewall Settings Using system-config-firewall or iptables

The **system-config-firewall** command starts a firewall configuration tool. While the look and feel of the tool varies depending on whether you're working from the console or the GUI, they have essentially the same functionality. In addition, these tools are front ends to the **iptables** command. As the effect of **iptables** is limited to IPv4 networks, you can limit your focus to firewalls as they relate to IPv4 networking.

TABLE 4-1	Switch	Description
Switches for the setfacl Command	-b (--remove-all)	Removes all ACL entries; retains standard ugo/rwx permissions
	-k	Deletes default ACL entries
	-m	Modifies the ACL of a file, normally with a specific user (u) or group (g)
	-n (--mask)	Omits the mask in recalculating permissions
	-R	Applies changes recursively
	-x	Removes a specific ACL entry

Although firewall rules are based on TCP/IP ports as defined in the /etc/services file, they can also be configured to limit access by transport-level protocol, IP address, network device, and more. The default firewall for RHEL 6 supports access to a local SSH server.

In most cases, all you need to use is the Firewall Configuration tool. In its Trusted Services section, it includes options that help you configure access to a variety of services on the local system. Other options in this tool are more closely associated with RHCE objectives. If you need to set up a specialized rule, the tool includes a Custom Rules section that supports access to a custom configuration file beyond /etc/sysconfig/iptables.

Some users know the **iptables** command inside and out. If you can configure firewall rules in your sleep, just remember to save any rules that you configure to the /etc/sysconfig/iptables file. The **iptables-save** command can list currently implemented rules. If you forward it to the noted file, the same rules will be run the next time your system is booted. Of course, you should remember that **iptables** is also another network service, and you need to make sure it runs when you boot into standard runlevels.

on the job

One way to test the characteristics of a firewall is with the nmap and telnet commands. The nmap command can test open ports from a remote system. The telnet command can test access to individual services on a specific port. Just be aware the use of such tools on systems administered by others may be subject to legal restrictions.

Set Enforcing and Permissive Modes for SELinux

SELinux has an undeserved reputation for difficulty. Red Hat has done a lot of work to make SELinux easier to manage. As someone who is studying the RHCSA objectives, you shouldn't be intimidated by SELinux. This first of five SELinux-based RHCSA objectives is straightforward. There are three modes available for SELinux: *enforcing, permissive,* and *disabled.*

In enforcing mode, rule violations can stop a service from working. For example, if the SELinux contexts on a file server described in Chapter 1 aren't appropriate, users can't download files over that server.

In permissive mode, users can download those files, but audit messages will be sent to the /var/log/audit directory. For current SELinux settings, run the **sestatus** command. Normally, you see the following output:

```
SELinux status:                 enabled
SELinuxfs mount:                /selinux
Current mode:                   enforcing
Mode from config file:          enforcing
Policy version:                 24
Policy from config file:        targeted
```

on the
(j) o b

If you have to change the SELinux status from disabled to enabled, you have to reboot to implement the change. The relabeling process associated with enabling SELinux may add several minutes to the time required to reboot the system.

You could change the post-reboot status of SELinux in the /etc/sysconfig/selinux file with the SELINUX directive. As noted in the file comments, it can be set to enforcing, permissive, or disabled. As the focus is on targeted policies, it's fair to expect SELINUXTYPE=targeted. If you want to change the status of SELinux before a reboot, you can run the **setenforce permissive** or **setenforce enforcing** commands.

If you want SELinux configuration and error analysis tools, install the associated packages. One way to do so is with the following command:

```
# yum install policycoreutils-gui setools-gui setroubleshoot-server
```

While the command focuses on GUI tools, it also installs related command-line tools. As with most other Linux GUI tools, they're front ends to what you'd run at the command-line interface.

List and Identify SELinux File and Process Context

The operation of SELinux is secured by its contexts. As suggested by the objective, SELinux contexts apply to both files and processes. To review the SELinux contexts of files in the current directory, run the **ls -Z** command. To review the SELinux contexts of all running processes, run the **ps -eZ** command.

Much of the work of SELinux is in the configuration of file contexts. As you can see from this sample output of the **ls -Z** command, there are four categories of file contexts: user, role, type, and level, as defined in Table 4-2.

```
drwxr-xr-x. root root system_u:object_r:httpd_sys_content_t:s0 html
```

While the output from the **ps -eZ** command may appear more complex, the output lists the same categories of SELinux contexts as shown in Table 4-2. While most desktop process contexts are not defined, service contexts are frequently defined with an appropriate file-type label. For example, kernel contexts may be associated with the kernel_t file type.

Restore Default File Contexts

Given the large number of SELinux file contexts, especially file types, it can be helpful to know how to restore a default file context. The key command for this objective is **restorecon**.

The default file contexts in most directories is defined in a file_contexts file, in the /etc/selinux/targeted/contexts directory. Although you could edit this file directly, it's customary to add special file contexts to the file_contexts.local file in the same directory. The SELinux Administration tool that you can start with the **system-config-selinux** command has a File Labeling section that implements changes in the file_contexts.local file. Alternately, you could use the **semanage fcontext -a** command to implement those changes, as described in one of the RHCE objectives in Chapter 11.

The **restorecon -F** command is frequently applied to individual files or the contents of entire directories. It looks for the contexts as defined in the aforementioned files in the /etc/selinux/targeted/contexts directory.

TABLE 4-2	Context	Description
SELinux File Contexts	user	Typically either **system_u** or **unconfined_u**.
	role	While intended for use as role-based access control, most files are set to the **object_r** role. Many processes are associated with a **system_r** role.
	type	Highly customized—different file types are normally configured for different services.
	level	Associated with multilevel security; expect many different levels of security sensitivity in the future.

While the file_contexts file doesn't directly address all directories, subdirectories are assumed to inherit the default context of higher level directories. For example, the /srv directory is configured with **system_u**, **object_r**, **var_t**, and **s0** contexts. If you create a /srv/www subdirectory, it inherits those same contexts.

Use Boolean Settings to Modify System SELinux Settings

Boolean settings are associated with the functionality of a number of services. To get a taste of what SELinux booleans can do, review the files in the /selinux/booleans directory. This is a virtual directory, filled with options that can be enabled. For example, the **virt_use_usb** boolean supports access from KVM-based VMs to USB devices that may be connected to the host system. Read the contents of that file with the following command:

```
$ getsebool virt_use_usb
```

Unless the default has been changed, you should see **virt_use_usb --> on** in the output, which means the boolean is active. If you want a full list of active and disabled booleans, run the **getsebool -a** command.

While some SELinux options are further explained in man pages such as ftpd_selinux, standard online documentation isn't available for all SELinux booleans. However, that's one area where the SELinux Administration tool, shown in Figure 4-1, can make life easier. In that figure, the Boolean category is highlighted, the file from the /selinux/booleans directory is shown, with a description and module. For example, the explanation for the **virt_use_usb** boolean is "Allow virt to use USB devices," on the virt module.

Diagnose and Address Routine SELinux Policy Violations

When a service has a problem, and you're certain that the configuration of the service is correct, the next step is to check the audit.log file in the /var/lib/audit directory. Files in this directory are filled when SELinux identifies actions that violate SELinux policies. The contents of this file may seem cryptic. And it includes all SELinux messages, successes along with failures. While the **seaudit** command, by default, opens a GUI view of recent "denied" messages, the contents are still cryptic.

FIGURE 4-1   The SELinux Administration tool

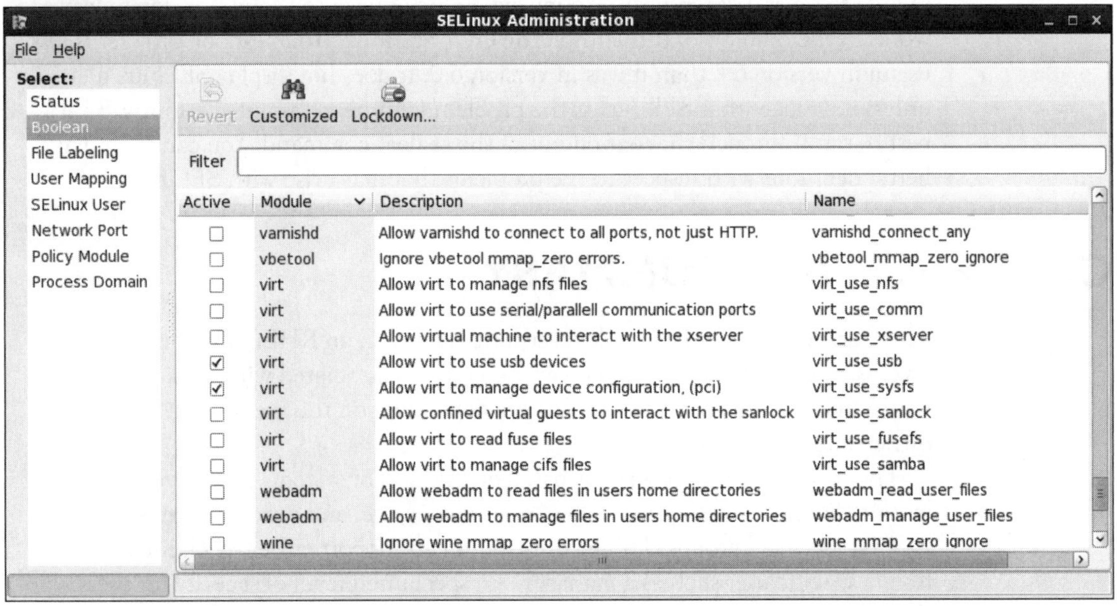

To help users manage SELinux, Red Hat has included the **sealert** command. The following variation on that command can be used to process the current audit.log file:

```
# sealert -a /var/log/audit/audit.log
```

Just be aware, the noted command may take a couple of minutes or so to process a *normal* SELinux audit.log file. The following is one useful excerpt, based on a failed network installation of RHEL 6. The last line even suggests one method for addressing the problem.

```
SELinux is preventing /usr/sbin/vsftpd from read access on the file /var/ftp/
pub/os/images/install.img.
*****  Plugin restorecon (85.9 confidence) suggests  *****************
If you want to fix the label.
/var/ftp/pub/os/images/install.img default label should be public_content_t.
Then you can run restorecon.
Do
# /sbin/restorecon -v /var/ftp/pub/os/images/install.img
```

Be aware, the output to the **sealert** command could easily include messages related to several dozen errors. In my experience, suggested solutions don't always work. In the opinion of this author, the GUI SELinux Troubleshoot Browser is less useful in version 6.2 than it was in version 6.0. It does not display SELinux alerts unless it deduces that SELinux is the problem with near absolute certainty. So it's best to scroll through the text output of the **sealert** command. You can then make better decisions with respect to the problems that may arise with SELinux.

CERTIFICATION SUMMARY

There are four basic RHCSA-level security layers on an RHEL 6 system. The first layer is based on the discretionary access controls associated with files. Those read, write, and execute permissions may vary depending on the user owner, the group owner, and other users.

The second layer of security is based on ACLs. For systems that have been mounted with the **acl** option, you can set read, write, and execute permissions for specific users and groups. Those permissions can support either specialized access from a specific user such as a manager or a specialized level of security for users who should have limited levels of access. Remember to set the appropriate execute bit on any directory for which you want to set an ACL.

The third layer of security is based on the firewall. By default, RHEL 6 blocks all but the most essential access from all external systems. The one service that is open through the default firewall is SSH. The Firewall Configuration tool makes it relatively easy to set up access to other ports.

The fourth layer of security described in this chapter relates to SELinux. One objective suggests that you must be ready to set up SELinux in enforcing or permissive mode. At the RHCSA level, the essence of SELinux is based on labels for each file, as well as boolean options. You can set labels with the **chcon** command and restore them to the default with the **restorecon** command. The key troubleshooting command is **sealert -a**, which can process the logs in the /var/log/audit directory into something more useful, often including suggested commands that may address any SELinux issues.

SELF TEST

The following fill-in-the-blank questions help you measure your understanding of the topics associated with this chapter. As there are no multiple-choice questions on the Red Hat exams, there are no multiple-choice questions in this book. If you have trouble with one or more of these questions, you may need to research associated topics further. However, there's almost always more than one way to solve a problem in Linux. Getting results, not memorizing trivia, is what counts on the Red Hat exams.

   As this is a practice book, the answers to these questions may or may not be found in the body of the chapter. For more information, see the *Study Guide*.

List, Set, and Change Standard ugo/rwx Permissions

   1. What command deactivates write permissions for all users on the file named readonly in the /home/testuser directory? Assume ACLs are not available for this filesystem.

   _____

Diagnose and Correct File Permission Problems

   2. When you create a script named admin in a text file, what command makes it executable for just the user who owns that file? Assume file admin is located in the current directory.

   _____

Create and Manage Access Control Lists (ACLs)

   3. Assume /home has been mounted with the **acl** option, and the executable bit has been set in the /home/testuser directory. What command allows user elizabeth, and only user elizabeth, read access to the file named secrets in that directory?

   _____

Configure Firewall Settings Using system-config-firewall or iptables

   4. What local service is accessible from remote systems, by default, on standard RHEL 6 systems?

   _____

Set Enforcing and Permissive Modes for SELinux

5. What file includes SELinux enforcing or permissive options that are read during the boot process?

_____

List and Identify SELinux File and Process Context

6. What command lists the SELinux context for all currently running processes?

_____

Restore Default File Contexts

7. What file includes the default SELinux file contexts for the /home directory?

_____

Use Boolean Settings to Modify System SELinux Settings

8. What GUI tool includes a description of each SELinux boolean setting?

_____

Diagnose and Address Routine SELinux Policy Violations

9. What file contains information logged from violations of SELinux policy? Specify the full path to this file.

_____

LAB QUESTIONS

Red Hat presents its exams electronically. For that reason, the labs in this and future chapters are available from the gamma.example.net system, from the ChapterLabs/ folder that appears in the GUI desktop. If you're running in a command-line console, you can find the labs in the /home/testuser/ Desktop/ChapterLabs directory.

The answers for each lab follow the Self Test Answers for the fill-in-the-blank questions.

SELF TEST ANSWERS

List, Set, and Change Standard ugo/rwx Permissions

1. Several variations on the following command are acceptable; if you run a different command, just make sure the write bit is not active for the readonly file.

```
# chmod -w /home/testuser/readonly
```

Diagnose and Correct File Permission Problems

2. While there are alternatives, the following command is the only sure way to avoid changing any other permission bits on the file for any other users.

```
# chmod u+x admin
```

Create and Manage Access Control Lists (ACLs)

3. The following **setfacl** command modifies (**-m**) the ACL settings for user (**u**) elizabeth, granting her read privileges on the noted file.

```
# setfacl -m u:elizabeth:r /home/testuser/secrets
```

Configure Firewall Settings Using system-config-firewall or iptables

4. Port 22 is the only port open in the default RHEL 6 firewall; it's associated with SSH. Also known as the Secure Shell service, SSH is accessible by default on standard RHEL 6 systems.

Set Enforcing and Permissive Modes for SELinux

5. The noted configuration file is /etc/sysconfig/selinux.

List and Identify SELinux File and Process Context

6. The **ps -eZ** command lists the SELinux context for all currently running processes.

Restore Default File Contexts

7. The file with SELinux file contexts for the /home directory is file_contexts.homedirs, in the /etc/selinux/targeted/contexts/files directory.

Use Boolean Settings to Modify System SELinux Settings

8. The SELinux configuration tool is the SELinux Management tool. One way to start it is with the **system-config-selinux** command.

Diagnose and Address Routine SELinux Policy Violations

9. The SELinux log file is /var/log/audit/audit.log.

LAB ANSWERS

Lab I

This is a straightforward lab testing your skills with ownership and permissions. If successful, you'll see something similar to the following output to the **ls -l /shared/test1** command:

```
-rw-r--r--. 1 testuser root 0 Feb 21 12:08 test1
```

Since I created the test1 file with the **touch** command, it has no content and is, therefore, 0 bytes, as shown in the output. It's acceptable if the file is of some different size. It's also acceptable if the group owner of the file is other than root. (Yes, the file is writable by the users named testuser and root, but it should be understood that the root user is all-powerful.)

Lab 2

To set up any filesystem for ACLs, you should set it up in the /etc/fstab directory. Technically, since /home is already mounted without ACLs in /etc/fstab, you could also set up a **mount -o remount /home** command in a file like /etc/rc.local. But the most efficient way to set up /home in the /etc/fstab for the gamma.example.net system is to set it up in /etc/fstab. In that file, you might see an entry like the following:

```
UUID=7f01c595-ecf7-4abf-b0fa-abc4c8b5234b /home    ext4   defaults   1 2
```

To set up ACLs, all you need to do is add **acl** to the fourth column:

```
UUID=7f01c595-ecf7-4abf-b0fa-abc4c8b5234b /home    ext4   defaults,acl   1 2
```

The next time the system boots, it automatically incorporates ACL capabilities into the /home directory filesystem. You could implement it prior to reboot with a command like the following:

```
# mount -o remount,acl /home
```

Yes, it's possible that the default configuration of the /home directory already has ACL as a default mount option. If /home is mounted on /dev/vda3, you could confirm that with the **dumpe2fs /dev/vda3 | grep acl** command. But you also need to know how to set up ACLs in /etc/fstab.

Lab 3

Assuming you've run Lab 2 as directed, ACLs are now available for the /home directory filesystem. In the /home/testuser/Desktop/ChapterLabs directory, you'll have a number of different files. If you want to focus on a specific file, focus on testaudit.log.

To support directory access from other users, you need to set the execute bit on all subdirectories. The /home directory already has that bit active for other users. One way to set up the execute bit for the other directories in line is with the following command, which sets the execute bit, recursively, for user testuser2, starting with the /home/testuser directory and all subdirectories.

```
# setfacl -R -m u:testuser2:x /home/testuser
```

Per the conditions stated in the lab, it is acceptable to set the regular execute bit on the noted directories with the regular **chmod** command. But that is a security risk as it allows all users to see what files exist in the /home/testuser directory.

Of course, you also need to set read privileges for the user named testuser2. One way to do so is with the following command:

```
setfacl -m u:testuser2:r /home/testuser/Desktop/ChapterLabs/testaudit.log
```

You should be able to test the result from the testuser2 account.

Lab 4

While **nmap** is not cited in the Red Hat objectives, it's an excellent way to verify active services and access through a firewall. Depending on what you have configured on the gamma.example.net system, the **nmap localhost** command on that system should reveal output similar to the following:

```
PORT     STATE SERVICE
21/tcp   open  ftp
22/tcp   open  ssh
25/tcp   open  smtp
111/tcp  open  rpcbind
631/tcp  open  ipp
```

Compare that to the output of the **nmap 192.168.122.20** command from the whitehat.example. net system. Depending on what you've already opened in the gamma.example.net firewall, it might look something like the following:

```
PORT    STATE SERVICE
21/tcp  open  ftp
22/tcp  open  ssh
```

In this case (yours may differ), you need to open TCP ports 25, 111, and 631. You can open all three through the Firewall Configuration tool. TCP ports 25 and 631 are easy to open in the Trusted Services section. You can set up TCP port 111 in the Other Ports section. When successful, the **nmap** commands from within the gamma.example.net system and from outside the whitehat.example.net system should match.

Lab 5

You should see two outputs from the **sestatus** command. When permissive mode is active, you see the following:

```
SELinux status:              enabled
SELinuxfs mount:             /selinux
Current mode:                permissive
Mode from config file:       enforcing
Policy version:              24
Policy from config file:     targeted
```

When you're done, the one difference is in the current mode:

```
SELinux status:              enabled
SELinuxfs mount:             /selinux
Current mode:                enforcing
Mode from config file:       enforcing
Policy version:              24
Policy from config file:     targeted
```

Lab 6

To set up files in the /srv/www directory with file contexts associated with the RHEL 6 FTP server, you need to set up the same contexts associated with the /var/ftp/pub directory. One method for doing so is with the following command:

```
# chcon /srv/www/* --reference /var/ftp/pub/
```

To confirm, run the **ls -Z /srv/www** and **ls -Z /var/ftp** commands. The SELinux contexts of the files shown should match.

Lab 7

One way to restore the default contexts in the /srv/www directory is with the following command:

```
# restorecon -R /srv/www
```

It uses the contexts defined in the file_contexts file in the /etc/selinux/targeted/contexts/files directory. By default, that means the SELinux contexts in the /srv/www directory should match those in the /var/www/html directory.

Lab 8

This lab assumes you've already installed the default FTP server, as suggested by one of the objectives cited in Chapter 1. Of course, you've made sure that server is running and will start after reboot. One way to do so is with the following commands:

```
# /etc/init.d/vsftpd start
# chkconfig vsftpd on
```

The default configuration file, vsftpd.conf, supports access to regular user accounts on the server. But such options are blocked by the SELinux **ftp_home_dir** boolean. One way to activate it is with the following command:

```
# setsebool -P ftp_home_dir 1
```

You should be able to verify it with an FTP client such as ftp or lftp, which you can install with a command like **yum install**.

If you're thorough, you also set up the ftpusers file in the /etc/vsftpd directory to prohibit access to all regular users except testuser. But that is a skill more closely associated with the RHCE objectives.

Lab 9

If you know how to analyze log files, you know that the following command can analyze and interpret the contents of the testaudit.log file:

```
$ sealert -a testaudit.log
```

Read the interpreted log file. You'll see from the "confidence" listings, the most likely problem relates to SELinux contexts in the /var/ftp/pub/os directory.

5

The Boot Process

As suggested by the title, the RHCSA objectives described in this chapter are based on various events that happen during the boot process and, by implication, the shutdown process as well. The chapter can be summed up by the first objective, based on what you can do to "boot, reboot, and shut down a system normally." Even though RHEL 6 incorporates the new Upstart system, it still uses elements known to the older SysVinit system, including runlevels. One key runlevel is known as single-user mode, which can be used to gain administrative-level access to a system.

You can configure network services to start any configured runlevel. Such services start when the boot process moves to that runlevel. Finally, this chapter also covers the system bootloader. Although other bootloaders exist for Linux, RHEL 6 is dedicated to the older version of the Grand Unified Bootloader (GRUB), 0.97.

Those of you who have read the *Study Guide* may have noticed the NTP coverage at the end of Chapter 5. Because of changes to the Red Hat objectives, that information is covered in Chapter 17. In addition, the *Study Guide* includes coverage of basic network configuration. Since it is not directly tied to a specific objective on the Red Hat exams, I've left that information out of this book.

Boot, Reboot, and Shut Down a System Normally

As suggested by the title, this objective includes three components. The boot process starts when a system is powered up. Once the Power-On Self-Test (POST) is complete, the boot process continues through the Basic Input/Output System (BIOS) or the newer Unified Extensible Firmware Interface (UEFI).

Next, the BIOS or UEFI looks for a bootloader on the Master Boot Record (MBR) of a connected hard drive. For RHEL 6, that's the Grand Unified Bootloader (GRUB). While some other Linux distributions use GRUB version 2.0, RHEL 6 uses GRUB version 0.97, controlled directly from the /boot/grub/grub.conf configuration file.

To understand how the Linux boot process works, you should understand the details of a GRUB configuration file. The following excerpt cites the contents of a GRUB configuration file:

```
default=0
timeout=5
```

```
splashimage=(hd0,0)/grub/splash.xpm.gz
hiddenmenu
title CentOS (2.6.32-220.el6.x86_64)
        root (hd0,0)
        kernel /vmlinuz-2.6.32-220.el6.x86_64 ro
root=UUID=3ed8058f-8a32-4c39-a3ca-3a54cf4852e2 rd_NO_LUKS
rd_NO_LVM LANG=en_US.UTF-8 rd_NO_MD quiet
SYSFONT=latarcyrheb-sun16 rhgb crashkernel=auto
KEYBOARDTYPE=pc KEYTABLE=us rd_NO_DM
        initrd /initramfs-2.6.32-220.el6.x86_64.img
```

The code between **kernel** and **rd_NO_DM** is one continuous line. It's broken in the text solely for formatting purposes.

If you understand each component of this file, you should be able to handle any issue that occurs during the boot process.

The other two components, reboot and shutdown, are relatively simple. You can reboot from the GNOME desktop by selecting System | Shut Down and clicking Reboot in the menu that appears. As documented in /etc/inittab, runlevel 6 reboots and runlevel 0 shuts down a system. Thus, you can start the reboot process with any of the following commands.

```
# reboot
# init 6
# telinit 6
# shutdown -r now
```

You can shut down an RHEL 6 system in a similar fashion. In the GNOME desktop, the Shut Down option is available after clicking System | Shut Down. Alternatively, you can run the **poweroff**, **halt**, **telinit 0**, or **init 0** commands.

Boot Systems into Different Runlevels Manually

The previous objective included some elements of how you can start a system in a different runlevel. The primary way to boot a system in this way is to use the GRUB menu. It allows access to the **kernel** command settings from the desired boot option. When accessed, you can enter the desired runlevel at the end of the line: the following excerpt boots into runlevel 3.

```
[ Minimal BASH-like line editing is supported.  For the first word,
TAB lists possible command completions.  Anywhere else TAB lists the
```

```
possible completions of a device/filename. ESC at any time cancels.
ENTER at any time accepts your changes.]
```

`>crashkernel=auto rhgb crashkernel=auto quiet rd_NO_LVM rd_NO_DM `**`3`**

Within Linux, you can "boot" into different runlevels with the help of the **init** or **telinit** commands. For example, if you're in runlevel 3, the following command boots the system into runlevel 5, which is the default for the GUI.

```
# init 5
```

The standard runlevels, along with the default, are shown in comments in the /etc/inittab file. While this is a now deprecated file from the obsolete SysVinit, it's still used to configure the default runlevel for RHEL 6. To confirm success, run the **runlevel** command. Two numbers appear:

```
3 5
```

This output means the system has moved from runlevel 3 to runlevel 5. An N in the output means that the system is still at the boot runlevel.

Use Single-User Mode to Gain Access to a System

This objective cites how you can access an RHEL 6 system without a user password. When successful, RHEL 6 automatically logs you into the root administrative account. You don't even need the root password. However, that assumes GRUB isn't also password protected.

The simplest way to boot in single-user mode is to access the GRUB menu. When you access the kernel command options just described, add a **1** or **single** to the end of that line. Boot the system with that modified option, and you'll soon see a prompt such as:

```
[root@gamma /] #
```

Once in single-user mode, you can even set the root password to just about whatever you want. Although blank passwords are not allowed, passwords with a single blank space are!

on the **!** job

As single-user mode supports password-free access with root administrative privileges, it's important to protect the bootloader with a password. You may also want to protect the system from other boot media such as Live DVDs and USBs.

Configure Systems to Boot Into a Specific Runlevel Automatically

This objective offers an excellent opportunity to review available runlevels. The major runlevels are listed in the /etc/inittab configuration file, which is also where you configure the boot runlevel. The following directive specifies normal system booting into runlevel 5:

```
id:5:initdefault
```

You can change 5 to any legal runlevel. Basic runlevels are shown in Table 5-1. Each of these runlevels is associated with scripts in the /etc/rc*n*.d directories, where *n* corresponds to the numeric runlevel.

If you're having trouble booting into RHEL 6, two other runlevels are available. When you reach the GRUB menu, you can append them to the kernel command options:

- **single**   Boots normally, but does not run the scripts in the /etc/rc1.d/ directory.
- **init=/bin/sh**   Boots without loading init-related options. It mounts only the top-level root directory (/) in read-only mode.

TABLE 5-1	Runlevel	Description
Red Hat Runlevels	0	Halt.
	1	Single-user mode, for maintenance and repair.
	2	Multiuser, with some network services.
	3	Multiuser, with networking.
	4	Normally unused (but available).
	5	X11, defaults to a GUI login screen; logins bring the user to a GUI desktop, with networking.
	6	Reboot (never set **initdefault** in /etc/inittab to this value).

Be aware of the files in the /etc/init directory and what they do. For those who are converting from RHEL 5, these files have taken over the functionality of everything but the default runlevel from the /etc/inittab file.

Configure Network Services to Start Automatically at Boot

In my opinion, this objective is not precise. Rarely would you want to start networking and a network service such as the FTP server when booting into single-user mode. On the other hand, you typically would want networking available in at least runlevels 3 and 5, which correspond to fully featured logins from the text and graphical-based consoles, respectively. In addition, for security, it's best to keep the number of active network services to a minimum.

The **chkconfig** command makes this process convenient. For example, if you want to configure the vsFTP network service to start automatically at boot, you could run the following command:

```
# chkconfig vsftpd on
```

This command applies to all reasonable runlevels; to confirm, run the **chkconfig --list vsftpd** command. You should see the following output, which suggests that the vsFTP server is a service that starts automatically during the boot process in runlevels 2, 3, 4, and 5. It is not started in runlevel 0 (shutdown), runlevel 1 (single-user mode), or runlevel 6 (reboot).

```
vsftpd          0:off  1:off  2:on  3:on  4:on  5:on  6:off
```

If you need to be more specific about the boot runlevel for network services, the **chkconfig** command still works. For example, the following commands set the noted service to start only in runlevels 3 and 5:

```
# chkconfig vsftpd off
# chkconfig --level 35 vsftpd on
```

Of course, you could use the console or GUI Service Configuration tool to make these changes to a variety of network services.

Modify the System Bootloader

The system bootloader is GRUB. To modify GRUB, you need the grub.conf configuration file in the /boot/grub directory. A soft link to this file is available in the /etc directory.

When you install a new kernel properly, it should automatically add a new stanza to the bootloader. That stanza will appear as a new option in the GRUB menu; this situation is covered in Chapter 7 of the *Study Guide*.

An excerpt of a GRUB configuration file was shown earlier in this chapter. If you know how to modify the system bootloader, you understand the implications of changing each line in the file. The implications are briefly described in Table 5-2; each line starts with a GRUB command, as shown in the left column.

TABLE 5-2	Command	Effect of a Change
Typical GRUB Commands	default	Points to a stanza to boot by default
	timeout	Specifies the time to wait before booting the default stanza
	splashimage	Notes the graphical splash screen to show during the boot process
	hiddenmenu	Hides the GRUB menu unless a key is pushed during the timeout period
	password	Specifies the password that protects the GRUB menu from changes
	title	Notes the stanza label shown from the main GRUB menu
	root	Points to the hard drive and partition with boot files
	kernel	Loads the kernel, specifies the file system with the top-level root directory, and adds boot options, potentially including the runlevel
	initrd	Loads the initial RAM disk

CERTIFICATION SUMMARY

This chapter focuses on exam objectives associated with all aspects of the boot process. It describes what happens during the boot process, along with the steps you can take to boot, reboot, and shut down a system. During the boot process, you can access the GRUB menu, and then add a desired runlevel to the end of the kernel command line. During the boot process, if you lose the root administrative password, you can add the terms **1** or **single** to the end of the kernel command line to boot a system into single-user mode.

Once a system is booted, you can use a command like **init** to boot a running system into a different runlevel. Runlevels 0 and 6 correspond to shut down and reboot, respectively. You can change the default runlevel by changing that variable in the /etc/inittab configuration file. With the proper use of the **chkconfig** command, you can configure various network services to start during the boot process in the default runlevel.

Finally, you need to know how to modify GRUB, the system bootloader. Each of the lines in the grub.conf configuration file starts with a command directive. You should know what happens when you revise the options associated with each of these directives.

SELF TEST

The following fill-in-the-blank questions help you measure your understanding of the topics associated with this chapter. As there are no multiple-choice questions on the Red Hat exams, there are no multiple-choice questions in this book. If you have trouble with one or more of these questions, you may need to research associated topics further. However, there's almost always more than one way to solve a problem in Linux. Getting results, not memorizing trivia, is what counts on the Red Hat exams.

   As this is a practice book, the answers to these questions may or may not be found in the body of the chapter. For more information, see the *Study Guide*.

Boot, Reboot, and Shut Down a System Normally

I. What runlevel is associated with shutting down a Linux system?

   _____

Boot Systems into Different Runlevels Manually

2. What runlevel is associated with the GUI?

   _____

Use Single-User Mode to Gain Access to a System

3. When do you enter a password during the boot process to enter single-user mode?

   _____

Configure Systems to Boot Into a Specific Runlevel Automatically

4. What is the full path to the configuration file with the default runlevel?

   _____

Configure Network Services to Start Automatically at Boot

5. What command ensures networking starts automatically in all normal runlevels?

   _____

6. What command ensures that networking does not start in any runlevel?

   _____

Modify the System Bootloader

7. What directive in the GRUB configuration file hides the boot menu?

   _____

8. What directive in the GRUB configuration file identifies the initial RAM disk?

   _____

LAB QUESTIONS

Red Hat presents its exams electronically. For that reason, the labs in this and future chapters are available from the gamma.example.net system, from the ChapterLabs/ folder that appears in the GUI desktop. If you're running in a command-line console, you can find the labs in the /home/testuser/ Desktop/ChapterLabs directory.

The answers for each lab follow the Self Test Answers for the fill-in-the-blank questions.

SELF TEST ANSWERS

Boot, Reboot, and Shut Down a System Normally

1. The runlevel associated with shutting down a Linux system is 0. In contrast, runlevel 6 is associated with rebooting.

Boot Systems into Different Runlevels Manually

2. The runlevel associated with the GUI is 5, but that's just the default, as configured in the prefdm.conf file in the /etc/init directory.

Use Single-User Mode to Gain Access to a System

3. No password is necessary to enter single-user mode during the boot process. It's a "backdoor" that may be a security issue, which is a good reason to password protect the GRUB bootloader.

Configure Systems to Boot Into a Specific Runlevel Automatically

4. The full path to the configuration file with the default runlevel is /etc/inittab. Although a legacy file, it's still in use for RHEL 6.

Configure Network Services to Start Automatically at Boot

5. The simplest command to ensure that networking starts automatically in all normal runlevels is **chkconfig network on**. Variations such as **chkconfig network --level 2345 on** are also acceptable.

6. The simplest command to ensure that networking does not start in any runlevel is **chkconfig network off**. As with question 5, there are variations that also work.

Modify the System Bootloader

7. The directive in the GRUB configuration file that hides the boot menu is **hiddenmenu**.

8. The directive in the GRUB configuration file that identifies the initial RAM disk is **initrd**.

LAB ANSWERS

Lab I

If you're successful in part 1, you won't see the splash screen, but you will see messages similar to the following.

```
readahead: starting
        Welcome to Scientific Linux
Starting udev:          [  ok  ]
```

The messages include most of what's saved in the /var/log/dmesg file, along with the services that are started in the configured runlevel. From the GRUB menu, you need to make sure all instances of **quiet** and **rhgb** are deleted from the kernel command options. Fortunately, changes at the GRUB boot menu are not saved, so you won't have to restore anything.

If you're successful in part 2, in 60 seconds, you'll begin to see messages associated with moving to runlevel 6, similar to the following:

```
Shutting down Avahi daemon       [  ok  ]
```

The system then reboots; it does not shut down.

If you're successful in part 3, the **shutdown** command won't shut down the system completely, but the **halt** command will.

Lab 2

The purpose of this lab is to show you that runlevel 4 is actually used and available, contrary to the comments in the /etc/inittab configuration file. When booting into this runlevel, you should be able to log into the console. Assuming the X Window server and GNOME desktop packages are installed, you'll be able to start the GUI with the **startx** command.

If you're unable to open the GUI normally, hopefully you'll now remember one other way to start the GUI desktop.

Lab 3

Now try to make runlevel 4 as fully featured as runlevel 5. Based on the hints described in the lab, one way to do so is with the following commands:

```
# chkconfig abrt-ccpp --level 4 on
# chkconfig abrtd --level 4 on
# chkconfig abrt-oops --level 4 on
# chkconfig spice-vdagentd --level 4 on
# chkconfig firstboot --level 4 on
```

There may be other discrepancies between runlevels 4 and 5 on your system; don't be too concerned about those. When you move to runlevel 4 with a command like **init 4**, you'll see that runlevel 4 still isn't equivalent to runlevel 5.

Lab 4

In the /etc/inittab file, the one active line should read as follows (before you restore it):

```
id:4:initdefault:
```

If you remember all details from the *Study Guide,* or just know the purpose of the prefdm.conf file in the /etc/init directory, you will also have changed the first two lines in that file to:

```
start on stopped rc RUNLEVEL=4
stop on starting rc RUNLEVEL=[!4]
```

Once changed, the next time you boot the system, it should move to the GUI in runlevel 4. Once you've completed this lab, don't forget to restore runlevel 5 to the /etc/inittab and the /etc/init/ prefdm.conf files.

Lab 5

If successful, you will see the following prompt, without having to log into the system:

```
[root@gamma /]#
```

As the root administrative user, you now have full privileges on the system; you can even change the root administrative password. If you use the same password, RHEL 6 won't object, except to note that the password is based on a dictionary word and is too simple.

Lab 6

If successful, you'll see two options from the GRUB menu. If you used a different value for the **title** directive, it'll be easy to identify when you call up the GRUB menu.

Given the way the gamma.example.net system has been configured, the simplest way to set up the new stanza is with the partition associated with the top-level root directory. That stanza may look something like the following:

```
title CentOS (2.6.32-220.el6.x86_64) lab 6
      root (hd0,0)
      kernel /vmlinuz-2.6.32-220.el6.x86_64 ro root=/dev/vda2
rd_NO_LUKS  KEYBOARDTYPE=pc KEYTABLE=us LANG=en_US.UTF-8
rd_NO_MD quiet SYSFONT=latarcyrheb-sun16 rhgb crashkernel=auto
```

```
rhgb crashkernel=auto quiet rd_NO_LVM rd_NO_DM
        initrd /initramfs-2.6.32-220.el6.x86_64.img
```

The code between kernel and rd_NO_DM is one continuous line. It's broken in the text solely for formatting purposes.

As noted by the bolding, I substituted **/dev/vda2** for **UUID=c55e95e0-bc00-4e40-8a9b-97e5d-34e3d09**. Your UUID may vary.

6

Linux Filesystem Administration

EXAM OBJECTIVES

- ❑ Add new partitions, logical volumes, and swap to a system non-destructively
- ❑ List, create, delete, and set partition type for primary, extended, and logical partitions
- ❑ Create and remove physical volumes, assign physical volumes to volume groups, and create and delete logical volumes
- ❑ Extend existing unencrypted ext4-formatted logical volumes
- ❑ Create, mount, and use ext2, ext3, and ext4 file systems
- ❑ Mount and unmount CIFS and NFS Network File Systems
- ❑ Configure systems to mount file systems at boot by Universally Unique ID (UUID) or label
- ❑ Create and configure LUKS-encrypted partitions and logical volumes to prompt for password and mount a decrypted file system at boot
- ❑ Mount, unmount, and use LUKS-encrypted file systems
- ❑ Configure systems to mount ext4, LUKS-encrypted, and Network File Systems automatically
- ❑ Self Test

A s suggested by the title, this chapter is all about filesystem management. Yes, there are ten objectives covered in this chapter. In general, they deal with the configuration of a hard drive into partitions, as well as the reconfiguration of such partitions into logical volumes. Once configured, those partitions and volumes can be formatted to the ext2, ext3, and ext4 file systems. If desired, such partitions can be set up in encrypted format.

Formatted file systems can be mounted temporarily with commands. Formatted file systems can also be mounted automatically during the boot process through the /etc/fstab configuration file. To minimize the risks of confusion on systems with multiple drives, Linux allocates Universally Unique IDs (UUIDs) or labels to each volume. Such volumes can then be mounted locally, or shared via Samba or the Network File System.

While this chapter addresses ten different objectives, these objectives are interactive. For example, to add a new partition, you need to use a tool like **fdisk** or **parted**. To set the partition type, you need to know what to change in those utilities. To create an ext2, ext3, or ext4 file system, you need to know how to format a partition or logical volume. To configure that file system to be mounted automatically, you need to configure it in /etc/fstab.

So if some of the instructions in one section seem incomplete, read the rest of the chapter. Of course, as this is a *Practice Exams* book, all explanations are minimal.

While there's some free space available on the VMs for additional partitions, some of you may prefer to use an entirely separate storage device. From the gamma.tar.gz archive on the DVD, you may have noted a second virtual disk file, gamma.example.net-1.img. It's a 1GB file intended for use as a second virtual hard disk. You can set it up as "existing storage" in the GUI Virtual Machine Manager console for that system. Alternatively, you could just create your own second virtual drive. The next time you boot, it will be available for configuration. You can use this drive with less fear of damaging the current VM. Of course, if something goes badly wrong, you could delete and then reimport the gamma.example.net system, using the techniques described in Chapter 1.

Some of you may note the lack of coverage of the automounter in this chapter. It's not covered in the RHCSA objectives and is not listed in the relevant Red Hat course outlines.

e x a m

ⓦ a t c h

Although RAID was included in Red Hat objectives for RHEL 5, it is not included in the objectives associated with the RHCSA or RHCE exams for RHEL 6.

Add New Partitions, Logical Volumes, and Swap to a System Non-Destructively

Since this objective is associated with *adding* space to a system *non-destructively*, it's fair to assume you need to know how to configure space on storage media that is unallocated and unpartitioned. Creating partitions is a straightforward process.

Logical volumes can be built from partitions, as described later in this chapter. Swap space can be configured from either a partition or a logical volume. In other words, to learn this objective, you need to know how to

- Run a utility such as **fdisk**, **parted**, or the GUI Disk Utility to create a partition from empty space.
- Configure partitions appropriately for logical volumes and swap space.
- Set up physical volumes, volume groups, and logical volumes from existing empty partitions.

Users of GParted may be disappointed, as it is not included with RHEL 6. But in my opinion, the Disk Utility tool available with the **palimpsest** command is at least as good. Other objectives address what you need to do to change partition types, to set up logical volumes, to configure swap space, to format partitions and volumes, and finally, to set them up to boot automatically.

List, Create, Delete, and Set Partition Type for Primary, Extended, and Logical Partitions

The objective listed in the title is a mouthful. But it makes sense. Before you make any changes, you should know what partitions have already been configured. To list currently configured partitions, you could run either of the following commands. Just be sure to do so as the administrative user, as regular users don't have such privileges.

```
# fdisk -l
# parted -l
```

To create a partition, you need access with **fdisk**, **parted**, or the GUI Disk Utility, as the root administrative user. You can configure up to four primary partitions on most storage devices. One primary partition can be reallocated as an extended partition. That extended partition can then be subdivided into logical partitions.

The same tools that allow you to create a partition also allow you to delete partitions. Just protect and back up any important data before deleting any partition.

on the job

Be careful with parted and the GUI Disk Utility. Any changes made with these tools are immediately written to disk.

Create and Remove Physical Volumes, Assign Physical Volumes to Volume Groups, and Create and Delete Logical Volumes

This objective lists the sequence associated with the configuration of a logical volume. Briefly, to create a logical volume, you take the following general steps:

1. Create a partition; make sure the LVM partition type is set.

2. Initialize that partition for use by a volume group with the **pvcreate** command. That command creates a physical volume (PV).

3. Assign one or more PVs to a volume group (VG) with the **vgcreate** command.

4. Create a logical volume with the **lvcreate** command. You can create it from available space in the VG, based on a size with the **-L** switch.

Of course, the objective suggests you should also know how to reverse the process. To delete an LV, you can use the **lvremove** command.

Before you can remove a PV, you need to unassign it from an existing VG. One way to do so is with the **vgreduce** command. You can then remove the PV with the **pvremove** command. That partition is then available for other purposes.

You can also use the GUI Logical Volume Management tool, available from the System | Administration menu (or the **system-config-lvm** command). It's an excellent tool that supports the functionality of each of these commands.

Extend Existing Unencrypted ext4-formatted Logical Volumes

Sometimes, you've just got to increase the space available to an LV. If you're working with a production system, it's important to back up things first. Life is simpler, however, if the data isn't that important. In that case, you take the following general steps to extend an LV:

1. Unmount the current file system. If the file system is mounted on /abc, run the following command:

   ```
   # umount /abc
   ```

2. Run the **vgs** command. If sufficient space is available in the VG, skip to step 6.
3. Create a new partition, and set it to the LVM partition type.
4. Set up the PV with the **pvcreate** command.
5. Use the **vgextend** command to include the new PV in the VG.
6. Use the **lvextend -L** command to extend the LV to the amount of space required. The following example extends the LV on the noted device to 3GB. (You can substitute /dev/mapper/vg_00-lv_00 if desired.)

   ```
   # lvextend -L 3000M /dev/vg_00/lv_00
   ```

7. Now you can resize the formatted volume. To resize the format to match the new size of the LV on this particular device, run the following command:

   ```
   # resize2fs /dev/vg_00/lv_00
   ```

8. You may be prompted to check the file system with the **e2fsck** command. In this case, first run the **e2fsck -f /dev/vg_00/lv_00** command to force a filesystem check.
9. Finally, you can remount the filesystem device on the original directory (/abc) that you unmounted in step 1.

Create, Mount, and Use ext2, ext3, and ext4 File Systems

As suggested by the title, this objective requires three basic steps. To create a file system, you need to format it. To make a file system useful, you need to mount it. Once mounted, you should be able to use normal commands to read from and write to that file system.

There's one basic command associated with creating a file system: **mkfs**. Variations on this command support the creation of the ext2, ext3, ext4, and other file systems. RHEL 6 supports the use of the **mkfs.ext2**, **mkfs.ext3**, and **mkfs.ext4** commands for that purpose. Alternatively, the **mkfs -t ext4** command works just as well for the default ext4 file system. For example, if you've just created a /dev/sda9 partition, you can create an ext4 file system on that partition with the following command:

```
# mkfs -t ext4 /dev/sda9
```

You can then mount a file system with the **mount** command. You can mount that freshly formatted file system on a hypothetical /shared directory as follows:

```
# mount /dev/sda9 /shared
```

While technically you're supposed to specify the filesystem format with the **mount -t ext4** command, the ext4 file system is the default for RHEL 6. You can mount it with other options; for example, the following command mounts the noted file system in read-only mode:

```
# mount -o ro /dev/sda9 /shared
```

Once mounted on a directory, you should be able to use the formatted file system in the same way as you use any other directory.

An implicit part of this objective is the preparation of additional swap space. As an example, if you've configured a partition or LV for swap space, the **mkswap** command formats and the **swapon** command activates the space. Of course, you should remember to configure all of these systems in /etc/fstab to ensure they're active after reboot.

Mount and Unmount CIFS and NFS Network File Systems

Before you can mount a shared CIFS (Common Internet File System) or an NFS (Network File System), it actually has to be shared. The configuration of these services are an RHCE skill discussed in Chapters 15 and 16 of the *Study Guide*. If you do share a directory using one of these services, you need to make sure the appropriate ports are open in any existing firewall. That process has been simplified in the Firewall Configuration tool, as the Trusted Services section supports "one-click" configuration of appropriate ports for each service.

Before you mount a CIFS or NFS directory, you need to know what's being shared. The following commands list shared directories from the noted system:

```
$ smbclient -L gamma.example.net
$ showmount -e gamma.example.net
```

Once an appropriate directory is shared, you can connect to it from a remote location with a specific **mount** command. The following commands mount a /test directory shared via CIFS and NFS from the noted remote system:

```
# mount -t cifs //gamma.example.net/test /mnt -o
username=testuser
# mount -t nfs gamma.example.net:/test /net
```

The CIFS share assumes that user testuser has an account on the gamma.example. net system and has been included in the CIFS user database. The associated command prompts for a password.

The **umount** command works on CIFSs and NFSs too. If the **umount** command doesn't work, the **-l** switch can sometimes help.

Configure Systems to Mount File Systems at Boot by Universally Unique ID (UUID) or Label

To mount a file system during the boot process, you should make sure it's configured in the /etc/fstab file. The simplest mount is by device; for example, the following line in /etc/fstab is one way to set up the top-level root directory (/) in that file:

```
/dev/vda2    /    ext4    defaults    1    1
```

Of course, the objective specifies UUIDs or labels. A UUID is what you see by default in RHEL 6. It may appear similar to the following:

```
UUID=c55e95e0-bc00-4e40-8a9b-97e5d34e3d09    /    ext4    defaults   1 1
```

If you've just formatted a new file system, the **dumpe2fs** command can help identify the UUID for the associated device. The following command isolates the UUID for the noted /dev/vda2 device:

```
# dumpe2fs /dev/vda2 | grep UUID
```

The "label" included in the objective refers to the way /etc/fstab was normally configured for RHEL 5. You can set up labels for RHEL 6 with the help of the **e2label** command. For example, the following command sets up a label for the /dev/vda2 partition:

```
# e2label /dev/vda2 /top
```

You can then change the noted entry in /etc/fstab to

```
LABEL=/top    /    ext4    defaults    1 1
```

It doesn't matter if the /top directory actually exists, as it's just a label.

Create and Configure LUKS-encrypted Partitions and Logical Volumes to Prompt for Password and Mount a Decrypted File System at Boot

Black-hat hackers have been known to steal or copy computer storage devices. The Linux Unified Key Setup (LUKS) is a disk encryption specification that can help protect the data on such devices. When configuring a partition or LV for LUKS, be prepared with a passphrase. While it's easiest to install a LUKS-encrypted partition/ LV during the installation process, you may not get that opportunity during an exam.

The first step is to load the dm_crypt and dm_mod modules. One way to do so is with the **modprobe dm_crypt** command. If successful, you should see the following modules in the output to the **lsmod | grep dm_** command:

```
dm_crypt     13022  0
dm_mod       81500  3 dm_crypt,dm_mirror,dm_log
```

To create a LUKS-encrypted partition, take the following basic steps:

1. Create a new partition. If directed to set up an LV, take the steps required to set it up from empty space on available PVs and VGs. Add the partition to PVs if necessary.

2. Apply the **cryptsetup** command to the partition; enter a passphrase when prompted.

   ```
   # cryptsetup luksFormat /dev/sda1
   ```

3. If required, set up a UUID for the encrypted device; the following example writes the UUID to a text file:

   ```
   # cryptsetup luksUUID /dev/sda1 > textfile
   ```

4. The following command, which prompts for a passphrase, maps the encrypted partition to the UUID. If you're not using UUIDs, skip to step 5.

   ```
   # cryptsetup luksOpen /dev/sda1 `cat textfile`
   ```

5. Alternatively, the following command skips UUIDs and sets up a device label:

   ```
   # cryptsetup luksOpen /dev/sda1 notUUID
   ```

6. Now format the encrypted device with a command like **mkfs.ext4**; the device file should be available in the /dev/mapper directory.

Your LUKS volume is now ready for the next two objectives. Don't reboot yet, or you'll lose the work that you've done to create this volume.

Mount, Unmount, and Use LUKS-encrypted File Systems

On the surface, this objective is simple. If you've already created a LUKS-encrypted file system in the previous objective, all you need to do is apply the **mount** and **umount** commands to the associated device file in the /dev/mapper directory.

However, that's not enough. If you rebooted now, the dm_crypt module wouldn't even be loaded. To set up the LUKS-encrypted file system properly, you need to configure the /etc/crypttab file. Each encrypted volume gets one line in that file, using the following format:

```
device      unformatted volume      passphrase_file      options
```

The device is the file created earlier in the /dev/mapper directory. The unformatted volume may be the partition or the LV that has been encrypted. The passphrase_file can be configured with 600 permissions; if you substitute **none** in this column, RHEL 6 prompts for the passphrase during the boot process. No options are required; I normally keep this entry blank. If you want to go beyond "basic operation" the crypttab man page details available options.

For the device, you use either the UUID created with the **cryptsetup luksUUID** command or the plain device filename created with the **cryptsetup luksOpen** command.

on the
() o b
If you want to practice creating encrypted volumes, and want to reuse a device currently configured in the /dev/mapper directory, run the cryptsetup luksClose device command, where device is the name of a file in that /dev/ mapper. You can then rerun the cryptsetup commands on the same partition or volume.

Configure Systems to Mount ext4, LUKS-encrypted, and Network File Systems Automatically

Automatic mounts are associated with the /etc/fstab configuration file, so for this objective, you need to know how to configure all three types of file systems in /etc/fstab. First, a standard ext4 file system is straightforward. You could set it up with partitions or LV devices:

```
/dev/sda1       /dir1       ext4        defaults      1 2
/dev/vg_00/lv_00     /dir2       ext4        defaults      1 2
```

Of course, you could substitute the UUID for each device. A similar configuration works for newly configured swap space; for example, if you've run **mkswap /dev/ sda2**, the following line ensures space is used after the next boot:

```
/dev/sda2     swap       swap       defaults      0 0
```

As for LUKS-encrypted file systems, the process is similar. You could use the UUID, or you could specify the device file from the /dev/mapper directory. The following is one example of how it would appear in /etc/fstab:

```
/dev/mapper/test    /dir3       ext4        defaults      1 2
```

There are two types of networked file systems: NFS and CIFS. The following line specifies an NFS version 4 share, /shared1 from server srv1, mounted on /dir4, with 8192 blocks of data to be read and written per transmission, with a client that waits 1.4 seconds for the connection to be completed, with a connection that may be interrupted. The 0 0 disables archiving and filesystem checks.

```
svr1:/share1  /dir4  nfs4  rsize=8192,wsize=8192,timeo=14,intr  0 0
```

The format for a shared CIFS directory is a bit different. Using the same parameters, the following supports access over a properly shared CIFS connection. Yes, the username and password are shown in clear text, which is why you can substitute an option like **credentials=/etc/cifs** for the noted username and password.

```
//svr1/share1  /dir4  cifs  rw,username=testuser,password=rhcert  0 0
```

on the **Job**

If you boot and forget the passphrase for the encrypted volume, add the init=/bin/sh option to the end of the kernel command line in the GRUB menu. You should then be able, with a few tricks, to mount volumes and make changes in read/write mode.

CERTIFICATION SUMMARY

This chapter is focused on the file system. If you're a master of the topics in this chapter, you know how to create a regular Linux partition, a swap partition, and space that can be built into an LV. That means you know how to set up these partition types, as well as primary, extended, and logical partitions.

Of course, LVs go further. You should know that partitions can be set up in PVs, which can then be assembled into VGs. You can then allocate desired space to the LV. If that LV is not big enough, you can add more PVs, include them in a larger VG, and allocate the additional space in a larger LV.

Whatever file systems you configure, you need to know how to format them to the ext2, ext3, ext4, and even the Linux swap file systems. Once formatted, you should be able to set them, as well as networked NFSs/CIFSs, in /etc/fstab. In that vein, you may substitute a label or a UUID for the filesystem device file.

Finally, you should be able to handle LUKS-encrypted volumes. When you use the **cryptsetup** command on a partition or LV and set up the /dev/mapper device file in the /etc/cryptsetup file, you can then configure that device in /etc/fstab. When successful, you'll be prompted for an associated passphrase during the boot process.

SELF TEST

The following fill-in-the-blank questions help you measure your understanding of the topics associated with this chapter. As there are no multiple-choice questions on the Red Hat exams, there are no multiple-choice questions in this book. If you have trouble with one or more of these questions, you may need to research associated topics further. However, there's almost always more than one way to solve a problem in Linux. Getting results, not memorizing trivia, is what counts on the Red Hat exams.

As this is a practice book, the answers to these questions may or may not be found in the body of the chapter. For more information, see the *Study Guide*.

Add New Partitions, Logical Volumes, and Swap to a System Non-Destructively

1. Name three RHEL 6 utilities that can be used to configure a new partition from available empty space.

   _____   _____   _____

List, Create, Delete, and Set Partition Type for Primary, Extended, and Logical Partitions

2. Name three different partition types associated with Linux.

   _____   _____   _____

Create and Remove Physical Volumes, Assign Physical Volumes to Volume Groups, and Create and Delete Logical Volumes

3. Name the commands that create a physical volume, assign a physical volume to a volume group, and then create a logical volume.

   _____

Extend Existing Unencrypted ext4-formatted Logical Volumes

4. Name the command that can be used to change the amount of space a formatted file system uses in an LV.

   _____

Create, Mount, and Use ext2, ext3, and ext4 File Systems

5. What command mounts the hypothetical /dev/sda1 device on the /mnt directory in read-only mode?

_____

Mount and Unmount CIFS and NFS Network File Systems

6. What command mounts the /abc directory, shared via CIFS, from the gamma.example.net system, based on the default testuser?

_____

Configure Systems to Mount File Systems at Boot by Universally Unique ID (UUID) or Label

7. Name a command that can help identify the UUID associated with available volumes.

_____

Create and Configure LUKS-encrypted Partitions and Logical Volumes to Prompt for Password and Mount a Decrypted File System at Boot

8. Name a command that LUKS-encrypts the /dev/sdb1 partition.

_____

Mount, Unmount, and Use LUKS-encrypted File Systems

9. What two files do you have to edit before Linux will mount a LUKS-encrypted file system during the boot process?

_____   _____

Configure Systems to Mount ext4, LUKS-encrypted, and Network File Systems Automatically

10. You've just created a /dev/sda3 partition and formatted it to ext4. You've also created a /test1 directory to mount that file system. Using default settings, what would you add to the /etc/fstab file to ensure it's mounted the next time you boot that system?

_____

LAB QUESTIONS

Red Hat presents its exams electronically. For that reason, the labs in this and future chapters are available from the gamma.example.net system, from the ChapterLabs/ folder that appears in the GUI desktop. If you're running in a command-line console, you can find the labs in the /home/testuser/ Desktop/ChapterLabs directory.

For the labs in this chapter, it's assumed you've installed the second virtual hard drive on the gamma.example.net system. If you don't remember or mistype a passphrase, the system may appear unbootable. (It happened to me when some crumbs got stuck in my keyboard.) That happens when a system expects a passphrase in support of a LUKS-encrypted partition. If you encounter that situation, take the following basic steps (details may vary):

1. At the GRUB menu, open the kernel command line.

2. Add **init=/bin/sh** to the end of the kernel command line. The system will mount the top-level root directory (/) volume in read-only mode.

3. Run the **mount -o remount,rw /** command to make the top-level root directory writable.

4. Edit the /etc/fstab file to comment out or delete the entry associated with the LUKS-encrypted partition. Edit the /etc/crypttab file to comment out or delete the associated entry.

5. Power down the system. (Commands like **shutdown** and **reboot** don't work from the way the system was booted with **init=/bin/sh**.) In the Virtual Machine Manager for the system, click Virtual Machine | Shut Down | Force Off.

6. You should now be able to boot the system normally; you won't be prompted for the LUKS passphrase.

The answers for each lab follow the Self Test Answers for the fill-in-the-blank questions.

SELF TEST ANSWERS

Add New Partitions, Logical Volumes, and Swap to a System Non-Destructively

1. Three RHEL 6 utilities that can be used to configure a new partition from available empty space are **fdisk**, **parted**, and the (GNOME) Disk Utility. The **palimpsest** command is an acceptable substitute for the GNOME Disk Utility.

List, Create, Delete, and Set Partition Type for Primary, Extended, and Logical Partitions

2. There are several different partition types associated with Linux. From the options shown in **fdisk**, they include Linux swap, Linux, Linux extended, Linux plaintext, Linux LVM, and Linux raid auto. As some of these partition types are listed differently in **parted** and the Disk Utility, there are several other acceptable answers.

Create and Remove Physical Volumes, Assign Physical Volumes to Volume Groups, and Create and Delete Logical Volumes

3. The commands that create a physical volume, assign a physical volume to a volume group, and then create a logical volume are **pvcreate**, **vgcreate**, and **lvcreate**.

Extend Existing Unencrypted ext4-formatted Logical Volumes

4. The command that can be used to change the amount of space a formatted file system uses in an LV is **resize2fs**. Despite the name, it works on ext2, ext3, and ext4 file systems.

Create, Mount, and Use ext2, ext3, and ext4 File Systems

5. One command that mounts the hypothetical /dev/sda1 device on the /mnt directory in read-only mode is **mount -o ro /dev/sda1 /mnt**.

Mount and Unmount CIFS and NFS Network File Systems

6. The command that mounts the /abc directory shared via CIFS, on the local /dir1 directory, from the gamma.example.net system, in read-write mode, and based on the default testuser is

```
# mount -t cifs //gamma.example.net/abc  /dir1 -o username=testuser
```

This command prompts for the rhcert password. If you prefer, you could specify **username=testuser,password=rhcert** instead. (In either case, you'll be prompted for a password.)

Configure Systems to Mount File Systems at Boot by Universally Unique ID (UUID) or Label

7. The **blkid** command identifies the UUID associated with available volumes.

Create and Configure LUKS-encrypted Partitions and Logical Volumes to Prompt for Password and Mount a Decrypted File System at Boot

8. The **cryptsetup luksFormat /dev/sdb1** command encrypts the noted partition, also prompting for a passphrase.

Mount, Unmount, and Use LUKS-encrypted File Systems

9. The two files are /etc/crypttab and /etc/fstab.

Configure Systems to Mount ext4, LUKS-encrypted, and Network File Systems Automatically

10. One line that would work in /etc/fstab is the following; other options in the fourth, fifth, and sixth columns are also acceptable. However, because there is no information on the label or UUID, you need to specify the partition device file.

```
/dev/sda3    /test1    ext4    defaults    1 1
```

LAB ANSWERS

In general, when successful, you'll have met all of the requirements listed in the lab questions, after a reboot.

Lab 1

You could easily use **fdisk**, **parted**, or the GUI Disk Utility to start this lab by creating a partition of 400MB. It's understood that these tools are not that precise; for example, when I ran the **parted -l** command after creating a 400MB partition, I got the following output:

```
Number   Start   End     Size    Type      File system      Flags
  1      32.3kB  428MB   428MB   primary   linux-swap(v1)
```

The difference in size between 428MB and 400MB is trivial for these purposes. Of course, to set it up as additional swap space, you need to format it properly. If this is partition /dev/sda1, run the following commands:

```
# mkswap /dev/sda1
# swapon /dev/sda1
```

You can confirm success in the /proc/swaps file. Of course, to make sure the changes survive a reboot, you need to add an entry in /etc/fstab. If UUIDs are required, you can identify them with a command like **blkid**; otherwise, you can include a simple entry such as:

```
/dev/sda1    swap      swap      defaults     0 0
```

Lab 2

Yes, the remaining space on the second virtual drive is small, about 600MB. However, when you create two partitions on this drive, you get a chance to practice the steps required to configure an LV. You can use any of the three disk management tools described in Lab 1 to create the additional partitions. Although you can use the GUI Logical Volume Management tool to perform these tasks, I cite the command-line options that you can use to meet the requirements of this lab. I assume the two additional partitions are device files, /dev/sda2 and /dev/sda3. Your device files may be different. If so, substitute accordingly.

1. Create partitions /dev/sda2 and /dev/sda3 using one of the disk management tools described in Lab 1. Together, these two partitions should add up to at least 500MB. Make sure they're set to the LVM volume type.

2. Run the **pvcreate /dev/sda2 /dev/sda3** command to set up PVs. If desired, run **pvs** to confirm.

3. Run the **vgcreate vg1 /dev/sda2 /dev/sda3** command to allocate all of these PVs to the VG named vg1. If desired, run **vgs** to confirm.

4. Run the **lvcreate -L 200M -n lv1 vg1** command. Confirm the creation with the **lvs** command. Confirm the device file /dev/vg1/lv1 now exists.

5. Run the **mkfs.ext4 /dev/vg1/lv1** command to format it as directed.

6. Add the following entry to /etc/fstab; the /dev/mapper/vg1-lv1 file should also exist.

   ```
   /dev/mapper/vg1-lv1     /dir1     ext4      defaults     1 2
   ```

7. Don't create a label or UUID for the /dev/vg1/lv1 LV yet; wait for Lab 5.

Lab 3

Remember, there are two steps to this process. First, you need to expand the LV with the **lvextend** command, then you can expand the formatted space with the **resize2fs** command. Since there's sufficient space in the VG, you don't need to add a PV to this area. All you need to do is extend the LV with the following command:

```
# lvextend -L 500M /dev/mapper/vg1-lv1
```

You could also specify the /dev/vg1/lv1 device file. But first, you should check the associated file system with the following command:

```
# e2fsck -f /dev/mapper/vg1-lv1
```

You can then extend the formatted volume over the whole length of the file system with the following command:

```
# resize2fs /dev/mapper/vg1-lv
```

Lab 4

To unallocate the swap space created in Lab 1, run the **swapoff /dev/sda1** command. In addition, you wouldn't want Linux to look for that swap partition during the boot process, so you also want to delete the swap reference to that partition in the /etc/fstab file.

In addition, you'll want to change the flag on the partition from Linux swap space to a regular Linux partition. When complete, you'll see the following excerpt from the **fdisk -l** command:

```
   Device Boot    Start        End     Blocks    Id  System
   /dev/sda1          1         52     417658+   83  Linux
```

Now you can format /dev/sda1. If you're paying attention, note that the requirement is to format to the ext3 file system. One way to do this is with the following command:

```
# mkfs -t ext3 /dev/sda1
```

To set it up on a permanent basis, add a line like the following to /etc/fstab:

```
/dev/sda1    /dir2    ext3  defaults   1 2
```

Lab 5

To create a label for the LV (or for any volume), use the **e2label** command. It doesn't matter whether you use the /dev/mapper/vg1-lv1 or /dev/vg1/lv1 devices, as they're both soft-linked to the same file. I run the following command:

```
# e2label /dev/mapper/vg1-lv1 logvol
```

and then confirm with the **e2label /dev/vg1/lv1** command. I then set it up in /etc/fstab:

```
LABEL=logvol    /dir1    ext4     defaults     1 2
```

Next, I find the UUID of the /dev/sda1 partition that has been formatted to the ext3 file system. I could do this with the **blkid** or the **dumpe2fs /dev/sda1 | grep UUID** commands. I then set it up in /etc/fstab in the following entry:

```
UUID=550ad7db-0001-4ac5-bd14-c6f7ff9b943b     /dir2    ext3  defaults    1 2
```

This particular UUID is unique to my system; yours will be different.

Lab 6

Since you've been told not to worry about saving data, you can proceed to encrypt the LV device, /dev/mapper/vg1-lv1, with the following command:

```
# cryptsetup luksFormat /dev/mapper/vg1-lv1
```

During the execution process for this command, you're asked to confirm by typing an uppercase **YES**, along with the desired passphrase.

Because you haven't been told to set up a UUID, you can keep it simple and just set up a basic name. (You may not be told everything.) I've arbitrarily used the word **basic1** for this purpose. The following command sets up a device file named basic in the /dev/mapper directory:

```
# cryptsetup luksOpen /dev/mapper/vg1-lv1 basic1
```

You can then set up the encrypted device in /etc/crypttab; in this case, it would be:

```
basic1     /dev/mapper/vg1-lv1     none
```

Of course, you also have to set up the encrypted file system in /etc/fstab:

```
/dev/mapper/basic1      /dir1       ext4        defaults      1 2
```

If you're successful, you'll reboot, enter the passphrase when prompted, and then see the /dev/mapper/basic1 encrypted device mounted on /dir1.

7

Package Management

❑ Install and update software packages from Red Hat Network, a remote repository, or from the local file system

❑ Update the kernel package appropriately to ensure a bootable system

❑ Self Test

Although only two objectives are associated with this chapter, the first one is especially important. You may need to know how to install several different packages in support of other RHCSA objectives. To that end, it helps if you know how to use the **rpm** and **yum** commands in some detail. Implicitly, that also means you should know how to configure repositories in the /etc/yum.conf file and supporting directories (/etc/yum and /etc/yum.repos.d).

Install and Update Software Packages from Red Hat Network, a Remote Repository, or from the Local File System

Let's break this objective into different components. Install and update are two different methods for installing software packages. They both apply to the two commands associated with the management of Red Hat packages: **rpm** and **yum**. You can install and update with both commands; the options are straightforward. For **rpm**, the **-i** installs, the **-F** updates, and the **-U** does both; for **yum**, the **install** switch installs, and the **update** switch updates a package if it's already installed.

You don't need a connection to the Red Hat Network (RHN). The **yum** command works in the same way from the RHN and the remote repositories associated with Scientific Linux and CentOS. However, there are subtle differences in the configuration files. You can use the **rpm** command to install a package from the local file system. Alternatively, you can set up a local repository using the HTTP or FTP servers described in Chapter 1. All you need is a file named *file*.repo in the 4/etc/yum.repos.d directory. For example, if you have a default Apache HTTP server configured on the /var/www/html/os directory on IP address 192.168.122.1, you could include the following lines in the *file*.repo file:

```
[mine]
name=test repo
baseurl=http://192.168.122.1/os
```

You're welcome to substitute as desired for the italicized entries. When repositories for the RHN are configured through an account at rhn.redhat.com, subscribed systems are automatically connected to Red Hat's main repositories for installation packages and updates. That's functionally equivalent to the main and updates repositories common on many rebuild distributions.

The gamma.example.net VM is configured with an mh.repo file in the /etc/yum.repos.d directory. It includes options that activate access to the repository and takes advantage of GPG keys in the /etc/pki/rpm-gpg directory to verify the authenticity of such packages. If you want to deactivate the mh.repo repository, set **enabled=0**.

ⓦatch *For all objectives, you can refer to a more in-depth discussion in the* Study Guide, *also known as the* **RHCSA/ RHCE Red Hat Linux Certification Study Guide (Exams EX200 & EX300), 6th Edition.**

As I'm limited to a one-page description of each objective in this book, make sure you know the **yum install, yum update, yum search, yum info, yum clean, yum erase, yum grouplist, yum groupinfo,** and **yum groupinstall** commands. In addition, the **yum-config-manager** command displays all current parameters for each repository. Finally, the GNOME Add/Remove Software tool is a front-end to the **yum** command.

Update the Kernel Package Appropriately to Ensure a Bootable System

This objective, as written, is just a little tricky. To ensure a bootable system, you should always install and never update a kernel package. Updated kernels don't work with every system 100 percent of the time. However, if you run the **rpm -U** option with an existing kernel, it overwrites that kernel. So if that updated kernel does not work, for whatever reason, then you're out of luck. (Actually, you could use the rescue mode from the Installation DVD and reinstall an older version of the kernel, but the process is intricate.)

If successful, you'll see at least two kernels in the /boot directory, along with at least two boot options in the GRUB bootloader. That information is reflected in the GRUB configuration file: /boot/grub/grub.conf. You can confirm it from the version numbers of the kernels that are listed, in the two stanzas associated with booting.

Fortunately, the default settings for the **yum update kernel** command installs kernels as well. That's because the default **installonlypkgs** option for **yum** is set to prevent upgrades. Nevertheless, it's a better practice to run the **yum install kernel** command to update a kernel. You never know when someone might disable this particular default.

If you want to practice the **rpm** command on a new kernel, use the **yumdownloader kernel** command. It downloads the RPM for the latest available version of the **kernel** to the local directory. You may also want to download a specific, perhaps an older, version; the **yumdownloader kernel-2.6.32-220.el6.x86_64** command downloads the RPM for that particular version of the kernel.

CERTIFICATION SUMMARY

While this chapter covers only two objectives, it's a foundation for other objectives. You need to know that the right way to update a kernel is by installing it. If successful, you'll see two options in the GRUB menu, along with two sets of boot files in the /boot directory.

SELF TEST

The following fill-in-the-blank questions will help you measure your understanding of the topics associated with this chapter. As there are no multiple-choice questions on the Red Hat exams, there are no multiple-choice questions in this book. If you have trouble with one or more of these questions, you may need to research associated topics further. However, there's almost always more than one way to solve a problem in Linux. Getting results, not memorizing trivia, is what counts on the Red Hat exams.

As this is a practice book, the answers to these questions may or may not be found in the body of the chapter. For more information, see the *Study Guide*.

Install and Update Software Packages from Red Hat Network, a Remote Repository, or from the Local File System

1. What command uses the local abc-1.2.3-x86_64.rpm to upgrade the current version of the abc package?

   _____

2. What command would you use to install the latest available version of the package named def from the RHN? What command would you use to install the latest version of that same def package on Scientific Linux? Assume both systems have a high-speed network connection.

   _____

3. What is the main configuration file for **yum**?

   _____

4. What command would install the **FTP server** package group? Hint: FTP server is listed in the output to the **yum grouplist** command.

   _____

Update the Kernel Package Appropriately to Ensure a Bootable System

5. You know there's a kernel update available from the FTP server on IP address 192.168.122.50, with a filename of kernel-2.6.32-220-99.el6.x86_64.rpm, in the pub/os/Packages/ subdirectory. What command can you use to install that kernel?

   _____

6. Once a new kernel is installed, you should see at least two stanzas, each with a separate boot option. What two files cited in each stanza will have different version numbers?

_____

LAB QUESTIONS

Red Hat presents its exams electronically. For that reason, the labs in this and future chapters are available from the gamma.example.net system, from the ChapterLabs/ folder that appears in the GUI desktop. If you're running in a command-line console, you can find the labs in the /home/testuser/ Desktop/ChapterLabs directory.

The answers for each lab follow the Self Test Answers for the fill-in-the-blank questions.

SELF TEST ANSWERS

Install and Update Software Packages from Red Hat Network, a Remote Repository, or from the Local File System

1. The command that upgrades the current version of the abc package with the specified RPM is **rpm -U abc-1.2.3-x86_64.rpm**. The **rpm -F abc-1.2.3-x86_64.rpm** command is also acceptable.

2. The simplest command that installs the latest available version of the package named def from either the RHN or Scientific Linux repositories is **yum install def**.

3. The main configuration file for **yum** is /etc/yum.conf. It pulls in configuration files from the /etc/yum.repos.d directory and additional information from files in the /etc/yum directory.

4. The simplest command that installs the **FTP server** package group is **yum groupinstall "FTP server"**. The **yum groupinstall FTP\ Server** command is also acceptable. (Variations such as single quotes are acceptable. This is a rare command where capitalization of the package group does not matter.)

Update the Kernel Package Appropriately to Ensure a Bootable System

5. One command that installs the noted kernel package from the specified FTP server is **rpm -ivh ftp://192.168.122.50/pub/os/Packages/kernel-2.6.32-220-99.el6.x86_64.rpm**. While the **-v** and the **-h** switches are not required, the **-U** or the **-F** switches are unacceptable answers, as they would overwrite existing kernels.

6. The difference between the two stanzas will be the version numbers of the kernel and the initramfs files. It's also acceptable to refer to these files as the Kernel and the Initial RAM disk.

LAB ANSWERS

Lab 1

If successful, you'll see the version of the kernel that you installed in the output to the **uname -r** command. (Other **uname** commands, such as **uname -a**, also work.) For example, if you've just installed the kernel-2.6.32-220.4.el6.x86_64.rpm package, you see the following output to the **uname -r** command:

```
2.6.32-220.4.el6.x86_64
```

If you want to expand your skills, here's one more task. On the gamma.example.net system, make sure the files in the /root/boot directory match those in the /boot directory. Delete the files from that /boot directory. Reboot the system. What happens?

Reboot the system from the installation DVD, and boot into rescue mode. Restore the files from the /root/boot directory to /boot. Reboot the system again. The system should boot normally into the default kernel.

If something goes wrong and all else fails, a compressed version of the gamma.example.net VM is still available from the gamma.tar.gz file on the DVD. If you have to restore the VM, don't forget to ensure the hardware address of the network card is set to 52:54:00:b8:a7:ea, as discussed in previous chapters.

Lab 2

This lab is just slightly tricky. If you run the **yum groupinstall "Backup Server"** command, you install just one of the three packages in that group. You need to install the other packages in that group individually. One way to identify the packages in that group is to use the **yum groupinfo "Backup Server"** command.

Lab 3

Given the standard configuration of yum-related packages, all you need to do is add three lines to a file in the /etc/yum.repos.d directory. You can give any legal name to that file, as long as it has a .repo extension. Assuming you've set up the installation FTP server on the physical host system, one example of the three lines in that file would be:

```
[anything]
name=something
baseurl=ftp://192.168.122.1/pub/os
```

As long as you keep the same format, you can substitute for *anything* and *something* in the lines shown here. If successful, you'll see the word in the first line (*anything*) in the output to the **yum update** command.

Lab 4

To meet the requirements of this lab, run the **yum grouplist** command, and isolate those groups listed under Installed Groups. It's understood that the contents of the packagegroups.txt file will vary.

8

User
Administration

A s suggested by the title, this chapter is focused on the administration of users and groups. The objective associated with multiuser logins is tangentially related to user configuration. If you've mastered the objectives associated with this chapter, you understand how to manage users and associated passwords. You know how to set up specialized groups, along with dedicated directories configured for collaboration. Finally, you know how to configure a client to refer to a remote LDAP service for user and group information.

Although the focus here is on the command line, you can perform most of these tasks with the GUI User Manager tool. One way to start the tool from a command line in the GUI is with the **system-config-users** command.

Log In and Switch Users in Multiuser Runlevels

This objective should be straightforward even for users with a few days of Linux experience at the command line. First, there are four standard runlevels associated with logins of multiple users: 2, 3, 4, and 5. If a GUI login manager (and associated GUI desktop) is installed, user/password logins are straightforward for any computer user. Such logins are associated with runlevel 5. By default, these logins are associated with the first virtual terminal. In general, you can access different virtual terminals with the CTRL+ALT+F*n* key, where *n* is a number between 1 and 6. The CTRL key is not required if you're already in a console login screen, with a prompt similar to what's shown here:

```
Scientific Linux release 6.2 (Carbon)
Kernel 2.6.32-220.el6.x86_64 on an x86_64

gamma login:
```

You can log in on this screen, just as you would log into the GUI with a configured username and password.

To switch users in the GNOME desktop, click System | Log Out *user*. In the window that appears, click Switch User. You're taken to the original GUI login manager. Despite what you just clicked, you see that the current user is still logged in. Any jobs currently being run by that user continue.

To switch users at the command line, switch to a different console. You see another login screen for the second user. The first user is still logged in.

Create, Delete, and Modify Local Users Accounts

The essence of user (and group) accounts on a Linux system rests in the shadow password suite. The information from that suite is contained in the passwd, shadow, group, and gshadow files in the /etc directory. To verify characteristics for users and groups, it can help to know each component in these files.

You can create new users with the **useradd** command. When you run a command like **useradd user1**, default options are set in the /etc/login.defs file. If you know the options for these commands, you can set users for nonstandard groups, set up temporary accounts, define different default shells, and more.

You can delete users with the **userdel** command. As the home directories of deleted users are retained by default, you should be aware of the **userdel -r** command, which deletes those home directories and their contents, along with any mailbox file that might exist in the /var/mail directory.

You can modify user information directly from the shadow password suite files or with the **usermod** command. With the right options, you can modify the information contained within the files of the shadow password suite. In many cases, it's better to use commands, as multiple files can be affected.

Just remember, when you create a new user, the user private group scheme means that user is the exclusive member of his or her own group. By default, the user and group have the same name and ID number.

One implicit part of this objective is the way regular users are given administrative privileges in the /etc/sudoers file.

Change Passwords and Adjust Password Aging for Local User Accounts

Every user has the right to change the password for his or her account with the **passwd** command. The administrative user has the right to change the password for any user with the **passwd** *username* command.

Password aging is a security component. If a black-hat hacker gets hold of your password database, or applies social engineering techniques to specific users, passwords may eventually be compromised. Aging can be employed to force users to change their passwords on a periodic basis.

To review current password aging for a user, run the **chage -l *user*** command. When applied to the testuser account, I get the following output:

```
Last password change                              : Jan 30, 2012
Password expires                                  : never
Password inactive                                 : never
Account expires                                   : never
Minimum number of days between password change    : 0
Maximum number of days between password change    : 99999
Number of days of warning before password expires : 7
```

Know how to modify each of these settings, as each plays a part in password aging policies. You can make changes with the **chage** command or the GUI User Manager tool.

Create, Delete, and Modify Local Groups and Group Memberships

People frequently work in groups. In Linux, a group can be configured as an owner of a file. Users who are members of that group may be allowed to read, write, or execute that file. So administrators may need to create special groups, as well as modify those groups to add or delete users. Of course, when the group has finished its tasks, you as an administrator may need to delete that group.

The associated commands are **groupadd**, **usermod**, **groupmod**, and **groupdel**. Be aware, when you create a group, it takes the next available group ID number. If you like to keep the same user and group ID numbers for new users, that would mess up things. To that end, the following command specifies a local group number typically out of range of standard group IDs:

```
# groupadd -g 4000000 special
```

But no user is a member of that group, yet. To add members, you can add usernames to the appropriate lines in /etc/group and /etc/gshadow. Alternatively, you can specify users to add to a specific group; the following **usermod** command adds user testuser to group special:

```
# usermod -G special testuser
```

Unfortunately, the **usermod** command is less flexible with respect to deleting secondary users from a specific group. It's often easiest to delete those users directly in both the /etc/group and /etc/gshadow files or with the help of the GUI User Manager.

Create and Configure set-GID Directories for Collaboration

If you've created a specialized group, you can also create a dedicated directory for that group with specialized permissions. When done correctly, users who are members of that group have full access to files in that specialized directory.

For example, if you've created the group named *special* earlier in this chapter, you could take steps similar to the following ones to create and configure a "set-GID" directory.

1. Create an appropriate dedicated directory. As it would be configured like a regular user's home directory, it would be appropriate to set it up as a /home subdirectory. One way to do this is with the **mkdir /home/special** command.

2. Set appropriate group ownership. The following command gives a user such as promgr1 ownership of that directory, with privileges for members of that group:

```
# chown promgr1:special /home/special
```

3. Configure appropriate permissions; the following command sets up the set-GID bit, along with full read/write/execute permissions for the group owner of that directory:

```
# chmod 2770 /home/special
```

An alternative to the first 2 in the **chmod 2770** is **chmod g+s**. In other words, the noted **chmod** command activates the set-GID bit. Any files created in that directory automatically are assigned group ownership based on the group owner of that directory.

In other words, if a member of the group named *special* saves a work file to the /home/special directory, *special* becomes the group owner of that file. The directory is now ready for collaboration among the members of the *special* group.

Configure a System to Use an Existing LDAP Directory Service for User and Group Information

Not every Linux administrator understands LDAP, the Lightweight Directory Access Protocol. And that's acceptable, as network-based directory services require specialized knowledge. It's consistent with the objectives for both the RHCSA and RHCE certifications, as there is no current requirement in either exam to configure an LDAP server. (Of course, that is subject to change.)

To configure a system as an LDAP client, you need to configure three files: /etc/nsswitch.conf, /etc/pam_ldap.conf, and /etc/openldap/ldap.conf. As LDAP databases can include user and group information, you may need to make sure it is included with appropriate entries in the /etc/nsswitch.conf file, such as:

```
passwd: files ldap
shadow: files ldap
group: files ldap
```

If you configured the System Security Services Daemon (**sssd**) to start automatically during the boot process, substitute **sss** for **ldap**.

The /etc/pam_ldap.conf file comes from the pam_ldap RPM, which you may need to install. (You also need the nss-pam-ldapd package.) It helps enforce consistent password policies across a network. Pay attention to at least the **host** and **base** directives, as the LDAP server is probably located on a remote system, and the distinguished name may be something other than example.com.

Four directives of interest in the /etc/openldap/ldap.conf file are: BASE, URI, HOST, and, possibly, TLS_CACERTDIR, as they relate to the distinguished name, location of the LDAP server, hostname of the LDAP server, and the directory path to the appropriate certificate authorities, respectively:

```
URI ldap://127.0.0.1
HOST tester1.example.com
BASE dc=example,dc=com
TLS_CACERTDIR /etc/openldap/cacerts
```

In most cases, it's simpler to configure an LDAP client with the Authentication Configuration tool. You can access it with the **system-config-authentication** or the **authconfig-tui** command. Any changes you make with that tool are reflected in the noted configuration files.

CERTIFICATION SUMMARY |

This chapter addressed objectives related to the administration of groups and users. Logging in is a basic skill. If you know how to switch users in the GUI or in different consoles, different users can run programs simultaneously on the same system.

But you first need to create those users, locally. Commands like **useradd**, **userdel**, and **usermod** can help you create, delete, and modify local accounts. Selected accounts can be configured with varying administrative privileges based on options in the /etc/sudoers file. The **passwd** and **chage** commands can be used to change passwords and modify password aging requirements. The **groupadd**, **groupdel**, and **groupmod** commands can help you create, delete, and modify groups. You can also edit the /etc/group and /etc/gshadow files to configure group membership.

For a specialized group of users, you can create a dedicated group directory. When configured with the set-GID bit, it supports collaboration between members of that group. That set-GID bit assigns group ownership to any files copied to that dedicated group directory.

Finally, you need to know how to set up a system as an LDAP client. The Authentication Configuration tool may be the most efficient way to make that happen.

SELF TEST

The following fill-in-the-blank questions help you measure your understanding of the topics associated with this chapter. As there are no multiple-choice questions on the Red Hat exams, there are no multiple-choice questions in this book. If you have trouble with one or more of these questions, you may need to research associated topics further. However, there's almost always more than one way to solve a problem in Linux. Getting results, not memorizing trivia, is what counts on the Red Hat exams.

As this is a practice book, the answers to these questions may or may not be found in the body of the chapter. For more information, see the *Study Guide*.

Log In and Switch Users in Multiuser Runlevels

1. What standard runlevels support access from multiple users?

   _____

Create, Delete, and Modify Local Users Accounts

2. Specify the command that deletes the account for user testuser4, while preserving the files in that user's home directory.

   _____

Change Passwords and Adjust Password Aging for Local User Accounts

3. For user testuser3, what command sets the maximum password life to seven days?

   _____

Create, Delete, and Modify Local Groups and Group Memberships

4. Name all files, associated with the shadow password suite, with information about additional groups to which a user may belong.

   _____

Create and Configure set-GID Directories for Collaboration

5. What command configures just the set-GID bit on the /home/group1 directory? Assume proper ownership and access modes have already been set.

_____

6. Assume the set-GID bit is set on /home/group1, and ownership is given to user supervisor and group group1. What happens to the ownership of the status.doc file, when it is copied to the /home/group1 directory?

_____

Configure a System to Use an Existing LDAP Directory Service for User and Group Information.

7. When properly configured, what file forces the system to look for LDAP directory services?

_____

LAB QUESTIONS

Red Hat presents its exams electronically. For that reason, the labs in this and future chapters are available from the gamma.example.net system, from the ChapterLabs/ folder that appears in the GUI desktop. If you're running in a command-line console, you can find the labs in the /home/testuser/Desktop/ChapterLabs directory.

The answers for each lab follow the Self Test Answers for the fill-in-the-blank questions.

SELF TEST ANSWERS

Log In and Switch Users in Multiuser Runlevels

1. The standard runlevels that support access from multiple users are 2, 3, 4, and 5.

Create, Delete, and Modify Local Users Accounts

2. The command that deletes the account for user testuser4, while preserving the files in that user's home directory, is

```
userdel testuser4
```

Change Passwords and Adjust Password Aging for Local User Accounts

3. The command that sets the maximum password life to seven days for testuser3 is

```
chage -M 7 testuser3
```

Create, Delete, and Modify Local Groups and Group Memberships

4. The shadow password suite files with information about additional groups are /etc/group and /etc/gshadow. The /etc/passwd file contains information only about a user's main group.

Create and Configure set-GID Directories for Collaboration

5. Under the given conditions, the command that configures just the set-GID bit on the /home/group1 directory is

```
chmod g+s /home/group1
```

6. Courtesy of the set-GID bit, ownership of the status.doc file, when copied to the /home/group1 directory, is assigned to group group1.

Configure a System to Use an Existing LDAP Directory Service for User and Group Information

7. When properly configured, the file that forces the system to look for LDAP directory services is /etc/nsswitch.conf.

LAB ANSWERS

Lab 1

Since all users (including test1, test2, and test3) are supposed to get a copy of the ChapterLabs/ subdirectory, add that to the /etc/skel directory. One way to do so is with the following command:

```
# cp -ar /home/testuser/Desktop/ChapterLabs /etc/skel
```

Make sure to leave out the trailing slash to the ChapterLabs/ directory, so the directory container is also copied to /etc/skel. For completeness, you should also assign ownership of that directory (and the files therein) to the root user and group. One way to do this is with the following command:

```
# chown -R root.root /etc/skel/ChapterLabs
```

Now create the specified users. Remember, these accounts should be set to expire in 90 days. If today is November 1, 2012, the expiration date would be February 1, 2013. One way to do this is with the following commands:

```
# useradd -e 2013-02-01 temp1
# useradd -e 2013-02-01 temp2
# useradd -e 2013-02-01 temp3
```

Configure a password for all three users. Yes, the password should be temp1, temp2, and temp3, respectively. And make sure to get the password right; you do want to make it as easy as possible for a proctor to grade your exam. One way to set up those passwords is with the following commands:

```
# passwd temp1
# passwd temp2
# passwd temp3
```

While there are a number of methods available to create new users and groups, they should all come to the same result. You should be able to verify the account expiration date in the output to the **chage -l** *username* command.

Lab 2

Settings for future users are configured in /etc/login.defs. To meet the requirements of the lab, change two directives in that file to

```
PASS_MAX_DAYS    14
PASS_MIN_DAYS    2
```

But the settings for users temp1, temp2, and temp3 are different. You have to set minimum and maximum password lifetimes with a command such as **chage**. For example, the following command sets these parameters for user temp1.

```
# chage -m 2 -M 7 temp1
```

Of course, you have to repeat this process with users temp2 and temp3. To verify for the first temporary user, run the **chage -l temp1** command. Repeat the command to verify desired changes for users temp2 and temp3.

Lab 3

Administrative privileges associated with "sudo" are based on the /etc/sudoers file. For the user named testuser, I'll describe two ways to set up full sudo-based administrative privileges. First, you could set up a line similar to the one used for the root administrative user:

```
testuser    ALL=(ALL)    ALL
```

Alternatively, you could activate the line associated with the wheel group:

```
%wheel    ALL=(ALL)    ALL
```

Then you make testuser a member of the wheel group, as configured in the /etc/group and /etc/gshadow files.

For system shutdowns, there's already a group configured in /etc/sudoers for this purpose, based on the following line:

```
# %users  localhost=/sbin/shutdown -h now
```

Activate this line, and make user temp1 a member of the users group in the /etc/group and /etc/gshadow files. To make that line valid from local and remote systems, change it to:

```
%users  ALL=/sbin/shutdown -h now
```

To test the result, try running a regular administrative command as testuser; for example, try **sudo fdisk /dev/vda**. (The /dev/vda device is the standard for the gamma.example.net VM.) You should be prompted for the testuser password, rhcert.

To test the result from the temp1 account, run the **sudo /sbin/shutdown -h now** command, and enter the temp1 password when prompted. If successful, the system should begin shutting down.

Lab 4

Although there are several ways to meet the requirements of the lab, the results are the same in the /etc/group and /etc/gshadow file. In the /etc/group file, you should see the following entry:

```
temps:x:123456:temp1,temp2,temp3
```

In the /etc/gshadow file, you should see this:

```
temps:!::temp1,temp2,temp3
```

Lab 5

In previous labs, you've already created the temp1, temp2, and temp3 users, as well as the temps group. Now you need to create the /home/temps directory and give it appropriate permissions, along with the set-GID bit. One way to do this is with the following commands:

```
# mkdir /home/temps
# chown nobody.temps
# chmod 2770 /home/temps
```

Lab 6

If you haven't configured an LDAP server, you just have to inspect appropriate configuration files for the right entries. First, the /etc/nsswitch.conf should include either **ldap** or **sss** in the entries for **passwd**, **shadow**, and **group** directives. The Authentication Configuration tool normally uses the **sssd** daemon.

In either case, you see the following active entries in the /etc/openldap/ldap.conf file:

```
URI ldap://192.168.122.1/
BASE dc=example,dc=net
```

In addition, you see the following active entries in the /etc/pam_ldap.conf file:

```
base dc=example,dc=net
uri ldap://192.168.122.1/
ssl no
pam_password md5
```

While you also see an entry for certificate authority directory in both files, (TLS_CACERTDIR), it's not used based on the conditions for the lab.

Unless you have an LDAP server for the network, don't forget to disable the LDAP client, by reversing the steps you took in this lab.

9

RHCSA-Level System Administration Tasks

T
his is the final chapter associated with RHCSA exam objectives. As such, it's a "catch-all" chapter of sorts that addresses those administrative tasks not covered in other chapters. While most remote administration is done at the command line, there are times when the GUI access associated with Virtual Network Computing (VNC) can help. Other tasks include package and process management, administrative task scheduling, and local system log file management.

Access Remote Systems Using VNC

If you've read the objectives carefully, you'll note the objective includes SSH. Well, that part of the objective was covered in Chapter 2. In addition, you may already know more about VNC than you think, as it's the standard viewer for KVM-based virtual machines.

When properly configured, you can use VNC to see the GUI that a user sees. With that window, you can even help that user from a remote location. One way to set it up on a client is with the vinagre, tigervnc, and tigervnc-server packages.

To enable access to a VNC server, you should open at least TCP ports 5900 and 5901. If you're setting up VNC for a second user, you also need to open up TCP port 5902; a third user requires TCP port 5903, and so on.

If you want to demonstrate the use of VNC on a system such as gamma.example. net, close any existing graphical window for that system. The gamma.example.net client is still running; closing that graphical window prevents "feedback" issues.

This is one task where you'll want to run a client from the physical host system. Although you can run a VNC client from within a KVM system, it can lead to strange effects.

Archive, Compress, Unpack, and Uncompress Files Using tar, star, gzip, and bzip2

Before there were RPMs, Linux software packages were delivered via compressed archives. Files were collected in a single archive with the **tar** command and then compressed with the **gzip** or **bzip2** commands. Of course, you can incorporate either compression algorithms into the **tar** command.

For example, the following command creates a **gzip** compressed **tar** archive from the PracExams/ subdirectory, along with its contents:

```
$ tar czvf PracExams.tar.gz PracExams/
```

As most of you already know, to set up a bzip2 compressed archive, you substitute a j for the z. If you're unpacking an archive, substitute an x (extract) for the c (create). If you've created an archive with absolute path names, you can unpack that archive in the same way with the **P** switch.

One weakness of the **tar** command is that it does not preserve SELinux file contexts or Access Control List (ACL) attributes. That's the reason for the **star** command. Unfortunately, it includes a different set of switches. The following example saves the contents of the /home/testuser directory with both SELinux and ACL features:

```
# star -xattr -H=exustar -c -f=testuser.star /home/testuser
```

You have to compress separately with the **gzip** or **bzip2** commands. You can unpack the noted archive with the following command:

```
# star -x -f=testuser.star
```

Identify CPU/Memory Intensive Processes; Adjust Process Priority with renice, kill Processes

The essence of this objective is contained within the **ps**, **top**, **nice**, **renice**, **kill**, and **killall** commands. With those commands, you can identify running processes, find which process is consuming the most resources, reprioritize what process should have more resources, and stop processes that are ready to end.

Although the **ps** command just lists processes associated with the current console, you can go further. The **ps u** command lists processes for the current user; the **ps x** command includes those processes not associated with a terminal. The **ps l** command includes the parent process identifier (PPID).

The **top** command sets up a console browser that orders those processes in a sortable fashion, normally focused on CPU and RAM memory usage. The **nice** command allows you to start a process with a nonstandard priority; the **renice** command reprioritizes a running process. The priorities seem reversed, as they range from –20 (highest) to +19 (lowest).

When you identify a process that simply must be stopped, the **kill** command can help. It can be called indirectly from the **top** browser, or it can affect a process by PID. Some **kill** options can restart, gracefully stop, or even halt a process uncleanly. There are servers that normally run several processes automatically. If you know the process name, you can use the **killall** command to stop all instances of that service.

Schedule Tasks Using cron

The cron daemon is typically used by administrators to run scheduled tasks on a periodic basis. It works hand-in-hand with the anacron service, for those systems that may be subject to power outages. As configured, it's set up to search for jobs in several basic locations:

- Administrative jobs in the /etc/cron.d directory
- Hourly administrative jobs specified via /etc/cron.d/0hourly in the /etc/cron.hourly directory
- User-defined jobs in the /var/spool/cron directory
- Administrative jobs defined via /etc/anacrontab, in the /etc/cron.daily, /etc/cron.weekly, and the /etc/cron.monthly directories.

Consider these files when creating scripts for your own cron jobs. Each of these jobs is scheduled based on the following format, as defined in Table 9-1.

```
minute   hour   day of month     day of week   command
```

TABLE 9-1	Field	Value
Columns in a cron Configuration File	minute	0–59
	hour	Based on a 24-hour clock, for example, 23 = 11 P.M.
	day of month	1–31
	month	1–12, or jan, feb, mar, etc.
	day of week	0–7, where 0 and 7 are both Sunday, or sun, mon, tue, etc.
	command	The command to be executed, sometimes listed with the username to run the command

Cron jobs don't carry environmental variables from the current shell; most scripts start with a directive such as:

```
#!/bin/bash
```

Locate and Interpret System Log Files

The RHCSA objective is associated with local logs, as configured with the rsyslog daemon. There are corresponding objectives for the RHCE exam that address system log files transmitted and received over a network.

For all logs, you need to understand the basic logging facilities (authpriv, cron, kern, mail, news, user, and uucp), and their associated services. Logging data from each facility may be collected from one or more priorities (in ascending order): **debug, info, notice, warn, err, crit, alert, emerg**.

Although standard system logs are stored in the /var/log directory, each service can be configured to control its own log files. You should at least understand the functionality of each log file. A few significant log files and directories are described in Table 9-2.

TABLE 9-2	Log Files	Description
Standard Red Hat Log Files	audit/	Includes the audit.log file, associated with SELinux
	boot.log	Associated with services that start and shut down processes
	btmp	Lists failed login attempts; readable with the **utmpdump btmp** command
	cron	Collects information from scripts run by the cron daemon
	dmesg	Includes basic boot messages
	maillog	Collects log messages related to e-mail servers
	messages	Includes messages from other services as defined in /etc/syslog.conf
	rpmpkgs	Current list of installed RPM packages
	secure	Lists login and access messages
	setroubleshoot/	Directory of messages associated with the SELinux troubleshooting tool
	spooler	Shows a log file that might include critical messages
	Xorg.0.log	Notes setup messages for the X Window System; may include configuration problems
	yum.log	Specifies logs packages installed, updated, and erased with **yum**

CERTIFICATION SUMMARY

A systems administrator works on a variety of tasks. VNC makes it possible for that administrator to see what a user is doing remotely on a GUI system, assuming open TCP ports 5900 and 5901.

Different systems administration commands relate to packages, including **tar**, **star**, **gzip**, and **bzip2**. As an administrator, you need to know how to identify processes that are using too much memory or CPU with commands like **ps** and **top**. Once identified, you can reprioritize them with **renice**, stop them with **kill** and **killall**, and restart them in a more appropriate priority with **nice**.

Automated administration is still possible with the cron daemon. Jobs can be stored in the /etc/cron.d directory, time-sensitive directories such as /etc/cron.hourly and /etc/cron.monthly, as well as user-specified jobs in the /var/spool/cron directory.

When problems arise, you may need to refer to log files. Most local system log files can be found in the /var/log directory. File locations and facilities, as well as log levels to be collected, are defined in the /etc/rsyslog.conf file. Service-related log files may be configured in their own specialized directories.

SELF TEST

The following fill-in-the-blank questions help you measure your understanding of the topics associated with this chapter. As there are no multiple-choice questions on the Red Hat exams, there are no multiple-choice questions in this book. If you have trouble with one or more of these questions, you may need to research associated topics further. However, there's almost always more than one way to solve a problem in Linux. Getting results, not memorizing trivia, is what counts on the Red Hat exams.

   As this is a practice book, the answers to these questions may or may not be found in the body of the chapter. For more information, see the *Study Guide*.

Access Remote Systems Using VNC

1. Name one of two VNC client packages.

   _____

Archive, Compress, Unpack, and Uncompress Files Using tar, star, gzip, and bzip2

2. What command compresses and archives the contents of the /test/remote directory in bzip2 format with absolute paths? Set up the archive in a file named remotearchive.

   _____

Identify CPU/Memory Intensive Processes; Adjust Process Priority with renice, kill Processes

3. What command changes a process with a PID of 2020 to the lowest possible priority?

   _____

Schedule Tasks Using cron

4. Write a simple cron script that writes a list of the files in the /var/log directory to a file named loglist in the testuser home directory.

   _____

5. Where would you locate that script if you want it to be run on an hourly basis?

   _____

Locate and Interpret System Log Files

6. In what directory can you find system log files associated with SELinux?

_____

LAB QUESTIONS

Red Hat presents its exams electronically. For that reason, the labs in this and future chapters are available from the gamma.example.net system, from the ChapterLabs/ folder that appears in the GUI desktop. If you're running in a command-line console, you can find the labs in the /home/testuser/ Desktop/ChapterLabs directory.

The answers for each lab follow the Self Test Answers for the fill-in-the-blank questions.

SELF TEST ANSWERS

Access Remote Systems Using VNC

1. The two basic VNC client packages available for RHEL 6 are vinagre and tigervnc. In addition, as the vnc-viewer package uses VNC, it is also a correct answer.

Archive, Compress, Unpack, and Uncompress Files Using tar, star, gzip, and bzip2

2. The command that compresses and archives the contents of the /test/remote directory in bzip2 format with absolute paths in a file named remotearchive is

```
tar cjf remotearchive.tar.bz2 /test/remote
```

Identify CPU/Memory Intensive Processes; Adjust Process Priority with renice, kill Processes

3. The **renice 19 2020** command changes a process with a PID of 2020 to the lowest possible priority.

Schedule Tasks Using cron

4. One simple way to write such a script is to include the following line in a text file and make it executable:

```
/bin/ls /var/log > /home/testuser/loglist
```

5. Variations on this script, as long as it meets the requirements of this question, are acceptable. To set up a script to run on an hourly basis, set it up in the /etc/cron.hourly directory.

Locate and Interpret System Log Files

6. System log files associated with SELinux can be found in the /var/log/audit directory.

LAB ANSWERS

Lab 1

To minimize confusion, you could start the gamma.example.net system without opening the standard KVM window. One way to do this is with the **virsh start gamma.example.net** command. You can then connect to and administer the gamma system via SSH.

You can verify success in this lab by running a VNC client such as the Remote Desktop Viewer or the TigerVNC Viewer from the physical host system to show the active GUI from the gamma. example.net system.

To do so, you need to make sure the following conditions are met:

- The VNC server is running from the target user account.
- Appropriate TCP ports are open, at least 5900 and 5901 for the first user.
- The VNC server is configured in the /etc/sysconfig/vncservers file.
- You've started the VNC server from a target user's account. For example, from the testuser account, you could run the **vncserver :1** command to enable access over the given TCP ports.

Be aware, the Remote Desktop Preferences server configuration tool has problems with KVM-based VMs. That is not a bug, at least in my personal opinion, as KVM-based VMs already use VNC for normal operation. For the purpose of this lab, the TigerVNC server is the preferred method for configuring VNC on a KVM-based VM. If successful, you should be able to connect from the physical host with the TigerVNC client. Based on the conditions stated, you connect to the GUI on the testuser account by navigating to 192.168.122.20:1.

Lab 2

Before starting this lab, you may need to install the **star** command, available from an RPM of the same name. While the **star** command preserves ACL and SELinux settings, the **tar** command does not.

You can create the archive with the **star** command; one command that saves both ACLs and SELinux contexts is:

```
# star -xattr -H=exustar -c -f=homebackup /home/
```

You can then compress the archive with the **gzip** or **bzip2** commands and then transfer that archive to the /var/backup directory. The **gzip** and **bzip2** commands each add appropriate extensions (.gz or .bz2) to the given file.

Lab 3

The simplest place to create such a script is in the /etc/cron.monthly directory. The script can be simple; I would add the following two lines to some file in that directory:

```
#!/bin/bash
ps aux > /root/ps1
```

Make sure the root user can execute that script.

Lab 4

For this purpose, I created a script named break in the /etc/cron.d directory, with the following lines:

```
# create a break time message at 9, 11, 1, and 3
0 9,11,13,15 * * * root /usr/bin/wall "Time for a break;
press Enter to continue."
```

Even though this line is wrapped in the book, it must remain on one continuous line to work.

Lab 5

This lab includes three relatively simple tasks with files in the /var/log file that help you verify your skills diagnosing problems that may exist.

You can identify the network settings configured during the installation process in the anaconda .ifcfg.log file. This file won't exist if you didn't configure networking during installation. As the hardware address is associated with the **HWADDR** variable, one way to save the noted address is with the following command:

```
# grep HWADDR /var/log/anaconda.ifcfg.log > /root/ifcfg_eth0
```

If you haven't changed the GRUB configuration file, you should be able to find the UUID associated with the top-level root directory in the /var/log/dmesg file. (You may have changed the GRUB configuration file in Chapter 5.) If the GRUB configuration file still has the UUID, you should be able to meet the requirements in step 3 of the lab with the following command:

```
# grep UUID /var/log/dmesg > /root/rootUUID
```

Errors in the X Server log file are marked with an (EE). One way to meet the requirement in step 4 of the lab is with the following command:

```
# grep \(EE\) /var/log/Xlog.0.log > /root/Xerror
```

For the VMs configured from the DVD, you should see the following lines in the Xerror file:

```
          (WW) warning, (EE) error, (NI) not implemented, (??) unknown.
[    23.951] (EE) open /dev/fb0: No such device
[    24.963] (EE) QEMU 0.12.1 QEMU USB Tablet: failed to initialize for
relative axes.
```

10

A Security Primer

T his chapter provides a brief summary of some of the firewall-based security options available for RHEL 6. Advanced SELinux concepts are addressed in Chapter 11.

These options start with **iptables**-based firewalls; **iptables** also helps protect systems within internal networks with the help of Network Address Translation (NAT).

Security goes beyond **iptables** to more dedicated user- and host-based options, however. These options include Pluggable Authentication Modules (PAM), TCP Wrappers, and options specific to dedicated services.

In principle, it's best to start with systems configured with a minimal number of services. Such bastion systems are easier to secure. With solutions such as KVM, it's easier than ever to set up custom secure systems for each major service.

Use iptables to Implement Packet Filtering and Configure Network Address Translation (NAT)

The current Linux implementation of firewalls is based on the **iptables** and **ip6tables** commands. Those commands include three basic options: **filter**, **nat**, and **mangle**. The **mangle** option can be ignored in the context of the RHCE objectives. The default **filter** option matches a pattern such as a protocol or IP address to a packet. When the pattern matches, the associated **iptables** command specifies the action to take with that packet.

The **nat** option configures Network Address Translation, which modifies the headers of networked packets so a request from an internal system looks like it's coming from another system, normally a router.

Most **iptables**-based firewall rules are based on the **filter** option, where rules are taken together in *chains*. To list the currently active firewall rules, list them with the **iptables -L** command. If you want to empty firewall rules from the current system, *flush* them with the **iptables -F** command. You can add a rule to the end of a chain with the **iptables -A** command; when a rule number or pattern is specified, you can delete a rule with the **iptables -D** command. (The **ip6tables** command works in a similar fashion.)

Of course, you'll want to specify a pattern; options like **-s *ip_address*** can specify the source IP address (or network address). In the same fashion, an option like **-d *ip_address*** can set a pattern for the destination IP address.

You can also specify protocols and port numbers. For example, **-m tcp -p tcp --dport 22** looks for Transmission Control Protocol (TCP) packets sent to port 22. In fact, that's one default rule for RHEL 6, which supports remote access to the Secure Shell (SSH) service. Putting it all together, take this option from the /etc/sysconfig/iptables file:

```
-A INPUT -m state --state NEW -m tcp -p tcp --dport 22 -j ACCEPT
```

This is an input rule for new packets that match the TCP protocol over port 22. In this case, such packets are accepted (**ACCEPT**). Alternatively, they could be dropped (**DROP**) or rejected (**REJECT**). They can also be logged (**LOG**).

If you use the Firewall Configuration tool, use it for all **iptables**-based rules. It is worth taking some time to learn how to set up custom rules with this tool. One hint: set up custom rules in files other than iptables and ip6tables in the /etc/sysconfig directory.

Configure Host-Based and User-Based Security for the Service

The RHCE objectives cover the following services: HTTP/HTTPS, DNS, FTP, NFS, SMB, SMTP, SSH, and NTP. You can limit access to each of these services by host. Several of these services can be secured by user. You get a chance to configure such security in the labs in later chapters.

Host- and user-based security can also be configured in other ways. You can set up host-based security on specific ports based on **iptables** firewall rules. Some services include configuration files in the /etc/xinetd.d directory and can be regulated with the help of the Extended Internet Services Daemon, xinetd. Other services are associated with the TCP Wrappers library file, libwrap.so.0, and can be regulated with the help of the hosts.allow and hosts.deny files in the /etc directory.

To see if TCP Wrappers can be used to help secure a service, the library dependencies command (**ldd**) can help. For example, if you run the **ldd /usr/sbin/vsftpd grep libwrap.so.0** command, you should see the following 64-bit output to confirm:

```
libwrap.so.0 => /lib64/libwrap.so.0
```

Remember, TCP Wrappers searches /etc/hosts.allow first. If a rule that allows access is configured there, any related rule in /etc/hosts.deny is ignored. The following is a simple example of a rule that might be configured in either file:

```
sshd : ALL EXCEPT 192.168.122.130
```

If you added this rule to /etc/hosts.deny, access would be allowed only from the noted IP address, which corresponds to the whitehat.example.net system.

User-based security can also be configured with the help of PAM, based on files in the /etc/pam.d directory. The following entry from /etc/pam.d/vsftpd illustrates the rule that denies access from users listed in the /etc/vsftpd/ftpusers file:

```
auth      required      pam_listfile.so item=user sense=deny     \
file=/etc/vsftpd/ftpusers onerr=succeed
```

on the
❗job

If you understand the command line, you'll realize that the backslash shown above escapes the meaning of the carriage return, which serves as the functional equivalent of a line break. Sure, the line is in a configuration file; fortunately, the backslash also works in that particular file.

To interpret, PAM uses an authentication management (**auth**) test. The system is required to pass the test to continue. The rule that follows is based on the pam_listfile.so library in the /lib64/security directory. Details on how the library works is available in the pam_listfile man page. The **item=user** option specifies that PAM will check for the user. If there is a match, that user should be denied access (**sense=deny**). The file is /etc/vsftpd/ftpusers. If the file can't be opened, the user is allowed access (**onerr=succeed**).

CERTIFICATION SUMMARY

The **iptables** command is a key security feature of Linux, based on IPv4 networks. Rules configured in the /etc/sysconfig/iptables file can be used to check the headers of each network packet. Depending on characteristics such as network device, protocol, IP address, and port number, packets can be accepted, rejected, or dropped. For IPv6 networks, the corresponding command is **ip6tables**, configured in the /etc/sysconfig/ip6tables file. These commands can also be used in Network Address Translation to help protect the identity of systems on a private network.

User- and host-based security is another Linux security feature. Most of the services associated with the RHCE can be configured with both user- and host-based security. Some services can be secured with the help of the Extended Internet Services Daemon, xinetd. Other services that depend on the TCP Wrappers library can be secured with rules in the /etc/hosts.allow and /etc/hosts.deny files, in that order. User-based security can be enhanced with PAM; one example of user-based security resides in the /etc/pam.d/vsftpd configuration file.

SELF TEST

The following fill-in-the-blank questions help you measure your understanding of the topics associated with this chapter. As there are no multiple-choice questions on the Red Hat exams, there are no multiple-choice questions in this book. If you have trouble with one or more of these questions, you may need to research associated topics further. However, there's almost always more than one way to solve a problem in Linux. Getting results, not memorizing trivia, is what counts on the Red Hat exams.

As this is a practice book, the answers to these questions may or may not be found in the body of the chapter. For more information, see the *Study Guide*.

Use iptables to Implement Packet Filtering and Configure Network Address Translation (NAT)

1. What command displays currently configured **iptables**-based firewall rules?

_____

2. If you want to allow access from TCP packets to port 2345 from IP address 192.168.122.130, what options would you add to the **iptables** command? Hint: use the same format found in the /etc/sysconfig/iptables file.

_____

3. If you want to reject all packets from IP address 192.168.122.240, what options would you add to the **iptables** command?

_____

4. What options to the **iptables** command would drop all ICMP-related packets, including those related to the **ping** command?

_____

Configure Host-Based and User-Based Security for the Service

5. If the /etc/hosts.allow file is empty, what entry in the /etc/hosts.deny file would block access to all services that use TCP Wrappers libraries?

_____

6. If the /etc/hosts.allow file is empty, what entry in the /etc/hosts.deny file would block access to all services that use TCP Wrappers libraries, except for the system on IP address 192.168.122.130?

_____

7. How would you change the following entry from the /etc/pam.d/vsftpd file, if you wanted to prevent users listed in the /etc/blackhatters file from accessing your FTP server?

```
auth       required      pam_listfile.so item=user sense=deny  \
file=/etc/vsftpd/ftpusers onerr=succeed
```

_____

8. What command verifies that the Samba daemon, /usr/sbin/smbd, does or does not rely on TCP Wrappers libraries?

_____

LAB QUESTIONS

Red Hat presents its exams electronically. For that reason, the labs in this and future chapters are available from the gamma.example.net system, from the ChapterLabs/ folder that appears in the GUI desktop. If you're running in a command-line console, you can find the labs in the /home/testuser/Desktop/ChapterLabs directory.

The answers for each lab follow the Self Test Answers for the fill-in-the-blank questions.

SELF TEST ANSWERS

Use iptables to Implement Packet Filtering and Configure Network Address Translation (NAT)

1. The command that displays currently configured **iptables**-based firewall rules is

```
iptables -L
```

2. One way to allow access from TCP packets to port 2345 from IP address 192.168.122.130 is to add the following options to the **iptables** command:

```
-A INPUT -s 192.168.122.130 -m state --state NEW -m tcp \
-p tcp --dport 2345 -j ACCEPT
```

Variations on these options are acceptable, as long as it meets the basic conditions of the question.

3. One way to reject all packets from IP address 192.168.122.240 is to add the following options to the **iptables** command:

```
-A INPUT -s 192.168.122.240 -j REJECT
```

4. One way to configure the **iptables** command to drop all ICMP-related packets is with the following options:

```
-A INPUT -p icmp -j DROP
```

As the **ping** command uses ICMP, related packets are automatically included. You may note that the default firewall already accepts ICMP-related packets with the following entry:

```
-A INPUT -p icmp -j ACCEPT
```

You'd have to comment out or delete that entry for ICMP messages to be blocked.

Configure Host-Based and User-Based Security for the Service

5. If the /etc/hosts.allow file is empty, the following entry in the /etc/hosts.deny file would block access to all services that use TCP Wrappers libraries:

```
ALL : ALL
```

6. If the /etc/hosts.allow file is empty, the following entry in the /etc/hosts.deny file would block access to all services that use TCP Wrappers libraries, except for the system on IP address 192.168.122.130:

   ```
   ALL : ALL EXCEPT 192.168.122.130
   ```

7. To prevent users listed in the /etc/blackhatters file from accessing the local FTP server, use the following directive in the /etc/pam.d/vsftpd file:

   ```
   auth      required     pam_listfile.so item=user sense=deny \
   file=/etc/blackhatters onerr=succeed
   ```

8. One command that checks whether that the Samba daemon, /usr/sbin/smbd, relies on TCP Wrappers libraries is

   ```
   # ldd /usr/sbin/smbd | grep libwrap.so
   ```

   For RHEL 6, the Samba daemon does not depend on any TCP Wrappers libraries; in other words, the output to the noted **ldd** command should be blank.

LAB ANSWERS

Lab I

The VMs configured for this book are on the 192.168.122.0/24 network. All of these packets are connected to the physical host system via a virtual network adapter. You can configure an **iptables**-based firewall to accept all packets from that network in one of two ways:

- Make the virtual network adapter a *Trusted Interface*; that option is available through the Trusted Interfaces section of the Firewall Configuration tool. The associated rule would be

  ```
  -A INPUT -i virbr0 -j ACCEPT
  ```

- Create an **iptables** rule that supports access from the noted network; the associated rule would be

  ```
  -A INPUT -m state --state NEW -s 192.168.122.0/24 -j ACCEPT
  ```

You just need to make sure this rule precedes any other that includes IP addresses on the noted network. Of course, what you do in a "real-world" situation such as one presented on an exam depends on the exact wording of the question.

Lab 2

One of the flaws with blocking all ICMP packets is that it blocks network monitoring. While blocking such traffic is sometimes desirable, you should know how to block just the **ping**. The simplest way to set up that kind of rule is with the Firewall Configuration tool in the ICMP Filter section. It allows you to set up the firewall to reject *Echo Requests*, which is the function of the **ping** command. When implemented, it adds the following rule to the local firewall:

```
-A INPUT -p icmp -m icmp --icmp-type echo-request -j REJECT \
--reject-with icmp-host-prohibited
```

Lab 3

Most of you know that port 22 is the standard port for the SSH service. Black-hat hackers may scan systems, looking for that open port. One way to promote security is through obscurity. One way to implement obscurity is to set up nonstandard ports for critical services.

While you could then set up SSH clients to use the nonstandard port automatically, that can be a pain to implement on a whole variety of clients. One simpler way to set up "obscurity" is by port forwarding. The Firewall Configuration tool makes it easy. If you set up port forwarding on the physical host system from the virtual network device, you can redirect traffic from port 22 to the designated port 13579. When implemented with the Firewall Configuration tool, it adds the following prerouting rules to the firewall:

```
-A PREROUTING -i eth0 -p tcp --dport 22 -j MARK --set-mark 0x64 COMMIT
-A PREROUTING -i eth0 -p tcp --dport 22 -m mark --mark 0x64 -j DNAT \
--to-destination :13579
```

It then modifies the standard input firewall rule to:

```
-A INPUT -i eth0 -m state --state NEW -m tcp -p tcp --dport 13579 \
-m mark --mark 0x64 -j ACCEPT
```

If you've made the specified changes to the SSH server configuration, you should now be able to log into the SSH server normally from other systems on the network.

For future labs, you may want to restore the original configuration. To do so, you would:

- Delete the specified three rules that forward traffic from port 22 to port 13579 in the local firewall.

- Delete the **Port 13579** directive in the sshd_config file in the /etc/ssh directory, and then reload the service with a command like **/etc/init.d/sshd reload**.

Lab 4

First, you can confirm that access to the SSH server is regulated by TCP Wrappers with the following command:

```
# ldd /usr/sbin/sshd | grep libwrap.so.0
```

The TCP Wrappers files that regulate access are /etc/hosts.allow and /etc/hosts.deny. There are several different combinations of directives that prohibit access from just the blackhat system. One way to do this is to add the following directive to the /etc/hosts.deny file on the gamma.example.net system:

```
sshd : 192.168.122.240
```

Of course, you could prohibit access via the iptables-based firewall. Assuming you've retained the default TCP port 22, you could add the following rule before the rule that accepts connections from other systems:

```
-A INPUT -m state --state NEW -m tcp -p tcp -s 192.168.122.240 \
--dport 22 -j REJECT
```

However, TCP Wrappers is also an important security tool. At some point, you may be asked to use both systems to create a layered security model.

Lab 5

There are two basic ways to meet the requirements of this lab. You could set up **DenyUsers** (or perhaps a **DenyGroups**) directives for the users listed in the /etc/vsftpd/ftpusers file. That is a longer, but straightforward process.

Using the method I personally prefer, I took the following steps:

1. Copy the /etc/vsftpd/ftpusers file to the /etc/ssh directory. While not required, I renamed that file to **sshusers**.

2. Navigate to the /etc/pam.d directory in two different consoles. Open the vsftpd and sshd files in that directory. The vsftpd file includes the following directive that points to the noted file:

```
auth     required    pam_listfile.so item=user sense=deny \
   file=/etc/vsftpd/ftpusers onerr=succeed
```

3. I copied the line shown to the /etc/pam.d/sshd file, as the second **auth** directive. Of course, I changed the file reference to **file=/etc/ssh/sshusers**.

4. As authentication proceeds via PAM, the changes should be implemented automatically. In this case, you can test the result with the root administrative user. If successful, that user won't be able to log into the SSH server, locally or remotely.

Lab 6

You can set this up either via **iptables** and/or TCP Wrappers. With **iptables**, you can do so with a reference to the standard FTP server port 21, with the following directives:

```
-A INPUT -m state --state NEW -m tcp -p tcp -s 192.168.122.240 \
--dport 21 -j REJECT

-A INPUT -m state --state NEW -m tcp -p tcp -s 192.168.122.0/24 \
--dport 21 -j ACCEPT
```

Remember, rules in **iptables** chains are considered in order. It is, therefore, important to set up the **REJECT** rule first.

Alternatively, you can set this up via TCP Wrappers in the /etc/hosts.allow and /etc/hosts.deny files. Add the following entry to /etc/hosts.allow:

```
vsftpd : 192.168.122. EXCEPT 192.168.122.240
```

and the following entry to /etc/hosts.deny:

```
vsftpd: ALL
```

11

System Services and SELinux

Throughout this chapter includes several objectives that apply to most of the services associated with the RHCE. For different services, you need to know how to install the right packages. Once installed, you need to make sure the system starts when RHEL 6 is booted. You also need to know how to configure SELinux to support proper operation of the service. In addition, you will configure each service for basic operation. Of course, details are covered in different chapters of the *Study Guide*.

This chapter also illustrates these options for the Secure Shell (SSH) service, along with key-based authentication and a catch-all objective: additional options described in documentation.

Install the Packages Needed to Provide the Service

You can install the packages needed to provide a service in four basic ways:

- Download the needed RPM packages, and install them with an appropriate **rpm** command. Given the number of "dependencies" associated with RPM packages, this process can sometimes be difficult.

- Use the **yum** command to download and install desired packages and dependencies. If you know exactly which packages to install, this method can be the most efficient.

- Use the **yum groupinstall** command to download and install mandatory and default packages from a target package group. You can identify the right package group(s) to install with the **yum grouplist** command. If needed, you can learn more about a package group; for example, the **yum groupinfo "Web Server"** command includes a description of the "Web Server" package group, along with mandatory, default, and optional packages.

- Open the Add/Remove Packages tool. If you know what package groups to install, you can find it in the list of Package Collections revealed in Figure 11-1. Alternately, you could identify specific packages in different categories shown in the lower-left pane. Just realize that the **yum** commands can provide more information about each package and package group.

FIGURE 11-1   Add/Remove Packages tool

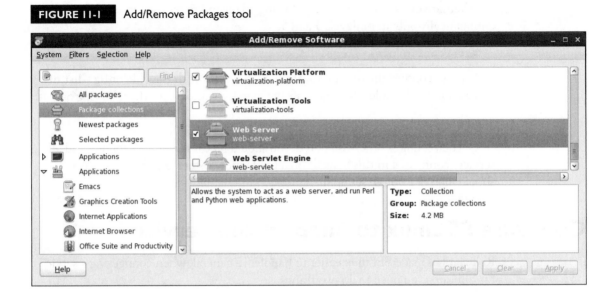

Configure the Service to Start When the System Is Booted

When configuring a service, make sure the service is active after the system is rebooted. After all, if it isn't running, how do you expect to get credit for your work?

To that end, run the **chkconfig --list** command. The output should include all services controlled from scripts in the /etc/init.d directory, including the action taken at each major runlevel. For example, the following line from the output suggests that the Network File System (NFS) service is currently set to stay off in all runlevels:

```
nfs    0:off  1:off  2:off  3:off  4:off  5:off  6:off
```

If you want to configure NFS to start in desired runlevels, you need to make sure these options are set to yes in the appropriate columns. As runlevels 0, 1, and 6 are associated with halt, single-user mode, and reboot, services should stay off in those runlevels. You could set the service to start automatically in runlevels 2 through 5 with the following command:

```
# chkconfig nfs on
```

Alternatively, you can run the following command to set the service to start automatically only in runlevels 3 and 5:

```
# chkconfig nfs --level 35 on
```

You can confirm the result for just the NFS service with the **chkconfig --list nfs** command. If only runlevels 3 and 5 are activated, you should see the following output:

```
nfs     0:off  1:off  2:off  3:on  4:off  5:on  6:off
```

Of course, unless otherwise noted, you should repeat the process for any and all services configured in this book or on a production system. Red Hat objectives should motivate you to set up such production-quality systems.

Configure SELinux to Support the Service

Red Hat has made SELinux easier to handle. In general, when configuring a service for SELinux, you need to do two things:

- Configure the file types associated with the service, normally the SELinux file types in directories being shared.
- Activate appropriate SELinux booleans in the /selinux/booleans directory.

Default file types are listed in the file_contexts file, in the /etc/selinux/targeted/contexts/files directory. In general, when sharing files from a nondefault directory, make sure the contexts match those of the default. For example, the following command matches the file contexts from the /var/www/html directory on the hypothetical /www/example.net directory:

```
# chcon -R --reference=/var/www/html /www/example.net
```

The booleans in the /selinux/booleans directory are often used to control the functionality of various services. For example, some Samba-related SELinux settings start with **samba_**. Most of these options are almost self-explanatory; for example, the **samba_enable_home_dirs** boolean controls the export of home directories over a Samba server. This option is disabled by default; to share home directories via Samba, you need to enable this boolean.

Some man pages include details for different SELinux booleans; one way to get a complete list of relevant man pages is to use the following command:

```
$ apropos _selinux
```

In addition, the SELinux Administration tool, accessible from the GUI with a **system-config-selinux** command, supports a view of booleans, easily grouped by service module, with a brief description of each boolean.

You can also get a database of these descriptions, along with their current status, by using the following command:

```
# semanage boolean -l
```

When searching through the database, be aware of the different names associated with certain services. For example, I run the following commands to identify all Samba-related booleans:

```
# semanage boolean -l | grep samba
# semanage boolean -l | grep cifs
```

Configure Key-Based Authentication

Key-based authentication is listed in the RHCE objectives as a part of the configuration of an SSH server. It's based on a pair of keys—one private, one public. The private key is kept on the SSH server, with **rw** permissions limited to the owner. The public key is available for others. For the host, the private and public keys are stored in the /etc/ssh directory. For users, the corresponding keys are stored in each user's home directory in the .ssh/ subdirectory.

When you first log into a remote system, log in with a username, using a command such as the following:

```
$ ssh testuser@gamma.example.net
```

The first time you make a connection between an SSH client and server, you're prompted with the following message:

```
The authenticity of host 'gamma.example.net (192.168.122.20)' can't be established.
RSA key fingerprint is 81:09:09:03:9e:c4:91:28:25:7c:f7:12:56:1a:05:bf.
Are you sure you want to continue connecting (yes/no)?
```

Once confirmed, the public RSA key of the remote SSH server from the /etc/ssh directory is copied to the SSH client, appended to the known_hosts file in the .ssh/ subdirectory of the client user's home directory. You're then prompted for the password of the target user on the SSH server.

When fully configured, key-based authentication supports secure connections without transmitting the password over any network. You can create a private/public user-based keypair with the **ssh-keygen** command, which prompts for a passphrase. By default, it creates a keypair with 2048 bits, which is much more secure than a standard password. You can find the private and public keys in the .ssh/ subdirectory of your home directory. By default, the keys are named id_rsa and id_rsa.pub.

You can then send the public key to the remote SSH server. The following **ssh-copy-id** command sends it to the gamma system:

```
$ ssh-copy-id -i.ssh/id_rsa.pub testuser@gamma.example.net
```

You'll find a copy of the local id_rsa.pub file appended to the end of the authorized_keys file on the SSH server, in the target user's ~/.ssh/ subdirectory. You can connect to the SSH server as before, but now you're prompted for the passphrase used to create the keypair.

Configure Additional Options Described in Documentation

Although this objective is limited to the SSH service, it is still pretty open-ended. To prepare, you really do need to understand at least those options shown in the SSH server configuration file sshd_config in the /etc/ssh directory. This section just covers a few of the major options; Chapter 10 suggested that you could set a different port number. The following directive sets up the SSH server on a nondefault port:

```
Port 13579
```

If there is more than one network card, you could use the following directive to limit access to the card on the noted IP address:

```
ListenAddress 192.168.122.20
```

While logins by the root user are enabled by default, you can prohibit them with the following directive:

```
PermitRootLogin no
```

To further promote user-based security, you could set up a list of users to allow in the configuration file, such as:

```
AllowUsers donna nancy randy mike
```

You can set up specific users on dedicated systems with directives such as:

```
AllowUsers donna@192.168.122.130
```

Related SSH server directives support customized configuration of users and groups (**AllowGroups, DenyUsers, DenyGroups**).

As noted earlier, public keys associated with passphrases are stored in the authorized_keys file in each user's .ssh/ subdirectory. That's associated with the following directive, which, of course, can be changed to help hide the file with those passphrases:

```
AuthorizedKeysFile .ssh/authorized_keys
```

When configuring just about any RHEL 6 service, you need to check appropriate SELinux settings. The **semanage boolean -l | grep ssh** command includes SELinux booleans that you may need to activate:

```
ssh_chroot_rw_homedirs  (off,off) Allow ssh with chroot env to read and write
files in the user home directories
ssh_sysadm_login  (off,off) Allow ssh logins as sysadm_r:sysadm_t
allow_ssh_keysign  (off,off) allow host key based authentication
fenced_can_ssh  (off,off) Allow fenced domain to execute ssh.
```

CERTIFICATION SUMMARY

The objectives covered in this chapter are general and specific. To install packages, you may need to use the **rpm** command on individual packages, the **yum** command to download and install one or more packages with dependencies, and the Add/ Remove Software tool to manage packages from the GUI.

Whatever you configure, you need to make sure a target service starts in appropriate runlevels the next time the system is booted. Part of the configuration process includes SELinux booleans and file contexts.

This chapter also addresses the configuration of SSH as a server. With private and public keys, you can set up authenticated connections that don't transmit passwords over a network. Additional options in the server configuration file, sshd_config, can regulate access by users, by hosts, by the root user, and for forwarding GUI applications and more.

SELF TEST

The following fill-in-the-blank questions help you measure your understanding of the topics associated with this chapter. As there are no multiple-choice questions on the Red Hat exams, there are no multiple-choice questions in this book. If you have trouble with one or more of these questions, you may need to research associated topics further. However, there's almost always more than one way to solve a problem in Linux. Getting results, not memorizing trivia, is what counts on the Red Hat exams.

As this is a practice book, the answers to these questions may or may not be found in the body of the chapter. For more information, see the *Study Guide*.

Install the Packages Needed to Provide the Service

1. What command installs the mandatory and default packages in the Web Server package group?

_____

2. What command starts the GUI Add/Remove Software tool?

_____

Configure the Service to Start When the System Is Booted

3. What command makes sure the smb service starts in runlevels 2, 3, 4, and 5?

_____

4. What command makes sure the Network Time Protocol service, ntpd, starts only in runlevel 5?

_____

Configure SELinux to Support the Service

5. In what directory would you find the SELinux booleans for the NFS directory-sharing service?

_____

6. What is the name of the file that includes the default SELinux contexts for standard directories? Just the filename is required; you don't need to spell out the directory path.

_____

Configure Key-Based Authentication

7. What permissions are associated with the private key when stored in your home directory in the .ssh/ subdirectory?

_____

8. What file in the .ssh/ subdirectory in your home directory includes the public keys from remote clients?

_____

Configure Additional Options Described in Documentation

9. What directive(s) in the SSH server configuration file support access from one or more specific users?

_____

LAB QUESTIONS

Red Hat presents its exams electronically. For that reason, the labs in this and future chapters are available from the gamma.example.net system, from the ChapterLabs/ folder that appears in the GUI desktop. If you're running in a command-line console, you can find the labs in the /home/testuser/ Desktop/ChapterLabs directory.

The answers for each lab follow the Self Test Answers for the fill-in-the-blank questions.

SELF TEST ANSWERS

Install the Packages Needed to Provide the Service

1. While there are alternatives, the one single command that installs the mandatory and default packages in the Web Server package group is:

   ```
   # yum groupinstall "Web Server"
   ```

2. The command that starts the GUI Add/Remove Software tool is:

   ```
   $ gpk-application
   ```

Configure the Service to Start When the System Is Booted

3. One command that makes sure the smb service starts in runlevels 2, 3, 4, and 5 is:

   ```
   # chkconfig smb on
   ```

   Alternatives such as **chkconfig --level 2345 smb on** are acceptable as well.

4. You need to run at least two commands to make sure the Network Time Protocol service, ntpd, starts only in runlevel 5. The following two commands serve the purpose:

   ```
   # chkconfig --level 234 ntpd off
   # chkconfig --level 5 ntpd on
   ```

Other commands may be acceptable, and the result can be confirmed with the **chkconfig --list ntpd** command.

Configure SELinux to Support the Service

5. The directory that contains all SELinux booleans, including those for NFS, is /selinux/booleans.

6. The file that includes the default SELinux contexts for standard directories is file_contexts. It happens to be in the /etc/selinux/targeted/contexts/files directory, something you can identify with the **locate file_contexts** command.

Configure Key-Based Authentication

7. The permissions are associated with the private key are 600, also known as read/write permissions for only the user owner of the file.

8. The file in the .ssh/ subdirectory in your home directory that includes the public keys from remote clients is authorized_keys.

Configure Additional Options Described in Documentation

9. You could use either the **AllowUsers** or **AllowGroups** directive in the sshd_config file to support access from one or more specific users.

LAB ANSWERS

Lab 1

If successful, you'll find the groupstatus, CIFSgroupinfo, CIFSinstall, and CIFSremove text files in the /root directory. While the contents of the groupstatus file vary, the file will list package groups in four categories:

- Installed groups
- Installed language groups
- Available groups
- Available language groups

If you've run the following command:

```
yum groupinfo "CIFS File Server" > CIFSgroupinfo
```

the contents of the CIFSgroupinfo file will include the following information:

```
Group: CIFS file server
 Description: Share files between Linux and Microsoft Windows systems.
 Mandatory Packages:
   samba
 Optional Packages:
   tdb-tools
```

As there is an optional package, the **yum -y groupinstall "CIFS file server" > CIFSinstall** command will not work. You need to run a command like the following:

```
# yum -y install samba tdb-tools > CIFSinstall
```

However, as the **yum groupremove** command is applied even to optional packages, the following command does work:

```
# yum -y groupremove "CIFS file server" > CIFSremove
```

Yes, the **yum -y remove samba tdb-tools > CIFSremove** command also works.

Lab 2

While the requirements of this lab are relatively trivial, it could be time consuming to run a command like **chkconfig** *service* **--level 4 off** on every applicable service. This is when the **ntsysv** tool, available from a package of the same name, can be helpful. The following command can help you toggle the default in runlevel 4:

```
# ntsysv --level 4
```

In the low-level graphical screen that appears, you can turn off each service at runlevel 4 relatively quickly. To confirm success, run the **chkconfig --list** command.

You should see the following entry associated with every service:

```
4:off
```

Lab 3

If successful, you'll see the following output when you run the **ls -Zd /ftp** and **ls -Zd /ftp/pub** commands:

```
drwxr-xr-x. root root system_u:object_r:public_content_t:s0 /ftp/
drwxr-xr-x. root root system_u:object_r:public_content_t:s0 /ftp/pub/
```

Perhaps the quickest way to set up these contexts on the noted directories is with the following command:

```
# chcon -R --reference=/var/ftp /ftp
```

Of course, you also need to change the default context. One way to do this is with the following commands:

```
# semanage fcontext -a -s system_u -t public_content_t /ftp
# semanage fcontext -a -s system_u -t public_content_t /ftp/pub
```

If successful, you'll see the following entries in the file_contexts.local file, in the /etc/selinux/targeted/ contexts/files directory:

```
/ftp     system_u:object_r:public_content_t:s0
/ftp/pub     system_u:object_r:public_content_t:s0
```

Lab 4

On the client system (whitehat.example.net) from the testuser account, run the **ssh-keygen** command to create the private/public keypair. Once complete, you'll see an id_rsa and id_rsa.pub file in the /home/testuser/.ssh directory. Use a command like **ssh-copy-id -i.ssh/id_rsa.pub 192.168.122.20** to send the public key to the gamma system. If you ran this lab properly, this command copied the contents of the public key file (id_rsa.pub) to the gamma.example.net system. (There are other methods that work, too.) You'll find those contents in gamma's /home/testuser/.ssh/authorized_keys file.

Of course, you should now be able to connect from whitehat to gamma and be prompted for the passphrase. If you properly enter

```
I will pass the RHCE exam!
```

the SSH server on the gamma.example.net system should allow you to connect.

Lab 5

In the /etc/ssh/sshd_config file on the gamma.example.net system, include the following entry:

```
PermitRootLogin no
```

In addition, to limiting access to the user named testuser from the noted system, include something like the following directive:

```
AllowUsers testuser@whitehat.example.net
```

In many cases, such as the default configuration for the example.net network used in this book, IP addresses are fixed. For this network, we know that whitehat.example.net is associated with IP address 192.168.122.130. In such cases, a directive like the following is also acceptable:

```
AllowUsers testuser@192.168.122.130
```

Once you run a command like **/etc/init.d/sshd reload**, logins to the root account will not be allowed through the SSH server. In addition, try using the **ssh** command from both the whitehat and the blackhat systems. You should have access from only the whitehat system.

Lab 6

This lab follows the same pattern as Lab 5. To disable GUI access over an SSH connection, you need to comment out the following directive:

```
X11Forwarding yes
```

Of course, you could include an **X11Forwarding no** line. But as that's the default, it isn't necessary. Once the SSH server is reloaded, remote users won't be able to access GUI tools over the SSH connection, even if they connect with the **ssh -X** command.

12
RHCE
Administrative
Tasks

While most of the RHCE objectives are focused on the configuration of different services, the objectives covered in this chapter are focused on different administrative tasks. As an administrator, you need to know how to create shell scripts. You can modify how the kernel interacts with other Linux components by modifying files in the /proc/sys directory and the /etc/sysctl.conf file.

To take full advantage of RHEL 6, you should know how to create an RPM. With that custom RPM, you can install custom files on the systems that you administer. RHEL 6 is built to work with remote storage. When you configure an iSCSI initiator, you demonstrate the ability to connect to one major type of network storage. When you set up a system as a Kerberos client, you're connecting it to a more secure network. And sometimes, you just need to set up a special route for network communications.

Use Shell Scripting to Automate System Maintenance Tasks

RHEL 6 includes examples of scripts that you can create to automate your own system maintenance tasks. You can find these scripts in various /etc/cron.* directories. You can see the format used to schedule a script in the /etc/crontab file (minute, hour, day of month, month, day of week, username, command). To set up a shell script, you should start that script with the desired shell, such as bash:

```
!#/bin/bash
```

The shell may not be required if you're using the script only to schedule a simple command. Just don't forget to use the full path to that command. Otherwise, you may need to set up operators of some sort, such as the following conditionals: if and test. Depending on whether the conditionals are met, the script may follow up with then and else. Some scripts include loops with do and done.

In general, scripts start by specifying some sort of condition, such as:

```
if [ ! -f /var/cache/man/whatis ]
```

The character that looks like an exclamation point (**!**) is known as a *bang,* which in Linux means "anything but." The **-f** checks for a regular file. In other words, the **if** conditional is satisfied, if the /var/cache/man/whatis file is not a regular file. You should know some of the other conditional operators, including those in Table 12-1.

TABLE 12-1	Operator	Description
Test Operators for Shell Scripts	-d	Looks to see if the file is a directory
	-e	Asks if the file exists
	-eq	Checks for equality of the noted variables or values
	-f	Works if the file is a regular file
	-ge	Looks to see if the first value is greater than or equal to the second
	-le	Looks to see if the first value is less than or equal to the second
	-lt	Looks to see if the first value is less than the second
	-ne	Looks to see if the first value is not equal to the second
	-r	Checks the file for read permissions
	-s	Checks to see if the size of the file is greater than zero
	-w	Inspects the file for write permissions
	-x	Looks to the file for execute permissions
	||	Asks if the previous expression is false
	&&	Asks if the previous expression is true

Use /proc/sys and sysctl to Modify and Set Kernel Run-Time Parameters

Kernel run-time parameters are dynamically loaded during the boot process, usually to the /proc/sys directory. You can edit specific files after the boot process is complete, or you can edit the /etc/sysctl.conf file to make sure preferred options are loaded during the boot process.

For example, you can set up IPv4 Forwarding in one of two ways. You could edit the appropriate file directly with the following command:

```
# echo "1" > /proc/sys/net/ipv4/ip_forward
```

Alternatively, you could edit the following directive in the /etc/sysctl.conf file, an action that would survive a reboot:

```
net.ipv4.ip_forward = 1
```

Other kernel run-time parameters of interest are listed in Table 12-2. If a parameter is not already in the /etc/sysctl.conf file, just add it. Remember, kernel parameters are stored in the /proc/sys directory. The parameters shown may be found in one or more of the following directories: /proc/sys/net/ipv4, /proc/sys/net/ipv4/conf/all, and /proc/sys/net/ipv4/conf/default. For example, to activate the **icmp_echo_ignore_broadcasts** parameter in the /proc/sys/net/ipv4 directory, include the following directive in /etc/sysctl.conf:

```
net.ipv4.icmp_echo_ignore_broadcasts = 1
```

You can implement any changes you make to the /etc/sysctl.conf file with the **sysctl -p** command.

Build a Simple RPM that Packages a Single File

To learn how to build an RPM package, download and install a source RPM. Many are available from ftp.redhat.com. Once installed, they can be found in the rpmbuild/ subdirectory. RPMs can be built based on .spec files in the rpmbuild/ SPECS subdirectory. To build a binary RPM, you need the **rpmbuild** command, which requires the installation of the rpm-build and rpmdevtools packages. Use the **rpmdev-setuptree** command to set up the rpmbuild/ subdirectory structure.

When you apply the **rpmbuild** command to a .spec file, the output may include dependencies that need to be installed before the binary RPM package can be built. Navigate to the rpmbuild/SPECS directory, and run the **rpmdev-newspec** command to set up a newpackage.spec template file in that directory. Copy the file to a desired package name. Examine the file. Pay attention to the directives listed in Table 12-3. Comment out any unused directives.

TABLE 12-2	Kernel Parameter	Description
Kernel Run-Time Parameters in /etc/sysctl.conf	log_martians	Activates logging of spoofed packets with impossible IP addresses
	accept_redirects	Determines access to routing tables; deactivate to deny access to black-hat hackers
	tcp_syncookies	Protects from the denial of service attack known as the SYN flood (SYN is an initial network transmission.)
	icmp_ignore_bogus_error_responses	Protects from mangled ICMP (Internet Control Message Protocol) messages
	icmp_echo_ignore_broadcasts	Stops replies to broadcasts such as those from a **ping -b** command

	Directive	Description
TABLE 12-3 Key Parameters in the newpackage .spec File	Name	Becomes the name of the RPM package
	Version	Sets the version number for the RPM, such as 1.0.
	Release	Appends to the version number; %1(?dist) represents 1.el6.
	Summary	Adds information about the RPM; actual verbiage is for documentation only.
	Group	Specifies the package group; can set to Miscellaneous.
	License	Lists the name of the license for the RPM, possibly the GPL.
	URL	Notes the website address associated with the package; usually lists the website of the developers.
	Source0	Specifies the compressed package to convert.
	BuildRoot	Specifies the assumed root directory for the RPM build; the defaults work.
	BuildArch	Includes the architecture, such as i686, x86_64, and noarch.
	BuildRequires Requires	Adds package dependencies, not required for an RPM with a single file; you may wish to comment them out.
	%description	Includes a developer-generated description.
	%prep	Notes commands associated with preparing the source code.
	%setup -q	Runs a macro that unpacks the archive from the rpmbuild/SOURCES directory.
	%build	Includes scripts to configure and make the source code (with the **%configure** and **make %{?_smp_mflags}** directives), which is not needed for an RPM with a single file; you'll likely comment these out.
	%install	Includes commands to clean and install; for this RPM, it applies to the single file; see related comments in this section.
	%clean	Cleans the source code after the RPM is built; no changes are required.
	%files	Defines the directory and file owner for the installed RPM.
	%changelog	Specifies the changes made between versions.

You'll want to add a couple of options to the %install and %files sections. The %install section in the newspec.spec template includes default commands; changes are shown in bold.

```
rm -rf $RPM_BUILD_ROOT
#make install DESTDIR=$RPM_BUILD_ROOT
```

```
install -m 0755 -d $RPM_BUILD_ROOT/opt/Chapter12
install -m 0644 onefile $RPM_BUILD_ROOT/opt/Chapter12/onefile
```

The **make install** command is not needed, as there's nothing to compile in a one-file RPM. Instead, the **install** commands set up the file in the /opt/Chapter12 directory, with 755 permissions, and the *onefile* in that directory, with 644 permissions.

You should be able to save the file, run the **rpmbuild** command to set up a binary RPM package based on the instructions in the .spec file, and then install the binary RPM, just like any other regular binary RPM.

Configure System as an iSCSI Initiator that Persistently Mounts an iSCSI Target

With an iSCSI (Internet Small Computer Systems Interface) initiator, you can set up RHEL 6 with network storage. You need the iscsi-initiator-utils package for that purpose. If you want to set up a target, you also need the scsi-target-utils package. (If you forget the names of these packages, run the **yum search scsi** command.)

Although the objectives suggest that you don't need to set up an existing target to be an RHCE, it can help you verify that you know how to mount that existing target. To do so, take the following steps:

1. Install the noted SCSI packages.

2. Start the tgtd service with the **/etc/init.d/tgtd start** command.

3. Create a /var/lib/tgtd/rhce directory; the /var/lib/tgtd directory already has default contexts.

4. Create a 100MB image file in the new directory with the **dd if=/dev/zero of=/var/lib/tgtd/rhce/iscsidev.img bs=1M count=100** command.

5. Set appropriate SELinux contexts with the **restorecon -R /var/lib/tgtd** command.

6. Add the following stanza to the /etc/tgt/targets.conf file; modify as needed for the date and system hostname.

   ```
   <target iqn.2012-05.net.example.gamma>
   backing-store /var/lib/tgtd/rhce/iscsidev.img
   write-cache off
   </target>
   ```

7. Restart the tgtd service with the **/etc/init.d/tgtd restart** command.

8. Load an appropriate module with the **modprobe iscsi_tcp** command.

9. Discover the new image file and start the iSCSI daemon with the **iscsiadm -m discoverydb -t st -p gamma.example.net -D** command. Review the first example on the **iscsiadm** man page. What are the differences? That can help you remember the command.

10. Start the iSCSI service with the **/etc/init.d/iscsi start** command.

11. Confirm the new iSCSI target with the **/etc/init.d/iscsi status** command.

12. Open TCP port 3260 in the local firewall, so you can test the result from another system.

13. Repeat steps 1, 8, 9, 10, and 11 on a remote system.

Of course, variations are possible. For more information on the process, see the *RHEL 6 Virtualization Administration Guide*. If successful, you'll see the iSCSI device from the remote system as if it were a local hard drive. You should be able to confirm with the **fdisk -l** command.

Configure System to Authenticate Using Kerberos

Unfortunately, it is not a simple matter to set up a Kerberos server on RHEL 6, as it requires the configuration of an authoritative DNS server. For the purpose of this book, it is sufficient to rely on the prompts available in the Authentication Configuration tool to understand how to authenticate and connect using Kerberos.

If you need to set up Kerberos without LDAP (Lightweight Directory Access Protocol), use the text-based console tool. The GUI tool forces you to set up Kerberos with LDAP. As LDAP clients are associated with the RHCSA, you may not necessarily see both requirements for the RHCE, as you can set up Kerberos with the reportedly insecure alternative, the Network Information Service (NIS).

To set up a Kerberos client, you need the following information:

- **Realm**   Normally set to the capitalized domain name, such as EXAMPLE.NET.

- **Key Distribution Center (KDC)**   Usually associated with the Fully Qualified Domain Name (FQDN) or IP address of the Kerberos server.

- **Kerberos Administrative Server**   While this server is frequently set to the same system as the KDC, it's where the kadmind daemon is running.

- **Whether to use DNS to resolve hosts to Kerberos Realms** If there's a trusted DNS server on the local network, activate this option. It takes over the search for the Realm.
- **Whether to use DNS to find a KDC for a Realm** If there's a trusted DNS server on the local network, activate this option. It takes over the search for the KDC and Kerberos administrative server.

The information, as configured, is added to the sssd.conf file in the /etc/sssd directory. It becomes part of the System Security Services Daemon, controlled by the /etc/init.d/sssd script. In addition, it adds sss (which represents *System Security Services*) to the passwd, shadow, and group directives in the /etc/nsswitch.conf file. When the local system looks for authentication information, it first checks local files and then the databases configured in the sssd.conf file.

Route IP Traffic and Create Static Routes

The titled objective implicitly includes two tasks:

- *Create a default route.* When more than one network card is available, you need to know how to set up a route over one specific card. Default routes typically carry traffic to larger networks such as the Internet.
- *Create a special route.* Sometimes you need to set up a specialized route between certain systems or networks.

Before proceeding, you should check the current routing table. One way to do so is with the **route -n** or **netstat -nr** commands. Both commands should present the same output. For IPv4 networks, the default route is associated with a destination address of 0.0.0.0. If that route does not yet exist, and you want to direct traffic through IP address 192.168.122.1 (which should correspond to the **virbr0** device on the physical host system), run the following command:

```
# route add default gw 192.168.122.1
```

On most systems, that information should already be embedded in the ifcfg-eth0 configuration file in the /etc/sysconfig/network-scripts directory (the device name may vary from eth0). Of course, you may have to discover that information through a bit of troubleshooting.

FIGURE 12-1

The Network
Manager
Connection
Editor

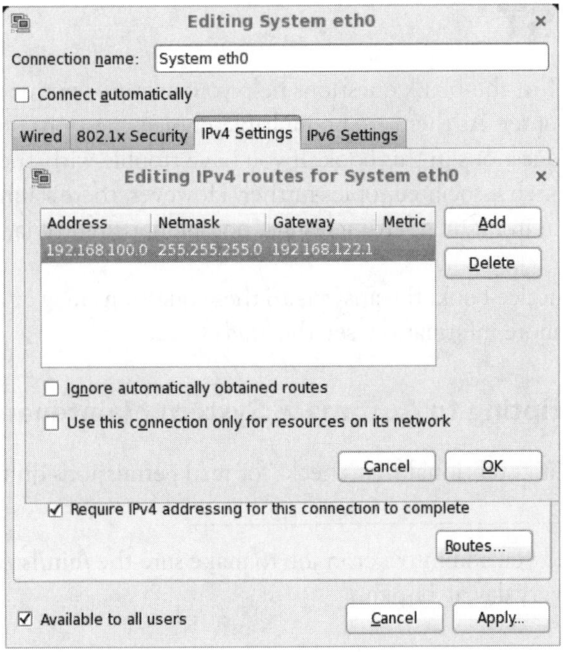

Editing System eth0

Connection name: System eth0

☐ Connect automatically

Wired | 802.1x Security | IPv4 Settings | IPv6 Settings

Editing IPv4 routes for System eth0

Address	Netmask	Gateway	Metric
192.168.100.0	255.255.255.0	192.168.122.1	

Add

Delete

☐ Ignore automatically obtained routes

☐ Use this connection only for resources on its network

Cancel   OK

☑ Require IPv4 addressing for this connection to complete

Routes...

☑ Available to all users   Cancel   Apply...

The simplest way to add a special route is with the GUI Network Connections tool, which you can start with the **nm-connection-editor** command. When you select the active network device, you can edit routes in the window shown in Figure 12-1. The information shown here is added to the route-eth0 file in the same /etc/sysconfig/network-scripts directory.

CERTIFICATION SUMMARY

As you aren't working 24 hours per day (at least I hope not!), you need to know how to set up scripts to automate system maintenance tasks with the help of the cron daemon. You can use the /etc/sysctl.conf file to optimize how the kernel works, primarily to better secure the system from the network.

When you learn how to configure the newpackage.spec file template, you'll know how to set up an RPM. To connect to an existing iSCSI target, use the first example on the **iscsiadm** man page. To configure system authentication via Kerberos, use the Authentication Configuration tool to set up the /etc/sssd/sssd.conf file. To create a new route, use the Network Connections tool to modify appropriate files in the /etc/sysconfig/network-scripts directory.

SELF TEST

The following fill-in-the-blank questions help you measure your understanding of the topics associated with this chapter. As there are no multiple-choice questions on the Red Hat exams, there are no multiple-choice questions in this book. If you have trouble with one or more of these questions, you may need to research associated topics further. However, there's almost always more than one way to solve a problem in Linux. Getting results, not memorizing trivia, is what counts on the Red Hat exams.

As this is a practice book, the answers to these questions may or may not be found in the body of the chapter. For more information, see the *Study Guide*.

Use Shell Scripting to Automate System Maintenance Tasks

1. Type in an **if** conditional that checks for read permissions on the /etc/something file.

   _____

2. What would you add into a cron job to make sure the **/bin/ls /home > /var/log/list** command is run once every day at 11 p.m.?

   _____

Use /proc/sys and sysctl to Modify and Set Kernel Run-Time Parameters

3. What would you add to the /etc/sysctl.conf file to make sure the /proc/sys/net/ipv4/conf/all/ arp_ignore boolean is activated the next time the system is booted?

   _____

Build a Simple RPM that Packages a Single File

4. What is the rpmbuild subdirectory that contains the archived and compressed source code?

   _____

5. What command creates the newpackage.spec file in the local directory?

   _____

Configure System as an iSCSI Initiator that Persistently Mounts an iSCSI Target

6. What command starts the iSCSI service and can also detect existing iSCSI targets? No switches are required.

_____

Configure System to Authenticate Using Kerberos

7. What is the standard configuration file associated with a client that authenticates through a Kerberos server?

_____

Route IP Traffic and Create Static Routes

8. Enter the command that sets the default gateway on device eth0 to IP address 192.168.0.1.

_____

LAB QUESTIONS

Red Hat presents its exams electronically. For that reason, the labs in this and future chapters are available from the gamma.example.net system, from the ChapterLabs/ folder that appears in the GUI desktop. If you're running in a command-line console, you can find the labs in the /home/testuser/ Desktop/ChapterLabs directory.

The answers for each lab follow the Self Test Answers for the fill-in-the-blank questions.

SELF TEST ANSWERS

Use Shell Scripting to Automate System Maintenance Tasks

1. One example of an if conditional that checks for read permissions on the /etc/something file is **if [-r /etc/something]**.

2. To make sure the noted command is run once every day at 11 p.m., you'd add the following line:

   ```
   0 23 * * * /bin/ls /home > /var/log/list
   ```

Use /proc/sys and sysctl to Modify and Set Kernel Run-Time Parameters

3. To make sure the /proc/sys/net/ipv4/conf/all/arp_ignore boolean is activated the next time the system is booted, you'd add the following to the /etc/sysctl.conf file:

   ```
   net.ipv4.conf.all.arp_ignore = 1
   ```

Build a Simple RPM that Packages a Single File

4. The rpmbuild subdirectory that contains the archived and compressed source code is SOURCES.

5. The **rpmdev-newspec** command creates the newpackage.spec file in the local directory.

Configure System as an iSCSI Initiator that Persistently Mounts an iSCSI Target

6. The **iscsiadm** command starts the iSCSI service and can also detect existing iSCSI targets.

Configure System to Authenticate Using Kerberos

7. The /etc/sssd/sssd.conf file is the standard configuration file associated with a client that authenticates through a Kerberos server.

Route IP Traffic and Create Static Routes

8. The **route add default gw eth0 192.168.0.1** command sets the default route to IP address 192.168.0.1.

LAB ANSWERS

Lab I

This is similar to the corresponding Lab 1 from the *Study Guide*. If you've run the **date** command as suggested in the body of the lab, the files from the /home/testuser directory should be copied to the /backup directory a minute later.

Although you could configure the script in the /etc/cron.hourly directory, that's set, by default, to one minute past the hour, per the /etc/cron.d/0hourly script. You could also configure it in the /etc/cron.d directory using the following lines:

```
SHELL=/bin/bash
45 * * * * root /bin/cp -ar /home/testuser /backup
```

Other lines could work, as long as they copy the files from the /home/testuser directory.

Given the importance of the system clock for Kerberos-based authentication, you should now restore the original time. If an NTP server has been configured for the network, you can do so with the **ntpdate** command.

Lab 2

If you've followed the instructions in this lab, the /etc/sysctl.conf file should now have the following entry:

```
net.ipv4.icmp_echo_ignore_broadcasts = 0
```

This entry makes sure the new setting survives a reboot. You may have also set the associated file, /proc/sys/net/ipv4/icmp_echo_ignore_broadcasts, to 1, or run the **sysctl -p** command to implement the change before the system was rebooted.

Of course, success can be confirmed with a **ping -b 192.168.122.255** command, both from local and remote systems. Because broadcasts are ignored by default, the gamma.example.net system at IP address 192.168.122.20 should be the only system that responds. If you want to restore the original configuration, return to the gamma.example.net system, and then remove the **net.ipv4.icmp_echo_ignore_broadcasts** option from the /etc/sysctl.conf file.

Lab 3

If successful, you have a dedicated .spec file in the rpmbuild/SPECS directory, and at least a binary RPM in the rpmbuild/RPMS/noarch directory. After copying and installing the binary RPM to the whitehat.example.net system, you should find the Chapter12-labs.txt file in the /opt/ChapterLabs directory.

If that doesn't work, you may need to refer back to Chapter 12 of the *Study Guide* for more information. To summarize, remember to perform the following steps:

1. Navigate to the /home/testuser/Desktop/ChapterLabs directory. Take the Chapter_12_labs.txt file and copy it to the Chapter12_labs-1.0/ subdirectory. Add a file named configure in that subdirectory, and give it user-executable permissions with the **chmod u+x configure** command.

2. Set up a compressed archive of those two files in that subdirectory with the **tar czvf Chapter12-labs.tar.gz Chapter12_labs-1.0/** command.

3. Install the rpm-build, rpmdevtools, and gcc packages.

4. Use the **rpmdev-setuptree** command to configure a directory tree to build the new RPM.

5. Use the **rpmdev-newspec** command to set up a newpackage.spec file to process the RPM source code.

6. In the .spec file, make sure to fill in the name, version, release number, summary, group, license, and a description. You should comment out the **BuildRequires** and **Requires** options, as there are no dependencies for this one file RPM. You should add a **BuildArch: noarch** line to disable architecture-specific references. You should also comment out or delete the **%configure** and **make** commands in the file, as there is nothing to "build" in a one-file RPM.

7. Make sure to set up **%install** directives at the end of the file; for example, the following directives make sure the binary RPM, when installed, sets up the file in the specified directory:

```
install -d -m 0755 $RPM_BUILD_ROOT/opt/ChapterLabs
install -m 0644 Chapter_12_labs.txt \ $RPM_BUILD_ROOT/opt/ChapterLabs
/Chapter_12_labs.txt
```

The second and third lines from the code shown above are intended to represent one continuous command.

8. Make sure the following directives confirm the noted directories, ownership, and filename from the source code. Of course, you can change the ownership of the loaded file with the help of the **defattr** directive.

```
%files
%dir /opt/ChapterLabs
%defattr(-,root,root,-)
%doc
/opt/ChapterLabs/Chapter_12_labs.txt
```

9. Save the file and apply the **rpmbuild -ba** command to the .spec file. If there are any dependencies, install those packages and try again.

10. Address any build errors that may appear in the **rpmbuild -ba** command output; errors are normally detailed in the newest rpm-tmp.* file in the /var/tmp directory.

11. Use the **rpm** command to install the newly configured RPM from the rpmbuild/RPMS/norarch subdirectory.

12. If successful, you'll see the Chapter12_labs.txt file in the /opt/ChapterLabs directory. Copy the RPM to the whitehat.example.net system, and repeat the installation there.

Lab 4

Before you exit the gamma.example.net system, run the **/etc/init.d/iscsi status** command to make sure the iSCSI targets are available. Then make sure TCP port 3260 is open on that system. Log into the remote whitehat.example.net system and connect to the newly created iSCSI target with the same **iscsiadm** command shown in the lab. If successful, you'll see the targets detected as if they were hard drives in the output to the **fdisk -l** command.

Lab 5

If successful, you'll be able to confirm the following elements on the whitehat.example.net system:

- The sssd service is running and is set to run the next time the system is booted. You can confirm this with commands like **/etc/init.d/sssd status** and **chkconfig --list sssd**.

- The /etc/nsswitch.conf file includes the following entries for the shadow password suite:

```
passwd:    files sss
shadow:    files sss
group:     files sss
netgroup: files sss
```

- The /etc/sssd/sssd.conf file should include the following entries, possibly at the end of the file:

```
[domain/default]
ldap_id_use_start_tls = False
ldap_search_base = dc=example,dc=net
krb5_realm = EXAMPLE.NET
krb5_kdcip = gamma.example.net
id_provider = ldap
auth_provider = krb5
chpass_provider = krb5
ldap_uri = ldap://192.168.100.1
krb5_kpasswd = gamma.example.net
cache_credentials = True
ldap_tls_cacertdir = /etc/openldap/cacerts
```

Lab 6

If you use the Network Connections tool to set up a special route, it should set up a special file in the /etc/sysconfig/network-scripts directory. If the specified network adapter is eth0, that special file is route-eth0. Given the parameters used in the lab, that file contains the following three lines:

```
ADDRESS0=192.168.100.0
NETMASK0=255.255.255.0
GATEWAY0=192.168.122.1
```

13

Electronic Mail Servers

T his and all remaining chapters cover various services. Each service is associated with five common objectives, which I cover in minimal detail. Of course, the details vary by service. In each case, this addresses what you install, how you configure SELinux, what you do to configure basic operation, the command you use that makes sure the service starts the next time the system is booted, as well as the service-specific host- and user-based security measures that you can take.

The focus of this chapter is on the Simple Mail Transfer Protocol (SMTP), associated with the transmission of e-mail over a network. RHEL 6 supports two SMTP services: Postfix and sendmail. (Yes, the capitalization of sendmail is correct.) While sendmail was the default e-mail service through RHEL 5, Postfix is the default for RHEL 6. For the purposes of the RHCE, it doesn't matter which service you configure, as long as it meets all requirements.

When you make changes to the Postfix or sendmail configuration, make sure the appropriate files are processed. For Postfix, you need to apply the **postmap** command to files that have been changed and then reload the service with the **/etc/init.d/postfix reload** command. For sendmail, you need to process the files in the /etc/mail directory by running the script named **make** from that directory. For either service, if you've edited the /etc/aliases file, you also need to run the **newaliases** command.

Install the Packages Needed to Provide the Service

The RPM required for the Postfix service (postfix) should already be included as part of even a minimal installation of RHEL 6. It's used to report errors internally by those systems so configured. It's not accessible remotely, even when TCP port 25 is open. If necessary, you can install the RPM with the following command:

```
# yum install postfix
```

If you prefer sendmail, you can install it with the following command:

```
# yum install sendmail sendmail-cf
```

If you plan to change the actual configuration of sendmail, you need to install the sendmail-cf package as well. It supports the conversion of the sendmail macro file, sendmail.mc, to the actual sendmail configuration file, sendmail.cf.

If you want to keep both services installed and switch between them, run the **alternatives --config mta** command. It brings up the following menu:

```
There are 2 programs which provide 'mta'.Selection      Command
-------------------------------------------------
+ 1             /usr/sbin/sendmail.postfix
  2             /usr/sbin/sendmail.sendmail
Enter to keep the current selection[+], or type selection number:
```

Configure SELinux to Support the Service

For RHEL 6, three booleans are related to SELinux:

- **allow_postfix_local_write_mail_spool**   Allows access from Postfix to files in the /var/spool/postfix directory. Active by default.
- **httpd_can_sendmail**   Supports e-mails from Apache modules through sendmail. Disabled by default to prevent spam attacks.
- **logging_syslogd_can_sendmail**   Enables e-mails from the system logging daemon (syslogd) through sendmail. Disabled by default.

If you use a nonstandard directory for Postfix, change the contexts of the associated files and directories to match those shown in the /var/spool/postfix directory.

Configure the Service to Start
When the System Is Booted

In even the minimal installation of RHEL 6, Postfix is already configured to start during the boot process, something that you can confirm with the following command:

```
# chkconfig --list postfix
```

However, if you install the sendmail RPM, Postfix is part of the boot process. If you later uninstall the sendmail RPM, Postfix is automatically reset to start in runlevels 2, 3, 4, and 5.

Of course, some other administrator (or perhaps someone who prepares an exam) could run the **chkconfig postfix off** command, which would keep Postfix from starting during the boot process.

Configure the Service for Basic Operation

Postfix's default configuration is already set up as an SMTP server. You can confirm the configuration from the local system with the following command:

```
# telnet localhost 25
```

On the main VM, it leads to the following output:

```
220 gamma.example.net ESMTP Postfix
```

The default configuration works only for the local system; configuration for a network is the topic for one of the SMTP-specific objectives, described shortly. If you're running sendmail instead, the same **telnet** command leads to the following output:

```
220 gamma.example.net ESMTP Sendmail 8.14.4/8.14.4; Wed 18 Apr 2012
09:30:02 -0700
```

Of course, the dates and version numbers may vary.

Configure Host-Based and User-Based Security for the Service

Host-based security is already configured for the default SMTP communications channel, TCP port 25. In other words, the default firewall blocks communications through that port. Of course, to allow access from a limited number of hosts, modify the firewall with an entry like the following in the /etc/sysconfig/iptables file:

```
-A INPUT -m state --state NEW -m tcp -p tcp -s 192.168.122.0/24
--dport 25 -j ACCEPT
```

If you use the Firewall Configuration tool, set up this line in its own file in the "Custom Rules" section, so it isn't overwritten if you make other changes with that tool.

For Postfix, you can set up user- and host-based security in the /etc/postfix/access file. The following sample entries show how you can set up Postfix to accept and reject access from users, IP address blocks, and domain names. Additional details are available in the default version of the file, which includes a commented version of the appropriate man page.

```
michael@ REJECT
192.168.122 OK
blackhat.example.net REJECT
```

In addition, you should modify a couple of directives in the main Postfix configuration file, /etc/postfix/main.cf. The following directives are suggestions based on the VMs configured for this book:

```
myhostname = gamma.example.net
mydomain = example.net
mydestination = $mydomain, $myhostname, localhost.$mydomain, localhost
mynetworks = 192.168.122.0/24, 127.0.0.0/8
```

In addition, you can limit access to authorized usernames with the following directive.

```
smtpd_sender_restrictions = permit_sasl_authenticated, reject
```

For more information, see the README-Postfix-SASL-RedHat.txt file in the /usr/share/doc/postfix-2.6.6 directory.

For sendmail, you can modify the /etc/mail/access file in a similar fashion to /etc/postfix/access. The default entries support access from the localhost system. To support access from a network, add an entry such as the following:

```
Connect:192.168.122     RELAY
```

In addition, you want to comment out the following directive in the main sendmail macro configuration file, /etc/mail/sendmail.cf. Doing this also limits access to the localhost system:

```
dnl DAEMON_OPTIONS(`Port=smtp,Addr=127.0.0.1, Name=MTA')dnl
```

If you've installed sendmail, you can also use the TCP Wrappers files to configure user-and host-based security, as discussed in Chapter 10 of the Study Guide.

Configure a Mail Transfer Agent (MTA) to Accept Inbound E-mail from Other Systems

For the most part, this section summarizes steps described earlier, with the focus on what you would do to configure Postfix or sendmail to accept inbound e-mail from other systems, meaning systems other than the localhost.

In both cases, you need to make sure to open TCP port 25 in any existing local firewall before either service can accept inbound e-mail from other systems.

Postfix is already configured for basic operation for the local system. To set it up to accept inbound e-mail from other systems, you also need to take the following steps.

1. Make sure Postfix (and not sendmail) is running.

2. Include the IP address(es)/address block(s) of desired systems in the /etc/postfix/access file, in the format suggested in the associated man page.

3. Edit the /etc/postfix/main.cf file, and edit the **myhostname**, **mydomain**, **inet_interfaces**, and **mynetworks** directives.

Also noted earlier is how sendmail is already configured for basic operation when installed. To set up that alternative service to accept inbound e-mail, you should take the following steps:

1. Make sure sendmail (and not Postfix) is running.

2. Include the IP address(es)/address block(s) of desired systems in the /etc/mail/access file, in the same format as shown for the localhost system.

3. Edit the /etc/mail/sendmail.mc file, and comment out the **DAEMON_OPTIONS(`Port=smtp,Addr=127.0.0.1, Name=MTA')dnl** directive.

4. Once the desired changes are made, execute the **/etc/mail/make** script to process all files in the /etc/mail directory. Doing this processes changes from sendmail.mc into the actual sendmail.cf configuration file, along with any other files that you've changed in the /etc/mail directory.

Configure an MTA to Forward (Relay) E-mail Through a Smart Host

A "smart host" MTA can forward e-mail to other e-mail services. If you want to rely on e-mail services configured by someone else such as an ISP, you'll want to configure the local MTA as a smart host.

To set up a smart host on a Postfix server, include a forwarding address in the main.cf file in the /etc/postfix directory. You can set up that address with the **relayhost** directive. Substitute accordingly for the external.example.com system:

```
relayhost = external.example.com
```

In addition, you want to make sure that all e-mail sent to users on the local system is properly forwarded through the /etc/aliases file. For example, the following line would forward administrative e-mails to a regular user on the example.net network:

```
root:        michael@example.net
```

The /etc/aliases file is used by both Postfix and sendmail. Don't forget to apply the **newaliases** command to process the file into a database read by either service. To configure a sendmail smart host, modify the following directive in the sendmail.mc file from the /etc/mail directory:

```
dnl define(`SMART_HOST', `smtp.your.provider')dnl
```

For the same external.example.com remote MTA, change the line to:

```
define(`SMART_HOST', `external.example.com')dnl
```

CERTIFICATION SUMMARY

The two SMTP services associated with RHEL 6 are Postfix and sendmail. You should not run them both on the same system. Fortunately, the installation of the standard RHEL 6 sendmail RPM disables Postfix; the uninstallation of that package restores it. If you need both services installed on the same system, use the **alternatives --config mta** command to switch active services. In either case, you need to open TCP port 25 in the local firewall.

You can find Postfix configuration files in the /etc/postfix directory. Basic configuration options are included in the main.cf file. Users and hosts can be regulated in the access file. Both Postfix and sendmail use the /etc/alias file for user aliases when hashed into a database with the **newaliases** command. Although already configured for basic operation for the local system, you can set up access to the local network through the access file. You can configure it as a relay with the **relayhost** directive.

Red Hat still supports sendmail on RHEL 6. When installed, it supersedes Postfix. You can configure it through a macro configuration file, sendmail.mc, in the /etc/mail directory. As with Postfix, it's already configured for basic operation for the local system. You can comment out one directive in sendmail.mc to open it up to other systems. To set it up as a smart host relay, you can define the **SMART_HOST** directive in that same macro file.

SELF TEST

The following fill-in-the-blank questions help you measure your understanding of the topics associated with this chapter. As there are no multiple-choice questions on the Red Hat exams, there are no multiple-choice questions in this book. If you have trouble with one or more of these questions, you may need to research associated topics further. However, there's almost always more than one way to solve a problem in Linux. Getting results, not memorizing trivia, is what counts on the Red Hat exams.

As this is a practice book, the answers to these questions may or may not be found in the body of the chapter. For more information, see the *Study Guide*.

Install the Packages Needed to Provide the Service

1. Name the two packages most closely associated with the sendmail and Postfix services.

   _____   _____

Configure SELinux to Support the Service

2. What is the function of the one SELinux boolean directly associated with Postfix?

   _____

Configure the Service to Start When the System Is Booted

3. What two commands would you run to make sure sendmail, and not Postfix, is started the next time you boot Linux? For this question, assume you've been told to keep both packages installed.

   _____

Configure the Service for Basic Operation

4. Name the primary configuration file for Postfix.

   _____

Configure Host-Based and User-Based Security for the Service

5. What file is designed to include users and hosts, along with access rules, for Postfix?

_____

Configure a Mail Transfer Agent (MTA) to Accept Inbound E-mail from Other Systems

6. When you change the sendmail.mc and other files in the /etc/mail directory, what command processes those files?

_____

7. What command lists all current Postfix settings?

_____

Configure an MTA to Forward (Relay) E-mail Through a Smart Host

8. What directive should you add to the Postfix configuration file to direct traffic to a smart host?

_____

LAB QUESTIONS

Red Hat presents its exams electronically. For that reason, the labs in this and future chapters are available from the gamma.example.net system, from the ChapterLabs/ folder that appears in the GUI desktop. If you're running in a command-line console, you can find the labs in the /home/testuser/ Desktop/ChapterLabs directory.

The answers for each lab follow the Self Test Answers for the fill-in-the-blank questions.

SELF TEST ANSWERS

Install the Packages Needed to Provide the Service

1. The packages associated with the sendmail and Postfix services are sendmail and postfix.

Configure SELinux to Support the Service

2. The function of the one boolean directly associated with Postfix, **allow_postfix_local_write_mail_spool**, is to support access to the /var/spool/postfix directory.

Configure the Service to Start When the System Is Booted

3. When both packages are installed, the two commands to make sure sendmail, and not Postfix, is started the next time you boot Linux are:

   ```
   # chkconfig sendmail on
   # chkconfig postfix off
   ```

   Variations on these commands, such as **chkconfig sendmail --level 35 on**, are acceptable. For standard configurations, levels 3 and 5 are the most common standard initial runlevels. (Yes, the **alternatives --config mta** command meets the requirements as well.)

Configure the Service for Basic Operation

4. The primary configuration file for Postfix is main.cf.

Configure Host-Based and User-Based Security for the Service

5. The file that is designed to include users and hosts, along with access rules for Postfix, is /etc/postfix/access.

Configure a Mail Transfer Agent (MTA) to Accept Inbound E-mail from Other Systems

6. The **/etc/mail/make** command processes the files in the **/etc/mail directory**. The script has been revised so you can run it from any directory.

7. The command that lists all current Postfix settings is **postconf**.

Configure an MTA to Forward (Relay) E-mail Through a Smart Host

8. The directive that redirects traffic from a local Postfix server to a remote smart host is **relayhost**.

LAB ANSWERS

Lab 1

This lab is slightly tricky, as it does not require any direct configuration of Postfix or sendmail. All it requires are changes to the /etc/aliases file, which is used by both SMTP services. Add the following entries to that file:

```
testuser:  genius@example.net
root:  genius@example.net
```

Of course, you also need to process the file with the **newaliases** command to create a new or updated /etc/aliases.db file.

If you want to check the result, you can use a command-line client such as **mutt** or **mail**. You'll need to create a user named **genius**. Then, if you send a test e-mail to the local root user, the message should be received by user genius, as the domain for the VMs is example.net.

Lab 2

First, to enable access from more than just the localhost, you should modify the **inet_interfaces** directive in /etc/postfix/main.cf to:

```
inet_interfaces = all
```

Next, to set up the limitations on the domains, open the /etc/postfix/access file and include the following lines:

```
blackhat.example.net   REJECT
example.net   OK
```

You could set up equivalent functionality with appropriate options in the firewall.

Lab 3

To configure a smart host in Postfix, you want to add the **relayhost** directive to the main.cf file in the /etc/postfix directory. For the parameters given in the Lab, if the physical host is located on system kauai.example.net, add the following directive:

```
relayhost = kauai.example.net
```

Lab 4

You can also set up user rules in the /etc/postfix/access file. With the following line, the user blackhat is disallowed from all systems:

```
blackhat@  REJECT
```

Lab 5

This lab is simpler than it seems. First, all you need to do to disable Postfix and enable sendmail is to install the sendmail RPM. If it's already installed, you can enable sendmail and disable Postfix with the help of the **alternatives --mta smtp** command.

From the default sendmail.mc file, you want to make two changes. First, you want to comment out the following directive to enable access to external IPv4 communication. Just add the **dnl** in the front of the line, as shown in bold:

```
dnl DAEMON_OPTIONS(`Port=smtp,Addr=127.0.0.1, Name=MTA')dnl
```

In addition, you want to activate the following directive by deleting the **dnl**:

```
dnlDAEMON_OPTIONS(`Port=submission, Name=MSA, M=Ea')dnl
```

If desired, you can confirm that the submission port is normally associated with port 587 in the /etc/services file.

Lab 6

This is a relatively open-ended lab, with two possible approaches to meeting the requirements:

■ Using iptables-based firewalls, prohibit access over port 25 from IP address 12.168.122.240. Make sure to include a rule afterward allowing access to the 192.168.122.0/24 network.

■ Using the /etc/mail/access file, add the following directives; make sure to process the file into a database with the /etc/mail/make script.

```
Connect: 192.168.122 OK
Connect: 192.168.122.240 REJECT
```

Both of these answers are acceptable, as they all perform the same function.

Lab 7

On the gamma.example.net system, open the sendmail macro file, /etc/mail/sendmail.mc. Activate the following directive, changing **smtp.*your.provider*** to the Fully Qualified Domain Name of the physical host system, kauai.example.net:

```
dnl define(`SMART_HOST', `kauai.example.net')dnl
```

Note the cross-out of the comment directive, **dnl**. Don't forget to process the sendmail.mc macro with the help of the make script in the /etc/mail directory.

14

The Apache
Web Server

T his chapter is focused on the Apache web server, which may be the most important server software on the Internet. According to the Netcraft (www.netcraft.com) survey, which tracks the web servers associated with virtually every site on the Internet, Apache is currently used by more sites than all other web servers combined.

While there are nine objectives related to Apache, this chapter is focused on the configuration of Apache at a relatively basic level. While a little knowledge of scripting is helpful to satisfy the Common Gateway Interface (CGI) scripting objective, it's not required. There are plenty of simple scripts available online (and even on a default RHEL 6 system) to demonstrate the basic concepts associated with Apache.

The main configuration files for Apache are httpd.conf and ssl.conf, which you can find in the /etc/httpd/conf and /etc/httpd/conf.d directories, respectively. When you make changes, run the **httpd -t** command to check file syntax and the **httpd -S** command to review virtual hosts.

If you use the **elinks** text-based browser to test a web page, just remember to include the http:// or https:// in front of the target IP address or uniform resource locator (URL).

Install the Packages Needed to Provide the Service

Although the Apache web server requires just one package (httpd), you need more. For secure web services, you need the **mod_ssl** package. For documentation, just in case you forget the code for a sample CGI script, you may want the **httpd-manual** package. For simplicity, it may be fastest to just install the Web Server package group with the following command:

```
# yum groupinstall "Web Server"
```

This command also installs other packages that might be useful under different circumstances; the relevant mandatory and default packages from the "Web Server" package group are shown in Table 14-1.

TABLE 14-1	Package	Description
Mandatory and Default Packages in the Web Server Group	httpd	Installs the main Apache web server
	httpd-manual	Includes a searchable Apache manual in the /var/www/manual directory
	crypto-utils	Adds tools to generate and manage SSL certificates and keys
	mod_perl	Incorporates a PERL language interpreter into Apache
	mod_ssl	Adds Secure Sockets Layer (SSL)/Transport Layer Security (TLS) support
	mod_wsgi	Supports a web server gateway interface for Python applications
	webalizer	Installs a web server log analysis program

Configure SELinux to Support the Service

As a service that is often used to interface with the public, Apache should always be considered a potential security risk. To limit that risk, a substantial number of SELinux options are associated with Apache, related to the file contexts of different directories as well as booleans, that permit or prohibit certain Apache-based functionality. The file contexts shown in Table 14-2 are somewhat descriptive. Just be prepared to set up the same contexts in other directories.

With 26 SELinux booleans related the Apache web server, you can do a lot to secure a system and prevent problems. These booleans are described briefly in Table 14-3. The first six in the list are active by default.

TABLE 14-2	Context	Description
SELinux File Types for Apache	**httpd_config_t**	Supports configuration files, such as those in the /etc/httpd directory
	httpd_modules_t	Supports directories with loadable modules, including those in the /usr/lib64/httpd/modules directory
	httpd_log_t	Works for files in log directories such as /var/log/httpd
	httpd_sys_context_t	Sets up the data files for a web server, such as HTML pages
	httpd_sys_content_ra_t	Supports data where Apache reads and appends to the file
	httpd_sys_content_rw_t	Supports data where Apache reads and writes to the file
	httpd_sys_script_exec_t	Allows the Apache service to access executable scripts

TABLE 14-3	SELinux Booleans for Apache
Boolean	**Description**
httpd_builtin_scripting	Supports the use of scripts in directories with the httpd_t process context associated with Apache
httpd_dbus_avahi	Allows Apache to work with automated IP address configuration
httpd_enable_cgi	Enables Apache to run CGI scripts, if the files are properly labeled with the httpd_sys_script_exec_t file type
httpd_tty_comm	Supports access to a terminal; needed by Apache to access SSL certificates
httpd_unified	Allows a single security domain for HTTP-related content
xguest_connect_network	Enables access from secured guest users
allow_httpd_anon_write	Supports writing to files labeled with the public_content_rw_t file type
allow_httpd_mod_auth_ntlm_winbind	Enables access to Microsoft authentication databases, in conjunction with the mod_auth_ntlm_winbind module
allow_httpd_mod_auth_pam	Enables access to PAM authentication modules, in cooperation with the mod_auth_pam module.
allow_httpd_sys_script_anon_write	Supports access by scripts to public_content_rw_t files
httpd_can_check_spam	Works with web-based e-mail applications to check for spam
httpd_can_network_connect	Supports access by Apache scripts/modules to remote connections
httpd_can_network_connect_cobbler	Enables access by Apache scripts/modules to the Cobbler installation server
httpd_can_network_connect_db	Allows Apache scripts/modules to connect to a database server
httpd_can_network_memcache	Enables HTTP memory caching access; originally set up for a translation server
httpd_can_network_relay	Supports the use of the HTTP service as a relay server
httpd_can_sendmail	Allows the use of HTTP-based e-mail services, such as (but not necessarily) sendmail
httpd_enable_homedirs	Configures access via HTTP to files in user home directories; requires the httpd_sys_content_t file context
httpd_execmem	Supports access from HTTP modules to executable memory regions
httpd_read_user_content	Enables access to scripts from user home directories
httpd_setrlimit	Allows Apache to modify maximum number of file descriptors
httpd_ssi_exec	Allows Apache to access Server Side Include (SSI) scripts; similar to httpd_enable_cgi

TABLE 14-3	SELinux Booleans for Apache (*continued*)
Boolean	**Description**
httpd_tmp_exec	Supports those Apache-based scripts that require access to the /tmp directory
httpd_use_cifs	Enables Apache access to shared Samba directories when labeled with the cifs_t file type
httpd_use_gpg	Allows access to systems that require GPG encryption
httpd_use_nfs	Enables Apache access to shared Samba directories when labeled with the nfs_t file type

Configure the Service to Start When the System Is Booted

As with other services, you want target services to start in standard runlevels. The following command makes sure the Apache web server starts in runlevels 3 and 5:

```
# chkconfig --level 35 httpd on
```

Alternatively, the following command makes sure Apache starts in runlevels 2, 3, 4, and 5:

```
# chkconfig httpd on
```

Configure the Service for Basic Operation

This requirement is essentially identical to that for the RHCSA exam, to "configure a system to run a default HTTP server." In some ways, basic operation is enabled by default. You can control Apache with either the **httpd** script in the /etc/init.d directory or the **apachectl** command.

You can confirm success with basic operation on the local system by running either of the following commands:

```
# /etc/init.d/httpd status
# apachectl status
```

You can set up different web site files, as long as those files associated with the web site are configured with the **httpd_sys_content_t** boolean. The same context can be applied to directories other than the default.

Configure Host-Based and User-Based Security for the Service

As with all other services, you can configure host-based security with the help of **iptables**-based firewalls. To allow access to Apache, you normally have to set up access through ports 80 and 443, which corresponds to regular (HTTP) and secure (HTTPS) services. These ports are configured with the following **Listen** directives in the httpd.conf and ssl.conf configuration files.

```
Listen 80
Listen 443
```

For systems with multiple network cards, you can further limit access by specifying the IP address of the target network card:

```
Listen 192.168.122.20:80
Listen 192.168.122.20:443
```

Host-based security can be configured more specifically in Apache configuration files. In stanzas that support access to directories and virtual sites, you can configure access limits starting with the **Order deny,allow** or **Order allow,deny** directive. You can then include directives such as the following for domain names:

```
Allow from admin.example.com
Deny from example.com
```

You could also apply such limits to IP addresses. One example is shown here:

```
Deny from 192.168.122.240
Allow from 192.168.122
```

In support of user-based security, you can set up different types of authentication based on the **AuthType Basic** directive. The following stanza configures an "Account Information Required" window that appears when users try to connect to the associated URL:

```
<Directory "/var/www/html/protect">
    AuthType Basic
    AuthName "Account Information Required"
    AuthUserFile /etc/httpd/acctinfo
    Require user testuser
</Directory>
```

You can set up the account file with the **htpasswd** command. If desired, you could organize such users into groups and use the **AuthGroupFile** and **Require group** directives as appropriate.

Configure a Virtual Host

Virtual hosts are used to configure multiple web sites on a single Apache server, using a single IP address. The default Apache configuration file includes the following sample virtual host container:

```
#<VirtualHost *:80>
#     ServerAdmin webmaster@dummy-host.example.com
#     DocumentRoot /www/docs/dummy-host.example.com
#     ServerName dummy-host.example.com
#     ErrorLog logs/dummy-host.example.com-error_log
#     CustomLog logs/dummy-host.example.com-access_log common
#</VirtualHost>
```

Of course, you need to activate the desired directives from this container and revise options such as the URL and directories per the requirements of the subject web site. In addition, make sure that target directories have the same SELinux contexts as the default /var/www/html directory and the same default contexts in the file_contexts file in the /etc/selinux/targeted/contexts/files directory. For the noted directories, the commands are:

```
# chcon -R -u system_u -t httpd_sys_content_t \
/www/docs/dummy-host.example.com
# semanage fcontext -a -s system_u -t httpd_sys_content_t
/www/docs/dummy-host.example.com
```

To activate name-based virtual hosts, you also need to activate the following directive:

```
#NameVirtualHost *:80
```

Yes, for secure virtual hosts, you would need to add a corresponding **NameVirtualHost *:443** directive. For clarity, you should include it in the ssl.conf file. Just be aware, all information in ssl.conf is automatically included in the Apache configuration courtesy of the **Include conf.d/*.conf** directive. A similar template for secure virtual hosts exists in the ssl.conf file in the **<VirtualHost _ default_:443>** container. Just remember to substitute an asterisk (*) for **_default_** in any such containers that you create.

If you need to generate a "self-signed" security certificate, navigate to the /etc/pki/tls/certs directory. The following command starts a console-based wizard that helps you generate a certificate for the gamma.example.net system:

```
# genkey gamma.example.net
```

To use the certificate that's generated, you need to modify the **SSLCertificateFile** and **SSLCertificateKeyFile** directives to the location of the gamma.example.net.crt and gamma.example.net.key files, respectively.

Configure Private Directories

In this context, private directories on a web site are configured for every individual user. As a model, a default stanza is already available to configure access to user home directories, in the following container:

```
#<Directory /home/*/public_html>
```

But before activating this stanza, you have to deal with two other directives. Access to user home directories is disabled, by default, in two ways. First, in the httpd.conf file, you find the following directive that disables such access directly:

```
UserDir Disabled
```

Second, the same stanza includes the following commented directive, which activates access to user home directories, in the public_html/ subdirectory:

```
#UserDir public_html
```

Normally CGI scripts are disabled by default when accessing home directories via Apache, with the **IncludesNoExec** directive at the end of this line:

```
Options MultiViews Indexes SymLinksIfOwnerMatch IncludesNoExec
```

To configure Apache-based private access to a home directory, give it 701 permissions. That makes file lists in that directory readable by all users. Alternatively, you could set up executable Access Control List (ACL) permissions for the Apache user. In either case, you also have to activate the **httpd_enable_homedirs** SELinux boolean.

Deploy a Basic CGI Application

If you don't know programming, don't panic. You don't need to know how to code to meet this objective. If you've installed the httpd-manual RPM described earlier, you can search for more information in Apache documentation. Of course, the httpd-manual RPM may or may not be available during a Red Hat exam.

Apache's use of CGI scripts for the default web site depends on two directives in the httpd.conf file:

```
LoadModule cgi_module modules/mod_cgi.so
ScriptAlias /cgi-bin/ "/var/www/cgi-bin/"
```

In the default Apache server configuration, on a gamma.example.net system, you could run scripts from the http://gamma.example.net/cgi-bin URL.

If you want to set up Perl scripts in a dedicated directory, or even on a virtual host, include the following directives in the appropriate directory container:

```
Options ExecCGI
AddHandler cgi-script .pl
```

I've selected Perl arbitrarily. I intend no disrespect to users who prefer other scripting languages. Scripts associated with different languages may have different file extensions. In the Apache documentation, in the "Writing a CGI Program" section, you can find code for a simple Perl script:

```
#!/usr/bin/perl
print "Content-type: text/html\n\n";
print "Hello, World!";
```

(While this script is the first one often used in some programming courses, it's not "real" coding. I've just shown you what to copy to meet the subject RHCE objective.)

Make sure the file has 755 permissions, supporting execution by all users; after all, it's a web site. If you want to limit access to the script, you can do so with user and group restrictions described elsewhere in this chapter.

Configure Group-Managed Content

The process used to set up private directories for a group in Apache is similar to the process used to set up a private group directory described in Chapter 8. Start with the stanza created earlier in the section on user- and host-based security.

You have to go just a bit further with a group directory shared via an Apache server. Set up a regular user as the owner. You can then create a group with the desired users. Make sure the group directory (and files therein) are set up with appropriate user and group ownership.

For this purpose, you can set up this directory in the httpd.conf configuration file in a fashion similar to a shared user home directory. After all, a shared group directory is normally also configured as a subdirectory of /home.

You want to set world-executable permissions on the directory, or at least executable ACL-based permissions accessible to the user named apache. You can then use the **htpasswd** command to set up users. Pointing to an authorized group requires an **AuthUserFile**, an **AuthGroupFile**, and a **Require group** directive. The format of the group file can be simple: the following entry sets up an analyst group made up of users nerd1 and nerd2:

```
analyst:  nerd1 nerd2
```

CERTIFICATION SUMMARY

The Apache web server is conceivably the most important server software associated with RHEL 6. As one of the requirements of the RHCSA is to configure Apache in its default configuration, the RHCE goes further. Associated packages are available in the "Web Server" package group. Apache can be controlled with the help of a number of different SELinux file contexts and booleans.

Although Apache is normally controlled with the help of the **apachectl** command, you can still use commands like **chkconfig** to make sure it starts during the boot process into normal runlevels. While host-based security can be controlled through the firewall, user- and host-based security can be enhanced within the Apache configuration files.

To see some of Apache's capabilities, you should know how to set up virtual hosts, using both the HTTP and HTTPS protocols. You need to know how to configure private directories protected by passwords. Those private directories can be extended to groups for group-managed content. Finally, options such as **ExecCGI** and **AddHandler cgi-script .pl** enable the use of Perl scripts in desired Apache directory containers.

SELF TEST

The following fill-in-the-blank questions help you measure your understanding of the topics associated with this chapter. As there are no multiple-choice questions on the Red Hat exams, there are no multiple-choice questions in this book. If you have trouble with one or more of these questions, you may need to research associated topics further. However, there's almost always more than one way to solve a problem in Linux. Getting results, not memorizing trivia, is what counts on the Red Hat exams.

As this is a practice book, the answers to these questions may or may not be found in the body of the chapter. For more information, see the *Study Guide*.

Install the Packages Needed to Provide the Service

1. What package is associated with Apache documentation?

_____

Configure SELinux to Support the Service

2. What SELinux boolean should you activate to enable access via Apache to user home directories?

_____

Configure the Service to Start When the System Is Booted

3. What commands make sure the Apache web server starts in only runlevel 3?

_____

_____

Configure the Service for Basic Operation

4. If you want to set up your own index.html web page for the default Apache server, as configured, what directory would you use?

_____

Configure Host-Based and User-Based Security for the Service

5. What three lines would you add to an Apache configuration stanza that limits access to all systems on the 192.168.0.0 network, except for IP address 192.168.0.100?

_____

_____

_____

Configure a Virtual Host

6. What command would you use to enable secure name-based virtual hosts for different web sites?

_____

Configure Private Directories

7. What directive in the Apache configuration file normally disables access to user home directories?

_____

Deploy a Basic CGI Application

8. What permissions are required for a CGI file configured in an appropriate directory?

_____

Configure Group-Managed Content

9. What account requires executable ACL permissions to a directory shared by multiple users and accessible via Apache?

_____

LAB QUESTIONS

Red Hat presents its exams electronically. For that reason, the labs in this and future chapters are available from the gamma.example.net system, from the ChapterLabs/ folder that appears in the GUI desktop. If you're running in a command-line console, you can find the labs in the /home/testuser/Desktop/ChapterLabs directory.

The answers for each lab follow the Self Test Answers for the fill-in-the-blank questions.

SELF TEST ANSWERS

Install the Packages Needed to Provide the Service

1. The package associated with Apache documentation is **httpd-manual**.

Configure SELinux to Support the Service

2. The SELinux boolean that enables access to user home directories via Apache is **httpd_enable_homedirs**.

Configure the Service to Start When the System Is Booted

3. Two commands are required to make sure the Apache web server starts in only runlevel 3 (variations on these commands that configure Apache to start only in runlevel 3 are acceptable answers):

```
# chkconfig httpd off
# chkconfig --level 3 httpd on
```

Configure the Service for Basic Operation

4. Based on the default Apache server, you can set up your own index.html page in the /var/www/html directory.

Configure Host-Based and User-Based Security for the Service

5. To set up access limits as specified in the question, you can include the following three lines in an appropriate stanza:

```
Order deny,allow
Deny from 192.168.0.100
Allow from 192.168.0.0/24
```

Variations on the IP address network used with the **Allow from** directive are acceptable, including 192.168.0 and 192.168.0.0/255.255.255.0.

Configure a Virtual Host

6. To enable secure name-based virtual hosts, include the **NameVirtualHost *:443** directive.

Configure Private Directories

7. The **UserDir disabled** directive in the Apache configuration file normally disables access to user home directories.

Deploy a Basic CGI Application

8. You need to set 755 permissions on a CGI file to make it executable from Apache when placed in an appropriate directory.

Configure Group-Managed Content

9. If you use ACLs for group-managed content, you need to set up executable permissions for the user named apache.

LAB ANSWERS

Lab 1

To meet the requirements of this lab, you need to do the following things:

- Install the **httpd** and **httpd-manual** packages; you could do this by installing individual packages or by installing the "Web Server" package group.
- Copy the index.html file from /var/www/manual to /var/www/html.
- Make sure the system is accessible from outside networks by making sure TCP port 80 is open in the firewall.
- Make sure Apache is running; the standard method to do this is with the **apachectl start** command.
- Make sure Apache starts in appropriate runlevels (at least runlevels 3 and 5).

Part of this lab is informational. First, you'll see the difference in how the index.html page appears. When you navigate to http://gamma.example.net/manual, all icons are shown. After that index.html page is copied to the /var/www/html directory, you won't see the icons when you navigate to http://gamma.example.net/.

In either case, it's helpful to review the documentation on at least CGI scripts. If you have to set up a Perl script in a pressure-filled situation such as an exam, you'll know what to do.

Lab 2

This is a multipart lab. While you could conceivably set up host-based access limits within the Apache configuration files, it's too easy to make a mistake and set the limit only on a certain directory. But if you can do that, great! It is one way to meet the requirements set out in this lab.

In my opinion, the most straightforward way to set up such host-based access limits is with the **iptables**-based firewall. The following rule rejects packets from the noted IP address on port 80 and then accepts them.

```
-A INPUT -m state --state NEW -m tcp -p tcp -s 192.168.122.240 --dport 80 -j REJECT
-A INPUT -m state --state NEW -m tcp -p tcp -s 192.168.122.0/24 --dport 80 -j ACCEPT
```

Of course, there are three ports in question. You could repeat these commands with ports 443 and 8080, or you could just specify **--dport 80,443,8080** in each of the commands shown here.

Yes, you also need to make sure that Apache is running and will start upon reboot. You also need to make sure the **Listen 80** and **Listen 443** directives are enabled in the httpd.conf and ssl.conf files, respectively. Of course, to set up port 8080, you want to add a **Listen 8080** directive in the httpd. conf file. A logical place is right after the **Listen 80** directive.

To confirm success, you could run the **nmap 192.168.122.20** command from both the whitehat and blackhat.example.net systems (which correspond to IP addresses 192.168.122.130 and 192.168.122.240). Of course, the ports should be visible only from the whitehat.example.net system.

Lab 3

This lab requires that you create two virtual hosts. One logical place to configure the containers for such hosts is in httpd.conf. The steps are similar to the corresponding lab in the *Study Guide*:

1. First, don't change the **ServerRoot** directive. It sets the default directory for the Apache server. Any files and directories not otherwise configured—or configured as a relative directory—are set relative to **ServerRoot**.

2. Set the **NameVirtualHost** directive to the port (80) associated with HTTP. For name-based virtual hosts, you wouldn't specify an IP address.

3. Create two **VirtualHost** containers with settings appropriate for the alpha.example.net and beta.example.net systems.

4. Assign the **ServerAdmin** to the e-mail address of the appropriate administrator, perhaps testuser@example.net.

5. Configure a unique **DocumentRoot** directory for each virtual host.

6. Set the first **ServerName** to alpha.example.net.

7. Add **ErrorLog** and **CustomLog** directives, and set them to unique filenames in the /etc/httpd/ logs directory (which is linked to the /var/logs/httpd directory). With the default **ServerRoot**, you can use a relative directory for this purpose, such as the following:

   ```
   ErrorLog logs/alpha.example.net-error_log
   ```

8. Make sure to close the **VirtualHost** container (with a **</VirtualHost>** directive at the end of the stanza).

9. Repeat the process for the second web site, making sure to set the second **ServerName** to beta. example.net.

10. Close and save the httpd.conf file with your changes.

11. Create any new directories that you configured with the **DocumentRoot** directives.

12. Create index.html text files in each directory defined by the associated new **DocumentRoot** directives. Remember the suggestion in the lab to include text such as

    ```
    This is the HTTP server for alpha.example.net.
    ```

13. Make sure these domain names are configured n the /etc/hosts file for each system (gamma, whitehat, and blackhat.example.net). For example, if the Apache server is configured on the gamma.example.net system, you could add the following lines to /etc/hosts:

    ```
    192.168.122.20 alpha.example.net
    192.168.122.20 beta.example.net
    ```

14. Use the Firewall Configuration tool (**system-config-firewall**) to allow access from remote systems to TCP port 80.

15. Configure appropriate SELinux file types on the directory associated with the **DocumentRoot** for each virtual host. If the directory is /virt/alpha.example.net, you can do so with the following command:

    ```
    # chcon -R -u system_u -t httpd_sys_content_t /virt/alpha.example.net
    ```

    In addition, one way to set up the file_contexts.local file in the /etc/selinux/targeted/contexts/ files directory is with the following command:

    ```
    # semanage fcontext -a -s system_u -t httpd_sys_content_t /virt/alpha.
    example.net
    ```

16. Make sure to run the **apachectl graceful** command (or something similar) to make Apache read the revised httpd.conf configuration file.

17. Now test the results. Try the web sites from the local gamma.example.net system. Repeat the process from the whitehat.example.net system.

Lab 4

This lab has two parts. First, you want to navigate to the /etc/pki/tls/certs directory. Then you can run the **genkey alpha.example.net** command to create appropriate certificates in the following files:

```
/etc/pki/tls/certs/alpha.example.net.crt
/etc/pki/tls/private/alpha.example.net.key
```

Second, you create a virtual host in the ssl.conf file in the /etc/httpd/conf.d directory. In a fashion similar to Lab 3, you want to first set up the following directives:

```
NameVirtualHost *:443
<VirtualHost *:443>
```

You can then set up the following SSL directives to point to the certificates:

```
SSLCertificateFile /etc/pki/tls/certs/alpha.example.net.crt
SSLCertificateKeyFile /etc/pki/tls/private/alpha.example.net.key
```

You also need to set up at least the **ServerName** and **DocumentRoot** directives within the virtual host container. It's helpful to also set up the **ErrorLog** and **CustomLog** directives, if problems arise.

The same criteria apply to rereading the configuration file, SELinux contexts based on the **chcon** and **semanage** commands, and opening up port 443 in the firewall.

Lab 5

This lab is similar to the corresponding lab in the *Study Guide*. Remember to create a /home/testuser/public_html directory and populate it with at least one file. Before user directories can be used, you need to change the **UserDir** directives. First comment out the following:

```
# UserDir disabled
```

and activate the following:

```
UserDir public_html
```

You can then set up access to user home directories in the commented stanza. You should add something like the following directives within the container:

```
AuthType Basic
AuthName "For the testuser user"
```

```
AuthUserFile /etc/httpd/user1
Require user testuser
```

The testuser home directory should have regular executable permissions for groups and other users (711 permissions). You need a /home/testuser/public_html directory with 755 permissions. You also need to make sure the **httpd_enable_homedirs** boolean is enabled. You can then use the following command to set up the **AuthUserFile**:

```
# htpasswd -c /etc/httpd/user1 testuser
```

Don't forget to specify the **rhcecert** password (different from the regular login password of rhcert) in response to the password prompts that appear. In addition, a **Require user testuser** directive limits access to that one user.

You can then test the result from a remote system, by navigating to http://gamma.example. net/~testuser. If successful, you're prompted for a username and password before getting access.

Lab 6

As discussed in the corresponding lab in the *Study Guide*, the process required to set up a group-managed directory is a hybrid. In general, you take the following basic steps:

1. Create a regular user and group named **candidates**. Although not required, it can be helpful to configure that user with a higher UID and GID to avoid interfering with other future users and groups.

2. Make the other users (eileen, jefferson, and charles) members of that group named candidates.

3. Create a /home/candidates directory, owned by the user and group named candidates.

4. Set up appropriate permissions on /home/candidates to support access by members of the candidates group and access by the Apache system user. Known as 2771 permissions, they include full permissions for the user and group owner, along with the Super Group ID bit.

5. To enable access by the Apache server, you need to set up executable permissions by other users or ACL-based executable permissions for the user named apache.

6. Create a /home/candidates/public_html/ subdirectory with 755 permissions.

7. Set up an index.html file in that subdirectory. It should already be set with ownership by the user and group named candidates.

8. To limit access, you need an **AuthUserFile**, **AuthGroupFile**, and **Require** group directive to limit access to the noted users as members of the candidates group.

Lab 7

You don't need absolutely need to set up CGI scripts in the alpha.example.net virtual host container, as the parameters are specified by the following general directives in the httpd.conf file:

```
ScriptAlias /cgi-bin/  "/var/www/cgi-bin/"
Options Indexes FollowSymLinks ExecCGI
AddHandler cgi-script  .pl
```

Ideally, it's best to set up these directives within a virtual host container, so as to not affect other containers. Although not required by this lab, it may be required on the job, or perhaps even on an exam.

The reference to Apache documentation alludes to what you saw in Lab 1, which includes the following code for a hello.pl script:

```
#!/usr/bin/perl
print "Content-type: text/html\n\n";
print "Hello World";
```

If you choose that script, remember to set 755 permissions. Don't forget to set the httpd_sys_script_exec_t file type on the script file (and the associated directory).

In addition, don't forget to run an appropriate **semanage fcontext -a** command to make the change permanent to the script directory designated for the alpha.example.net system.

15

The Samba File Server

W hen properly configured, Samba can make a Linux system work seamlessly on a Microsoft-based file-sharing network. Samba is the Linux implementation of current Microsoft file-sharing protocols, starting with the Server Message Block (SMB) system and upgraded to support the Common Internet File System (CIFS). Samba is used on all Unix-based operating systems, including Linux.

While Red Hat no longer includes a GUI tool to configure Samba, it does include a web-based tool in its optional repository, the Samba Web Administration Tool (SWAT). It's available from the samba-swat package.

Install the Packages Needed to Provide the Service

The Red Hat implementation of the Samba service is simple. There's one mandatory package associated with the CIFS file server package group: samba. So all you have to do to install the packages needed to provide the service is to run the following command:

```
# yum install samba
```

With dependencies, this command also installs the samba-client, samba-common, and samba-winbind-clients packages. Pay attention to the configuration files in the /etc/samba directory, along with commands like **smbstatus**, **smbcontrol**, **smbpasswd**, and the **smb** and **nmb** scripts in the /etc/init.d directory.

If you want to install SWAT, run the following command:

```
# yum install samba-swat
```

Just be aware that because it's part of the RHEL 6 optional repository, Red Hat is under no obligation to make this tool available during an exam. So focus your studies on the Samba configuration files, especially /etc/samba/smb.conf.

Configure SELinux to Support the Service

As with other network services, Samba comes with risks. The different booleans shown in Table 15-1 are designed to minimize the risks in case of a security breach.

Only one Samba-related boolean (**qemu_use_cifs**) is enabled by default. To get some of the features associated with Samba, you may need to activate some of the other booleans. The booleans in the table are grouped by functionality.

SELinux is also associated with file types. Normally, Samba can only share those files and directories labeled with the samba_share_t file type. The exception is when either the **samba_export_all_ro** or **samba_export_all_rw** boolean is enabled.

If you set up a shared directory with the samba_share_t type, you'll want to set up the file_contexts.local file in /etc/selinux/targeted/contexts/files directory with a command such as the following:

```
# semanage fcontext -a -t samba_share_t /share
```

TABLE 15-1	Boolean	Description
Samba SELinux Booleans	allow_smb_anon_write	Allows Samba clients to write to directories configured with the public_content_rw_t SELinux setting
	samba_export_all_ro	Enables read-only access to shared directories, including those without the samba_share_t file-type label
	samba_export_all_rw	Enables read/write access to shared directories, even those without the samba_share_t file-type label
	samba_create_home_dirs	Lets Samba create home directories, normally for outside users
	samba_enable_home_dirs	Supports the sharing of home directories
	use_samba_home_dirs	Supports the use of a remote server for Samba home directories
	samba_share_fusefs	Allows Samba to share fusefs-mounted file systems, common for the Microsoft NTFS file systems
	samba_share_nfs	Enables sharing of NFS file systems via Samba
	qemu_use_cifs	Enables virtual machine access to CIFS file systems
	virt_use_samba	Allows a VM to access files mounted to the CIFS file system
	cdrecord_read_content	Supports the use of the **cdrecord** command to read shared Samba directories
	samba_domain_controller	Allows Samba to act as a domain controller
	samba_run_unconfined	Allows execution of unconfined scripts from the /var/lib/samba/scripts directory

Configure the Service to Start When the System Is Booted

While this may seem repetitive, it's important to make sure every service that you configure is booted in standard runlevels. For Samba, two services are in question: the main Samba service controlled by the **/etc/init.d/smb** script and the NetBIOS Name Server controlled by the **/etc/init.d/nmb** script. The following commands make sure that Samba and the NetBIOS Name Server services start in runlevels 3 and 5:

```
# chkconfig --level 35 smb on
# chkconfig --level 35 nmb on
```

Alternatively, the following commands make sure that both services start in runlevels 2, 3, 4, and 5:

```
# chkconfig smb on
# chkconfig nmb on
```

Of course, you can make sure these services are running before a reboot with the following commands:

```
# /etc/init.d/smb start
# /etc/init.d/nmb start
```

Configure the Service for Basic Operation

Once Samba and the corresponding NetBIOS name services are running, the default configuration of Samba is already set up for basic operation—sort of. Given the basic **[printers]** stanza in the smb.conf configuration file, it supports access to printers configured via the Common Unix Printing System (CUPS) service.

But to actually access those printers, or any shared directory configured in Samba, you have to set up a user authentication database. The default "trivial database" is configured with the following directive:

```
passdb backend = tdbsam
```

You could connect the trivial database to a Lightweight Directory Access Protocol (LDAP) server, but the details go beyond the "basic operation" required by the objective. You can set up the default database with the **smbpasswd** command, based on users configured locally in /etc/passwd. The following command adds the user named testuser, prompting twice for a password (which may differ from the Linux password):

```
# smbpasswd -a testuser
```

This command sets up users and passwords in a binary file, passdb.tdb, in the /var/lib/samba/private directory. You can then review shares available to user testuser with the following command, which prompts for that password:

```
$ smbclient \\localhost -U testuser
```

You'll see the testuser share in the output. You can then mount the share on a directory such as /mnt with the following command, which prompts for the testuser Samba password:

```
# mount.cifs //localhost/testuser /mnt -o username=testuser
```

You might then see a "Permission denied" error when trying to read the **/mnt** directory. That's due to a SELinux boolean. Run the following command, and you'll be able to read the contents of the testuser home directory with the **ls /mnt** command:

```
# setsebool -P samba_enable_home_dirs 1
```

You can set up shares in other directories in a similar fashion; commented templates are available in the default smb.conf file. Just be aware that you may need to set up the samba_share_t file type and possibly one or more the booleans shown in Table 15-1.

If you make any changes to the Samba configuration file, run the testparm command to check the syntax. To see how it looks from a client such as blackhat.example.net, run the testparm /etc/samba/smb.conf client blackhat.example.net command. (You may substitute an IP address.)

on the **Job**

Configure Host-Based and User-Based Security for the Service

You've already reviewed the basics of user-based security on Samba. For access to user-based shares, those users have to be registered in some Samba-aware user database such as passwd.tdb. If you set up user-based security, don't forget to include such users with the **smbpasswd -a** *username* command. Just be aware, you could override user-based security with the following directive:

```
public = yes
```

If you do set up users, you can limit access among these users with the **valid users** directive. For example, the following directive limits access to users randy and nancy:

```
valid users = randy nancy
```

To set up access to outside systems, you have to open up four ports in the local firewall: UDP ports 137 and 138, along with TCP ports 139 and 445. The Firewall Configuration tool automates this process; when you select Samba as a "Trusted Service," the tool adds the following directives to the /etc/sysconfig/iptables file:

```
-A INPUT -m state --state NEW -m udp -p udp --dport 137 -j ACCEPT
-A INPUT -m state --state NEW -m udp -p udp --dport 138 -j ACCEPT
-A INPUT -m state --state NEW -m tcp -p tcp --dport 139 -j ACCEPT
-A INPUT -m state --state NEW -m tcp -p tcp --dport 445 -j ACCEPT
```

If desired, you can use these commands as a template for a custom firewall rule file that limits access by IP address. For example, to limit access to systems on the 192.168.122.0 network, you could include **-s 192.168.122.0/24** before the **--dport** option.

Alternatively, you can set up limits in appropriate stanzas in the smb.conf file. For example, the following directive limits access to all systems on the 192.168.122.0/24 network, except the system on IP address 192.168.122.240:

```
hosts allow = 192.168.122.
hosts deny = 192.168.122.240
```

Provide Network Shares to Specific Clients

This objective is about setting up a Samba share of some hypothetical directory, limited to certain hosts. For the purpose of this chapter, set up a share in the /linux directory. Populate it with a few files so you can verify success. Now set up a stanza in the smb.conf file. The following lines call it a share named **[linux]**, with a comment that appears in the output to a client-side **smbclient** command.

```
[linux]
comment = Shared samba directory
path = /linux
```

You'll want to add more to limit the share to a specific client. For example, the following line would limit access to systems on the .example.net network, except the blackhat.example.net system (feel free to substitute IP addresses):

```
hosts allow = .example.net EXCEPT blackhat.example.net
```

Of course, you also have to take the following actions with respect to local firewalls and SELinux booleans:

- Allow access through the firewall; if you've limited access in the Samba configuration file with the **hosts allow** directive, all you need to do is make Samba a "Trusted Service" in the Firewall Configuration tool.

- Set appropriate SELinux contexts on the shared directory, along with the files contained therein; one way to do this is with the **chcon -R -t samba_share_t /linux** command.

Provide Network Shares Suitable for Group Collaboration

While groups can be configured in a substantial number of ways on a Microsoft-based network, it's usually best to keep the requirements as simple as possible. The default smb.conf configuration file already includes a commented share stanza preconfigured for group collaboration. When combined with the configuration requirements associated with a group directory, you can set up a Samba network share suitable for group collaboration. You may use the following steps as a checklist to set up that share.

1. Set up a new group; make any desired users members of that group. For this example, call it group1. Set it up with standard user and group management commands described in Chapter 8. Don't forget to set up a stanza for the share, such as:

```
[testshare]
```

2. Create an appropriate /home directory such as /home/samba, configured with 2770 permissions. Limit access to and give group ownership of the directory to group1.

```
path = /home/samba
valid users = @group1
```

3. Alternatively, the following directives limit access if ownership has already been properly configured:

```
directory mask = 2770
create mask = 2770
```

4. Set up the samba_share_t file type on that directory, along with the files contained therein. Make sure that's reflected on a permanent basis with the **semanage fcontext** command. (For an explanation of how these commands are used, see Chapter 11 of the *Study Guide*.)

5. Check the syntax with the testparm command.

6. Make sure subject users are included in both the Linux and Samba password authentication databases.

7. Reload the revised Samba configuration file with the /etc/init.d/smb reload command.

CERTIFICATION SUMMARY

While the only package associated with the CIFS file server package group is samba, it also requires several other packages as dependencies, including samba-common for configuration files and samba-client for client utilities. Samba includes two service scripts in the /etc/init.d directory, smb and nmb, both of which must be set as active in appropriate runlevels during the boot process.

Shared Samba files can be configured with the samba_share_t file type. Shared Samba home directories can work if you activate the **samba_enable_home_dirs** boolean. Samba communicates over UDP ports 137 and 138, along with TCP ports 139 and 445.

Although Samba users must exist in a Linux user database, you also need to create a separate Samba database for each user with the **smbpasswd** command. Once you've configured the Samba configuration file /etc/samba/smb.conf, you can test the syntax with the **testparm** command. You can even test how the configuration file appears to external systems with the appropriate switches. If you're setting up a Samba share for a group, you can leverage an existing special group, if it's configured with appropriate ownership and permissions, as discussed in Chapter 8 of the *Study Guide*.

SELF TEST

The following fill-in-the-blank questions help you measure your understanding of the topics associated with this chapter. As there are no multiple-choice questions on the Red Hat exams, there are no multiple-choice questions in this book. If you have trouble with one or more of these questions, you may need to research associated topics further. However, there's almost always more than one way to solve a problem in Linux. Getting results, not memorizing trivia, is what counts on the Red Hat exams.

As this is a practice book, the answers to these questions may or may not be found in the body of the chapter. For more information, see the *Study Guide*.

Install the Packages Needed to Provide the Service

  1. What package includes the main Samba configuration file smb.conf in the /etc/samba directory?

  _____

Configure SELinux to Support the Service

  2. What SELinux file type supports Samba shares?

  _____

Configure the Service to Start When the System Is Booted

  3. Name the four port numbers that must be open for a Samba server to work with remote systems. Bonus: include the transport-layer protocol associated with each port.

  _____   _____   _____   _____

Configure the Service for Basic Operation

  4. What SELinux boolean should you activate to enable access to home directories, as defined in the default version of the smb.conf file?

  _____

  5. What command adds user windows1 to the Samba database? Assume that windows1 exists as a local user in the files of the Shadow Password Suite.

  _____

Configure Host-Based and User-Based Security for the Service

6. If you want to prevent connections from the system on IP address 192.168.1.24 to the local Samba server, what rule would you add to the **iptables**-based firewall?

_____

Provide Network Shares to Specific Clients

7. If you want to limit access to a certain shared directory to the whitehat.example.net system, what directive would you include in the associated stanza?

_____

Provide Network Shares Suitable for Group Collaboration

8. What permissions are required on a directory to be shared for a group of users?

_____

LAB QUESTIONS

Red Hat presents its exams electronically. For that reason, the labs in this and future chapters are available from the gamma.example.net system, from the ChapterLabs/ folder that appears in the GUI desktop. If you're running in a command-line console, you can find the labs in the /home/testuser/ Desktop/ChapterLabs directory.

The answers for each lab follow the Self Test Answers for the fill-in-the-blank questions.

SELF TEST ANSWERS

Install the Packages Needed to Provide the Service

1. The samba-common package includes the main Samba configuration file, smb.conf.

Configure SELinux to Support the Service

2. The samba_share_t SELinux file type supports Samba shares.

Configure the Service to Start When the System Is Booted

3. The four port numbers that must be open for a Samba server to work with remote systems, along with transport-layer protocols, are UDP 137, UDP 138, TCP 139, and TCP 445.

Configure the Service for Basic Operation

4. The **samba_enable_home_dirs** SELinux boolean enables access to home directories. Unless enabled, the [homes] stanza in the smb.conf file won't work.

5. The **smbpasswd -a windows1** command adds that user to the Samba database.

Configure Host-Based and User-Based Security for the Service

6. When added to a file like /etc/sysconfig/iptables, the following options to the **iptables** command would prevent connections from the system on IP address 192.168.1.24 to the local Samba server.

    ```
    -A INPUT -m state --state NEW -m tcp -p tcp -s 192.168.1.24 --dport 445
    -j REJECT
    ```

    Alternate options, such as **DROP** in place of **REJECT**, are acceptable. You could also specify other ports, such as 137, 138, and 139, as long as you specify the correct transport layer protocol (TCP or UDP). Of course, you don't even need options that specify transport layer protocols such as **-m state --state NEW**, **-m tcp**, or **-p tcp**.

Provide Network Shares to Specific Clients

7. To limit access to a certain shared directory to the whitehat.example.net system, find the stanza for that directory. Include the **hosts allow whitehat.example.net** directive in that stanza. Alternatives such as **allow hosts whitehat.example.net** are also acceptable.

Provide Network Shares Suitable for Group Collaboration

8. While not absolutely required, 2770 permissions are best on a directory to be shared by a group of users. The "2" represents the Super Group ID bit, which assigns group ownership to files copied to the directory therein, as described in Chapter 8 of the *Study Guide*.

LAB ANSWERS

Lab 1

This lab should be fairly simple. You can confirm success from a second system by mounting it with a command such as the following:

```
# mount.cifs //gamma.example.net/testuser /mnt -o username=testuser
```

Before this command is successful, you need to take the following actions:

■ Make sure both the **smb** and **nmb** services start in at least runlevels 3 and 5.

■ Activate the **samba_enable_home_dirs** boolean with the **-P** switch to make sure the change survives a reboot.

■ Add the testuser user to the Samba password database with the **smbpasswd -a testuser** command, and make sure to use the rhcecert password when prompted.

Lab 2

Once you've installed the samba-doc RPM, you can access it with a web browser. You'll find the main index.html file when navigating to file:///usr/share/doc/samba-doc-3.5.10/htmldocs/Samba3-ByExample/index.html. If that's too much to remember, navigate to file:///usr/share/doc. All subdirectories, including the subdirectory for Samba documentation, will appear in the browser.

Examples are available from the links near the bottom of the index.html page that appears.

Lab 3

This lab adds tasks to those already completed for Lab 1. To make sure it works, you may want to set up a second regular user. On the Samba server, add the following directives (or equivalent) to the **[homes]** share:

```
hosts allow = whitehat.example.net
browsable = yes
```

Lab 4

One way to set up /tmp share with the given parameters is with the following stanza:

```
[tmp]
   Comment = temp directory
   path = /tmp
   public = yes
   hosts allow = .example.net
```

Lab 5

Once you've set up the new user ceo and created the /ceo directory, copy the PDF files from the samba-doc package. Don't forget to set up user ceo in the Samba authentication database with the **smbpasswd -a ceo** command. You can identify the full path to these files with the help of the **rpm -ql samba-doc | grep pdf** command.

You'll also want to assign the samba_share_t file type to the files and the /ceo directory, making sure that file type is documented in the appropriate file_contexts.* file in the /etc/selinux/targeted/contexts/files directory. One way to do so is with the following command:

```
# semanage fcontext -a -t samba_share_t /ceo
```

When you set up the /ceo share in the Samba configuration file, include the following directives (or equivalent):

```
valid users = ceo
hosts allow = whitehat.example.net
```

Of course, you want to test the share from remote systems, both whitehat.example.net and another system, to make sure the share is available only from whitehat.

Lab 6

The actions you take here are similar to those required for Lab 5. However, you want to create a special group named cert to take group ownership of the /certnotes directory. After copying the contents of the /home/testuser/Desktop/ChapterLabs directory, take the following steps:

1. Configure users redhat1 and redhat2 as members of the cert group. Assign them Samba passwords with the help of the **smbpasswd -a username** command.

2. Set up the group named cert as the owner of the /certnotes directory, with 2770 permissions.

3. Include the **directory mask = 2770** and **create mask = 2770** directives in the appropriate Samba configuration stanza.

4. Although you may specify users redhat1 and redhat2 with a **valid users** directive, that directive is not required, as access to the shared directory is also controlled by permissions on the shared directory.

In this lab, you go even further and create a shared directory, with access limited to a group of two users. The basic steps are the same as for Lab 5; however, you need to create a directory with SGID permissions, along with full permissions to the group owner of that directory. The basic steps to create that shared directory are the same as for the directory created in Chapter 8.

This lab may take a significant amount of work. You need to set up a group of users, with group ownership of a dedicated directory. Since the discussion in Chapter 8 was based on an RHCSA requirement, you have to repeat that process in this lab. It is assumed that candidates for the RHCE have mastered RHCSA requirements.

Once complete, add the following directives to the stanza for the shared group directory:

```
create mask = 0770
directory mask = 2770
```

16

More File-Sharing Services

Thfis chapter covers two RHCE-level network services: the Network File System (NFS) and the File Transfer Protocol (FTP) server. As with other services, this chapter covers the five common objectives for network services. For the purposes of this chapter, I've added "NFS" and "FTP" to each objective as appropriate.

The requirements for FTP services are not that different from the corresponding objectives for the RHCSA. This chapter assumes you'll set up anonymous-only downloads from a nonstandard directory. The requirements for NFS services are functionally equivalent to those for Samba. As the NFS configuration file is simpler, the steps needed to meet those requirements are also simpler. Just be aware that RHEL 6 does not include GUI tools for these services.

Install the Packages Needed to Provide the Service

The packages associated with the NFS and FTP services are straightforward. The basic installation of the gamma.example.net system includes the nfs-utils and nfs4-acl-utils packages. The main NFS configuration file, /etc/exports, is included in the RPM named setup, which includes the files of the Shadow Password Suite, which is fundamental to Linux. So there's a good chance the packages required for version 4 of the NFS server are already installed. If necessary, just run the following command:

```
# yum install nfs-utils nfs4-acl-tools
```

If you're working with NFS versions 2 or 3, you want to install the portreserve, quota, and rpcbind packages.

RHEL 6 includes one package associated with FTP services, vsftpd. It's the default very secure FTP (vsFTP) service and is simple to install with the following command:

```
# yum install vsftpd
```

Configure SELinux to Support the Service

This is just the briefest of overviews of the SELinux booleans and file types associated with the NFS and FTP services. For NFS, no special SELinux file types are required on shared directories. For FTP, two file types are commonly used: public_content_t is for read-only files and public_content_rw_t is for read-write files. As read-write would apply to FTP uploads, that is beyond the scope of the related objective, to "configure anonymous-only download." So all you have to do when configuring a new directory for anonymous-only downloads is run a command such as the following:

```
# chcon -R -t public_content_t /new/dir
```

If you want a full list of NFS booleans, run the **ls /selinux/booleans | grep nfs** command. From this list, three NFS booleans, which are all enabled by default, are directly related to the configuration of the service:

- **nfs_export_all_ro**   Enables NFS sharing of directories in read-only mode
- **nfs_export_all_rw**   Enables NFS sharing of directories in read-write mode
- **use_nfs_home_dirs**   Supports the configuration of home directories mounted from a remote NFS server.

If a security administrator or an exam requires you to disable all read-write NFS shares, all you need to do is disable the **nfs_export_all_rw** boolean.

You can get a similar list of FTP server-related booleans with the **ls /selinux/booleans | grep ftp** command. Those that relate directly to the vsFTP server are described here. To preserve an "anonymous-only" download configuration for the FTP server, you may want to make sure that one or more of the following booleans stay disabled:

- **allow_ftp_anon_write**   Supports anonymous-only uploads on directories labeled with the public_content_rw_t file type.
- **allow_ftp_full_access**   Enables access by regular users configured on the FTP server
- **ftp_home_dir**   Allows regular users to log into their home directories on the FTP server

Configure the Service to Start When the System Is Booted

It's simple to set up both the FTP and NFS services to start when RHEL 6 is booted. All you need to do is run the following commands:

```
# chkconfig nfs on
# chkconfig vsftpd on
```

While other services are required to support NFS, the **/etc/init.d/nfs** script includes commands that start those other services.

Configure the Service for Basic Operation

For NFS, if the appropriate services are running, all you have to do is configure a shared directory in the /etc/exports file and then export the share. The default /etc/exports is blank; options are simple. For example, the following line shares the /test directory as read-only on all systems:

```
/test *(ro)
```

You can then run either the **/etc/init.d/nfs reload** or **exportfs -r** commands to implement the share. Of course, you need to set up the firewall and appropriate access restrictions, but those are subjects for other objectives.

Just be careful, as an extra space, such as after a comma, could invalidate some or all of the settings in a line in the /etc/exports file.

For the vsFTP service, the process is simpler, as the default configuration already works for basic operation. Anonymous-only users can log in and download files from the /var/ftp/pub directory. Be careful though. If you copy files to the /var/ftp/pub directory, those files might overwrite the root ownership and SELinux contexts of the directory. Unless those contexts are also set to **public_content_t** (or **public_content_rw_t**), that could even prevent FTP clients from reading the contents of that directory.

Nevertheless, the "user-based" security objective also applies to vsFTP. The default options within the /etc/vsftpd/vsftpd.conf file support authenticated access to user home directories.

e x a m

ⓦ a t c h

The reason anonymous FTP users are led to the /var/ftp directory is it's the home directory of the user named ftp, as defined in the /etc/passwd file.

Configure Host-Based and User-Based Security for the Service

For NFS, user-based security is based on a common set of users and groups on servers and clients. You can set this up with a little care in the files of the Shadow Password Suite, or with the help of an LDAP (Lightweight Directory Access Protocol) server, with is beyond the scope of either certification. The Shadow Password Suite and LDAP clients are covered in Chapter 8 of the *Study Guide*.

For host-based security, if you stick with NFS version 4, host-based security is relatively easy to configure. You can do so in the /etc/exports file; for example, the following line would limit the ability to mount the /test directory share to systems on the 192.168.122.0 network:

```
/test  192.168.122.0/24(ro)
```

Just be careful; if you have a space between the IP address and the (**ro**), access would be allowed to all hosts. If you prefer configuring host-based NFS security, activate the following directives in the /etc/sysconfig/nfs file:

```
MOUNTD_NFS_V2="no"
MOUNTD_NFS_V3="no"
RPCNFSDARGS="-N 2 -N 3"
```

You can then regulate access for NFSv4 over TCP port 2049.

For the vsFTP service, you can set up user-based security in the ftpusers file in the /etc/vsftpd directory. With the help of settings in /etc/pam.d/vsftpd, the ftpusers file includes all users who aren't allowed to access the service.

For vsFTP, you can set up host-based security fairly easily with the help of **iptables**-based firewalls, as communication proceeds over TCP port 21. As the /usr/sbin/vsftpd daemon also uses TCP Wrappers libraries, you can also set up security with the help of the /etc/hosts.allow and /etc/hosts.deny files.

Configure Anonymous-Only Download for an FTP Server

This objective is actually a bit more complex than it sounds. Anonymous downloads are enabled in the default vsftpd.conf file, courtesy of the following directive:

```
anonymous_enable = yes
```

Although anonymous downloads are enabled in the default configuration of vsFTP, access by regular users is also allowed. To disable access for regular users, delete the following directive from the vsftpd.conf file:

```
local_enable = yes
```

It is true, however, that user access to home directories isn't allowed unless you enable the following SELinux boolean:

```
ftp_home_dir
```

But in the system that you get in production (or on an exam), that boolean might already be active. And if you've been told to configure SELinux in permissive mode, vsFTP ignores this boolean.

Provide NFS Network Shares to Specific Clients

The steps you take to meet this objective have already been outlined in the section on host-based security. You can set up a shared directory with different parameters for each client. For example, the following line in the /etc/exports file shares the /common directory with two clients in different ways:

```
/common   whitehat.example.net(ro)   blackhat.example.net(rw)
```

You can share additional directories with other clients in a similar fashion; the following example shares the /share directory with two clients using IP addresses:

```
/share   192.168.122.130(rw)   192.168.122.240(ro)
```

Depending on the situation, you may be asked to specify something other than read-write or read-only limits. Several other parameters are included in Table 16-1.

TABLE 16-1	Parameter	Functional Description
NFS /etc/exports Options	no_subtree_check	Disables subtree checks, which prevents clients from checking higher-level directories of mounted shares
	sync	Syncs write operations on request
	no_wdelay	Forces immediate data writes
	hide	Hide subdirectories; if you export related directories such as /mnt and /mnt/inst, clients must mount /mnt/inst separately
	no_root_squash	Gives remote root user privileges locally on the shared directory
	all_squash	Maps all client users as anonymous
	anonuid=userid	Specifies a local user ID for anonymous users
	anongid=groupid	Specifies local group ID for anonymous groups

Provide **NFS Network Shares Suitable for Group Collaboration**

The configuration of an NFS network share for a group requires some coordination. You need to set up the same usernames and groups on both systems. Furthermore, you need to make sure the user ID and group ID numbers of the corresponding accounts match perfectly.

For that reason, it's best to have a network database of these users and groups. Such databases can be configured on an LDAP server. But since that's not part of either exam objective, that option may not be available to you.

In any case, this may provide the opportunity to practice what you learned in Chapter 8 of the *Study Guide*. Namely, it allows you to practice creating users, specialized groups, and dedicated directories with appropriate ownership and permissions.

When you've set that up on both the NFS server and client, you'll be ready to set up an NFS shared directory, suited for collaboration by the users who are members of the target group.

CERTIFICATION SUMMARY

The focus of this chapter is on two file-sharing services. As NFS is native to Linux and Unix computers, it's efficient. Although Linux supports NFSv2, NFSv3, and NFSv4, the latest version is actually simplest in several ways. NFSv4 only requires an open TCP port 2049; earlier versions of NFS required several other open ports. In any case, the main configuration file for sharing a directory via NFS is /etc/exports.

RHEL 6 uses one FTP server, vsFTP. While the RHCE objectives specify the configuration of anonymous-only downloads, they also specify host- and user-based security. So be prepared to configure vsFTP in both ways, based on the contents of the /etc/vsftpd/vsftpd.conf configuration file. Anonymous-only users are taken to the /var/ftp directory based on the configuration of the user named ftp. Special FTP directories should be configured with the public_content_t file type.

SELF TEST

The following fill-in-the-blank questions help you measure your understanding of the topics associated with this chapter. As there are no multiple-choice questions on the Red Hat exams, there are no multiple-choice questions in this book. If you have trouble with one or more of these questions, you may need to research associated topics further. However, there's almost always more than one way to solve a problem in Linux. Getting results, not memorizing trivia, is what counts on the Red Hat exams.

As this is a practice book, the answers to these questions may or may not be found in the body of the chapter. For more information, see the *Study Guide*.

Install the Packages Needed to Provide the Service

1. What is the name of the RPM package associated with the default RHEL 6 FTP server? Do not include a version number.

   _____

Configure SELinux to Support the Service

2. What SELinux boolean supports read-only access to shared NFS directories?

   _____

Configure the Service to Start When the System Is Booted

3. What command is required to make sure the NFS and rpc.mountd services are running the next time the system is booted?

   _____

Configure the Service for Basic Operation

4. What protocol and port number should you open in a firewall to access NFS version 4 services?

   _____

Configure Host-Based and User-Based Security for the Service

5. What file includes a list of users who are not allowed to access the vsFTP server?

   _____

Configure Anonymous-Only Download for an FTP Server

6. What directive would you remove from the /etc/vsftpd/vsftpd.conf file to make sure access to the vsFTP server is anonymous-only?

_____

Provide NFS Network Shares to Specific Clients

7. What would you add to the /etc/exports file to share the /tmp directory in read-write mode with the system on IP address 192.168.122.1?

_____

Provide NFS Network Shares Suitable for Group Collaboration

8. What permissions would you set on a directory associated with group collaboration?

_____

LAB QUESTIONS

Red Hat presents its exams electronically. For that reason, the labs in this and future chapters are available from the gamma.example.net system, from the ChapterLabs/ folder that appears in the GUI desktop. If you're running in a command-line console, you can find the labs in the /home/testuser/Desktop/ChapterLabs directory.

The answers for each lab follow the Self Test Answers for the fill-in-the-blank questions.

SELF TEST ANSWERS

Install the Packages Needed to Provide the Service

1. The default RHEL 6 FTP server RPM package is vsftpd.

Configure SELinux to Support the Service

2. The **nfs_export_all_ro boolean** supports read-only access to shared NFS directories.

Configure the Service to Start When the System Is Booted

3. The **chkconfig nfs on** command is sufficient to make sure the NFS and rpc.mountd services are running the next time the system is booted. Of course, variations on the **chkconfig** command that start NFS in runlevels 3 and 5 are also acceptable. No separate command is required for the rpc.mountd service.

Configure the Service for Basic Operation

4. To access NFS version 4 services, you need to open TCP port number 2049.

Configure Host-Based and User-Based Security for the Service

5. The ftpusers file in the /etc/vsftpd directory includes a list of users who are not allowed to access the vsFTP server. The user_list file in the same directory is also acceptable.

Configure Anonymous-Only Download for an FTP Server

6. To make the vsFTP server anonymous-only, delete or comment out the **local_enable=yes** directive. While disabling the **ftp_home_dir** boolean serves the same purpose, that's not sufficient, as you might be told to set SELinux in permissive mode.

Provide NFS Network Shares to Specific Clients

7. To share the /tmp directory in read-write mode with the system on IP address 192.168.122.1, add the following line to /etc/exports:

```
/tmp   192.168.122.1(rw)
```

Provide NFS Network Shares Suitable for Group Collaboration

8. For any directory associated with group collaboration, set 2770 permissions, also known as read, write, and executable permissions, for the user and group owner of that directory, along with the Super Group ID bit. Of course, that assumes either a network-based authentication scheme, or at least matching lists of users and groups on the server and client systems. But that detail is beyond the scope of this question.

LAB ANSWERS

Lab 1

This is something of an instructional lab to help you understand the impact of different options used when sharing a directory over an NFS server. This lab depends on the following assumptions:

- You've opened up appropriate ports in the NFS server (at least TCP ports 111 and 2049).
- You restart the NFS server each time after changing the /etc/exports file.
- You unmount the NFS shared directory once the new share is implemented, before remounting it.

With those assumptions in mind, you should perform the following in the steps listed in the Lab. (The commands listed are often not the only way to perform the task detailed in the Lab.)

1. Add the following line to /etc/exports, and start or restart the NFS service with the **/etc/init.d/nfs restart** command:

```
/home *(ro)
```

2. Run the following command as root from an NFS client such as whitehat.example.net:

```
# mount.nfs4 192.168.122.20:/home /mnt
```

You should get a "Permission denied" message when running the **ls /mnt/testuser** command.

3. The **su - testuser** command moves to the testuser account. When you run the **ls /mnt/testuser** command, you should be able to read the contents of the shared testuser home directory.

4. With the **no_root_squash** option, the root user from the NFS client should be able to read the contents of the shared testuser home directory.

5. With the **hide** option, access to the testuser home directory is blocked for all users.

6. To set executable permissions set for other users on the noted home directory, run the **chmod o+x /home/testuser** command on the NFS server. On the NFS client, you won't be able to read the contents of the /home/testuser directory. However, you will be able to read the contents of the /home/testuser/Desktop directory. From the gamma.example.net system, that should reveal the ChapterLabs/ and SampleExams/ subdirectories.

Lab 2

The solution to this lab is simple: the following command disables the SELinux boolean that supports the use of remote home directories:

```
# setsebool -P use_nfs_home_dirs 0
```

Of course, this lab works only if SELinux is active in enforcing mode.

Lab 3

This lab is also fairly simple; the system defined in /etc/exports is the system that is allowed to access the specified share. The following line in /etc/exports limits access to the noted system:

```
/home  whitehat.example.net(ro)
```

Variations may be acceptable; for example, given the conditions of the lab, you may substitute the 192.168.122.130 IP address for whitehat.example.net. You may also choose to include the sync option in the share.

Of course, to get this working, you have to re-enable the **use_nfs_home_dirs** boolean described in the answer to Lab 2.

Lab 4

The relevant entry in the /etc/passwd file for the RHEL 6 FTP server relates to the user named ftp, as shown here:

```
ftp:x:14:50:FTP User:/var/ftp:/sbin/nologin
```

Note the home directory for that user, /var/ftp. Files for the RHEL 6 FTP server are normally stored in the /var/ftp/pub directory; anonymous-only users have to navigate to that directory on login to see what files are available.

To help anonymous-only users avoid that step, you could change the noted entry in /etc/passwd to:

```
ftp:x:14:50:FTP User:/var/ftp/pub:/sbin/nologin
```

Of course, if you're using the FTP server for any other purpose, you may want to restore the original line, so any related scripts and more aren't affected.

Lab 5

To allow anonymous-only access and disable logging of transfers, you could comment out the following lines in the /etc/vsftpd/vsftpd.conf file, or change **YES** to **NO**:

```
local_enable=YES
xferlog_enable=YES
```

Commenting out these directives would work, as their default values, as confirmed in the man page for vsftpd.conf, are already set to **NO**. The simplest way to comment out a directive in most Linux configuration files is to add a pound sign (**#**) in front:

```
#xferlog_enable=YES
```

Lab 6

This lab goes a bit beyond anonymous-only access. Yes, the configuration of regular users, at least nominally, goes beyond the objective associated with the FTP server in the RHCE objectives. However, "user"- and "host"-based security is noted as a general requirement for all RHCE services.

To enable access by regular users, after the results of Lab 5, you want to make sure the following option is active:

```
local_enable=YES
```

To disable access from the user named testuser, you can add that name to the /etc/vsftpd/ftpusers file. As you can see in that file, restricted users are listed, one per line. To reiterate the process from the *Study Guide*, that file is called courtesy of Pluggable Authentication Modules, as defined in the /etc/pam.d/vsftpd file. Of course, you may need to create another regular user to confirm that other users can still access their home directories via this FTP server.

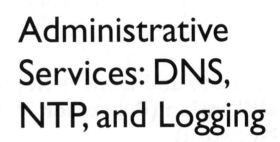

17

Administrative Services: DNS, NTP, and Logging

EXAM OBJECTIVES

❑   Produce and deliver reports on system utilization (processor, memory, disk, and network)

❑   Configure a system to log to a remote system

❑   Configure a system to accept logging from a remote system

❑   Install the packages needed to provide the service

❑   Configure SELinux to support the service

❑   Configure the service to start when the system is booted

❑   Configure the service for basic operation

❑   Configure host-based and user-based security for the service

❑   Configure a caching-only name server

❑   Configure a caching-only name server to forward DNS queries

❑   Synchronize time using other NTP peers

❑   Self Test

T his chapter gives you a chance to practice configuring four administrative services: the Domain Name System (DNS), the Network Time Protocol (NTP), system activity reports, and system logging services. The first two are listed as network services.

The DNS requirements for the RHCE aren't that complex, especially as the objectives suggest that "candidates are not expected to configure master or slave nameservers." The package associated with NTP works for servers and clients. System activity reports can be configured as a specialized cron job. System logging services support the configuration of a central logging server.

Produce and Deliver Reports on System Utilization (Processor, Memory, Disk, and Network)

One responsibility of many systems administrators is monitoring system utilization. In the context of the noted RHCE objective, that includes questions on CPU load, RAM memory utilization, free disk space, and network congestion. While you can get a snapshot of this information with commands like **top**, **df**, and **fdisk**, you can meet this objective by configuring the system status service, sysstat. The sysstat service collects relevant data in log files in the /var/log/sa directory.

Default system status reports are configured as a cron job in the sysstat file in the /etc/cron.d directory. The first line specifies a job that's run every ten minutes, collects statistics related to the use of swap space, and puts the information in a file named sa*dd* in the /var/log/sa directory, where *dd* is the numeric day of the month.

```
*/10 * * * * root /usr/lib64/sa/sa1 -S DISK 1 1
```

The last line, courtesy of the **sa2 -A** command, creates a daily report in a file named sar*dd*, also in the /var/log/sa directory. For example, the sar29 file would represent information collected on the 29th of the month. As it's in text format, open it up. Look at the information that's collected every day at 11:53 p.m.:

```
53 23 * * * root /usr/lib64/sa/sa2 -A
```

You could be asked to modify these system status jobs in some way. As noted in the man page for the **sar** command, the **-A** is equivalent to a whole host of options: "equivalent to specifying -bBdqrRSuvwWy -I SUM -I XALL -n ALL -u ALL -P ALL."

If you're asked to prepare a focused system status report, you can do this with the **sadf** command, which uses the reports generated by **sar** commands, such as **sa1** and **sa2**. One example is shown in the **sadf** man page; it takes the log file from the 21st of the month. The double-dash (**--**) uses **sar** command options, in this case for RAM (**-r**) and network device (**-n DEV**) usage.

```
# sadf -d /var/log/sa/sa21 -- -r -n DEV
```

In contrast, the following command includes CPU utilization (**-u**), with activity by block device associated with device names such as sda (**-dp**):

```
# sadf -d /var/log/sa/sa21 -- -u -r -dp -n DEV
```

Configure a System to Log to a Remote System

Whereas local logs are associated with the RHCSA, as described in Chapter 9, the RHCE includes two objectives associated with the transmission of log files over a network. This objective is based on the configuration of a system as a network logging client that transmits such information to a remote system, and assumes you've installed the rsyslog package, the system logging daemon.

The /etc/rsyslog.conf file includes a handy group of commented commands that can be used to configure a logging client as a client that forwards log information to some specified central logging server. As suggested by the comments in the file, these rules essentially belong together. To activate a logging client, remove the pound sign (**#**) from in front of all but the second to last line (that starts with **remote host is**):

```
#$WorkDirectory /var/spppl/rsyslog # where to place spool files
#$ActionQueueFileName fwdRule1 # unique name prefix for spool files
#$ActionQueueMaxDiskSpace 1g   # 1gb space limit (use as much as possible)
#$ActionQueueSaveOnShutdown on # save messages to disk on shutdown
#$ActionQueueType LinkedList   # run asynchronously
#$ActionResumeRetryCount -1    # infinite retries if host is down
# remote host is: name/ip:port, e.g. 192.168.0.1:514, port optional
#*.* @@remote-host:514
```

To set up a logging client, change the last line; the following example sends all logs (*.*), using TCP (@@), to IP address 192.168.122.1, over port 514:

```
*.* @@192.168.122.1:514
```

The following entry, in contrast, sends messages related to cron jobs, over UDP (@) port 514 to the same IP address:

```
cron.* @192.168.122.1:514
```

Configure a System to Accept Logging from a Remote System

The configuration of a system logging server is simpler, with respect to the changes required in the /etc/rsyslog.conf configuration file. All you need to do is activate one of the following two pairs of directives. As suggested by their names, the following commented directives, if activated, would listen on UDP port 514:

```
#$ModLoad imudp.so
#$UDPServerRun 514
```

In contrast, the following two commented directives are associated with TCP port 514:

```
#$ModLoad imtcp.so
#$InputTCPServerRun 514
```

Of course, you have to make sure the associated port in the local logging server firewall is open. If you use the Firewall Configuration tool, be aware that port 514 is not associated with any standard "trusted service." As such, you would need to set up a custom rule with a directive such as the following for TCP port 514:

```
-A INPUT -m state --state NEW -m tcp -p tcp --dport 514 -j ACCEPT
```

In production, system logging servers may require huge resources. For example, the logs from enterprise-level websites can easily consume gigabytes of data every day. Imagine the space required for a logging server associated with a group of web servers working in parallel.

Install the Packages Needed to Provide the Service

The packages associated with each of the services described in this chapter are summarized in Table 17-1. As with other packages, you can install them over a network with the help of the **yum install** *package* command.

Based on the default VMs available from the DVD, you only need to install the bind package. Of course, the system you administer, such as a test system, could be different.

Configure SELinux to Support the Service

All of the services discussed in this chapter have their own SELinux file contexts. However, they're largely irrelevant for our purposes. With the possible exception of DNS, none of the services include data files in any sort of specialized directories. Data files for DNS services apply to master and secondary name servers, which are explicitly excluded from the RHCE objectives.

In general, the only service covered in this chapter that's directly affected by SELinux booleans is DNS. The relevant boolean, **named_write_master_zones**, relates to the configuration of a master DNS server. So, for purposes of the RHCE, SELinux is not relevant to the services associated with this chapter.

TABLE 17-1	Package	Description
Relevant RPM Packages	sysstat	Provides commands and file structure that logs system activity
	rsyslog	Includes local and network logging configuration options
	ntp	Adds the Network Time Protocol (NTP) service
	ntpdate	Includes a client that retrieves the current time from an NTP server
	bind	Adds packages required for a DNS server
	bind-utils	Includes commands for querying DNS servers
	bind-chroot	Adds secure subdirectories for isolating black-hat hackers who break into a DNS service

Configure the Service to Start When the System Is Booted

By this point in the book, you should be quite familiar with the commands needed to activate a service in appropriate runlevels. For the purpose of this chapter, the following is a list of services that you should inspect to make sure they're appropriately configured to "start when the system is booted":

```
# chkconfig --list named
# chkconfig --list ntpd
# chkconfig --list ntpdate
# chkconfig --list rsyslog
# chkconfig --list sysstat
```

The output should show all of these services, at least those you're required to configure, active in at least runlevels 3 and 5.

Configure the Service for Basic Operation

Four services are covered in this chapter. When installed, the configuration files for each one of them are already configured for basic operation. Assuming you've set them to start at appropriate runlevels, they're already configured for basic operation under the following conditions:

- **System status service**   The sysstat service is configured to log system accounting every ten minutes. If you want a daily summary of the results a bit early, say within the couple of hours associated with an exam, you could modify the specified time for generating that report in the sysstat script in the /etc/cron.d directory.

- **System logging**   The RHEL 6 system logging service, rsyslog, is configured to log events from the local system. To configure it as a server or client, you need to make changes to the /etc/rsyslog.conf file described earlier in this chapter.

- **NTP services**   If you activate the **ntp** service, the default configuration in the /etc/ntp.conf file includes NTP servers to synchronize the local clock.

- **DNS**   The default /etc/named.conf file installed from the package named bind is configured as a caching-only name server.

Configure Host-Based and User-Based Security for the Service

User-based security is not supported for any of the services discussed in this chapter. On the other hand, host-based security is supported for the relevant network services: System logging, NTP, and DNS.

You can configure host-based security for these services with the help of standard **iptables**-based firewalls and the communication port defined for these services. The default port numbers for system logging, NTP, and DNS are 514, 123, and 53, respectively.

As discussed with other services in this book, you could set up host-based security in the Firewall Configuration tool, with the help of a custom rule. In fact, you might combine host-based security for all three of these services with the following lines in a single file:

```
-A INPUT -m state --state NEW -m tcp -p tcp -s 192.168.122.0/24 --dport 514 -j
ACCEPT
-A INPUT -m state --state NEW -m tcp -p tcp -s 192.168.122.0/24 --dport 123 -j
ACCEPT
-A INPUT -m state --state NEW -m tcp -p tcp -s 192.168.122.0/24 --dport 53 -j
ACCEPT
-A INPUT -m state --state NEW -m udp -p udp -s 192.168.122.0/24 --dport 53 -j
ACCEPT
```

Configure a Caching-Only Name Server

As suggested earlier, a caching-only name server is already configured based on the default installation of the bind package. But that installation is good only for the local system. Look at the /etc/named.conf file. The following directive specifies the IPv4 address to which the system listens:

```
listen-on port 53 { 127.0.0.1; };
```

To extend that directive to the network, you need to add the IP address of the network card. The following entry works for the gamma.example.net system:

```
listen-on port 53 { 127.0.0.1; 192.168.122.20; };
```

The noted entry also indicates why DNS servers are typically installed on systems with fixed IP addresses. If you were to specify a host name, it would have to look for a different DNS server for name resolution, which could get complicated. If IPv6 networking is in use, you could also include the IPv6 address of the appropriate network adapter in the **listen-on-v6** directive.

The other entry to change is **allow-query**; instead of limiting it to the localhost system, you could expand its reach to all systems on the 192.168.122.0/24 network as follows:

```
allow-query  { 127.0.0.1; 192.168.122.0/24; };
```

If successful, you'll see entries similar to the following in the output to the **rndc status** command:

```
CPUs found: 2
worker threads: 2
number of zones: 19
```

...

```
named (pid  7365) is running...
```

If you instead see an error message like "rndc: neither /etc/rndc.conf nor /etc/rndc. key was found," your system has been affected by a problem reported by Red Hat as bug 768798, documented at https://bugzilla.redhat.com. To get around this issue, run the following commands:

```
# rndc-confgen -a
# chgrp named /etc/rndc.key
# chmod g+r /etc/rndc.key
```

Restart the named service, and you should see the noted output to the **rndc status** command. You should be able to test the result from local and remote systems with commands like **dig** and **host**. Just don't forget to specify that you're using the caching-only DNS server on the local IP address. If you have RHEL 6.3, this issue may be resolved, as described in RHBA-2012:0830-1, a customer update described at http://rhn.redhat.com/errata/.

Configure a Caching-Only Name Server to Forward DNS Queries

Technically, the default caching-only name server already forwards DNS queries not already cached in the local database. The top-level root nameservers for the Internet are listed in the named.ca file in the /var/named directory. Queries not in the local cache are forwarded there. But in my opinion, that's not the intent of the objective. The **forwarders** directive allows you to configure requests from a local DNS server to use another (presumably) nearby server.

For example, the following directive specifies the noted IP addresses as the location of alternative DNS servers:

```
forwarders {
    192.168.122.1
    192.168.0.1
};
```

Despite appearances, the **forwarders** directive is seen as one line by the DNS server.

Synchronize Time Using Other NTP Peers

As suggested earlier, there are two NTP packages. The ntpdate package is the client. If that's all you need, you could conceivably even uninstall the server package, ntp. However, security packages such as the Identity, Policy, and Audit (IPA) system depend on the NTP server. In the default RHEL 6 configuration, both client and server use the ntp.conf file to identify external NTP servers. The relevant entries may look similar to the following:

```
server 0.rhel.pool.ntp.org
server 1.rhel.pool.ntp.org
server 2.rhel.pool.ntp.org
```

CentOS 6 systems include different URLs, based on centos.pool.ntp.org. If you have a system where the NTP server is not installed, you can still have the ntpdate client refer to such external servers in the /etc/ntp/step-tickers file. Just add these directive to that file. Assuming the ntpdate client is configured to start in at least runlevels 3 and 5, the client will automatically synchronize with those external NTP servers during the boot process.

Of course, some networks, such as those in exam rooms, may not have access to the Internet. In that case, you may need to set up other NTP servers, possibly even peers on the same network. It's fair to think that the word *peers* in the objective suggests that NTP servers are already configured on and accessible from other systems such as whitehat.example.net. To set up peers, replace the **server** directives with something like the following:

```
peer whitehat.example.net
peer somethingelse.example.net
```

To enable communication with peers, look at the first two directives in the file, and note the **nopeer** and **noquery** options, which, by default, apply to both IPv4 and IPv6 communication:

```
restrict default kod nomodify notrap nopeer noquery
restrict -6 default kod nomodify notrap nopeer noquery
```

To enable peers, you should remove the **nopeer** and **noquery** options:

```
restrict default kod nomodify notrap
restrict -6 default kod nomodify notrap
```

The next **restrict** directive provides unrestricted access to the local system:

```
restrict 127.0.0.1
restrict -6 ::1
```

Other **restrict** directives are allowed; you could add the following directive to support access from other systems on the local network:

```
restrict 192.168.122.0 mask 255.255.255.0 nomodify notrap
```

The **nomodify** option prevents clients on the noted network from modifying the local NTP server. The notrap option disables remote logging; if you're told to allow logging to remote systems, remove that option.

CERTIFICATION SUMMARY

This chapter briefly addresses the configuration of four different services. When the sysstat service is installed, you can get system utilization reports. Some are collected automatically with the help of the sysstat script in the /etc/cron.d directory.

When the rsyslog service is installed, you can set up logging clients and servers in the /etc/rsyslog.conf file. You can configure such communication over port 514; the file accommodates both TCP and UDP protocols.

If the ntpdate service is installed alone, you can set it up as an NTP client, synchronizing with servers listed in the /etc/ntp/step-tickers file. If the NTP server is also installed, the client defaults to the servers listed in /etc/ntp.conf. Alternatively, you can specify peer NTP servers with the **peer** directive. Just make sure to remove the **nopeer** option from the **restrict** directives at the beginning of the file.

The default installation of the DNS service supports a caching-only name server for the localhost system. It's configured in named.conf, normally in the /etc directory. To configure it for a network, you need to add the IP address of the local network card to the **listen-on** directive and the network address in the **allow-query** directive.

SELF TEST

The following fill-in-the-blank questions help you measure your understanding of the topics associated with this chapter. As there are no multiple-choice questions on the Red Hat exams, there are no multiple-choice questions in this book. If you have trouble with one or more of these questions, you may need to research associated topics further. However, there's almost always more than one way to solve a problem in Linux. Getting results, not memorizing trivia, is what counts on the Red Hat exams.

As this is a practice book, the answers to these questions may or may not be found in the body of the chapter. For more information, see the *Study Guide*.

Produce and Deliver Reports on System Utilization (Processor, Memory, Disk, and Network)

1. What is the full path to the script that delivers default system utilization reports?

   _____

Configure a System to Log to a Remote System

2. Based on the following entry at the end of the /etc/rsyslog.conf file, how would you configure mail log entries to be sent over UDP port 514 to a logging server on IP address 192.168.122.130?

   ```
   #*.* @@remote-host:514
   ```

   _____

Configure a System to Accept Logging from a Remote System

3. What default port number is used for communicating to a logging server?

   _____

Install the Packages Needed to Provide the Service

4. What is the name of the package associated with the DNS server?

   _____

Configure SELinux to Support the Service

5. What SELinux boolean relates to caching DNS services?

   _____

Configure the Service to Start When the System Is Booted

You get a break here. If you've made it this far in the book, you should already know how to configure every network service to start when a Red Hat system boots.

Configure the Service for Basic Operation

6. What standard port number is associated with the NTP service?

_____

Configure Host-Based and User-Based Security for the Service

7. What directive limits access, by host, to the NTP server in the /etc/ntp.conf file?

_____

Configure a Caching-Only Name Server

8. List all of the changes required to the named.conf file to set it up as a caching-only name server for the local system.

_____

Configure a Caching-Only Name Server to Forward DNS Queries

9. What directive would you add to the named.conf file to specify the IP address of a remote DNS server to forward queries?

_____

Synchronize Time Using Other NTP Peers

10. What directive in the /etc/ntp.conf file specifies other servers to synchronize with?

_____

LAB QUESTIONS

Red Hat presents its exams electronically. For that reason, the labs in this and future chapters are available from the gamma.example.net system, from the ChapterLabs/ folder that appears in the GUI desktop. If you're running in a command-line console, you can find the labs in the /home/testuser/ Desktop/ChapterLabs directory.

The answers for each lab follow the Self Test Answers for the fill-in-the-blank questions.

SELF TEST ANSWERS

Produce and Deliver Reports on System Utilization (Processor, Memory, Disk, and Network)

1. The full path to the script that delivers default system utilization reports is /etc/cron.d/sysstat.

Configure a System to Log to a Remote System

2. The following entry allows mail log items to be sent over UDP port 514 to a logging server on IP address 192.168.122.130:

```
mail.* @192.168.122.130:514
```

Configure a System to Accept Logging from a Remote System

3. The default port number used for communicating to a logging server is 514.

Install the Packages Needed to Provide the Service

4. The name of the package associated with the DNS server is bind.

Configure SELinux to Support the Service

5. This is a bit of a trick question, as the only SELinux boolean that relates to DNS services affects master servers, so the correct answer would be "none" or even to leave the answer blank.

Configure the Service to Start When the System Is Booted

You get a break here. You've made it this far—you know how to configure every network service to start when a Red Hat system boots.

Configure the Service for Basic Operation

6. Port 123 is the standard for the NTP service.

Configure Host-Based and User-Based Security for the Service

7. The **restrict** directive limits access, by host, to the NTP server in the /etc/ntp.conf file.

Configure a Caching-Only Name Server

8. This is another trick question, as the default named.conf file is already set up as a caching-only name server for the local system.

Configure a Caching-Only Name Server to Forward DNS Queries

9. The **forwarders** directive is used to specify the IP address of remote DNS servers to forward queries.

Synchronize Time Using Other NTP Peers

10. The **peer** directive in the /etc/ntp.conf file specifies other servers to synchronize with.

LAB ANSWERS

Lab I

If you understand this lab, the answer should be easy. If you understand the example on the **sadf** man page, you know to look at the **sar** man page for the switch related to CPU usage. The switch **-u** leads to the following command (you may need to substitute the report from a different day for the sa21):

```
# sadf -d /var/log/sa/sa21 -- -u ALL
```

Of course, to get that information into the noted file, the output must be redirected:

```
# sadf -d /var/log/sa/sa21 -- -u ALL > /root/cpu_report.txt
```

Lab 2

This lab is fairly simple; it requires that you edit the /etc/cron.d/sysstat file and change the last line to read as follows:

```
12 2 * * * root /usr/lib64/sa/sa2 -A
```

Don't forget to make sure that the sysstat service is running and set to start at appropriate runlevels on reboot with a command like **chkconfig sysstat on**.

Lab 3

Just a few changes are required to configure a system logging server. To set up UDP communications, open the /etc/rsyslog.conf file and activate the following directives:

```
$ModLoad imudp.so
$UDPServerRun 514
```

Of course, access requires an open port 514 in a local firewall. You can set up a custom rule, such as the following, with the Firewall Configuration tool, using the IP address for the whitehat.example.net system.

```
-A INPUT -m state --state NEW -m udp -p udp -s 192.168.122.130 --dport
514 -j ACCEPT
```

Don't forget to make sure the rsyslog service is running and set to start at appropriate runlevels on reboot with a command like **chkconfig rsyslog on**.

Lab 4

On the whitehat.example.net system, you can take advantage of the default version of the /etc/rsyslog.conf file. For the purpose of this lab, I've activated all lines, modified the final line to match that of the gamma.example.net system, and set a single @ symbol to match the use of the UDP protocol.

```
$WorkDirectory /var/spppl/rsyslog # where to place spool files
$ActionQueueFileName fwdRule1 # unique name prefix for spool files
$ActionQueueMaxDiskSpace 1g   # 1gb space limit (use as much as possible)
$ActionQueueSaveOnShutdown on # save messages to disk on shutdown
$ActionQueueType LinkedList   # run asynchronously
$ActionResumeRetryCount -1    # infinite retries if host is down
*.* @192.168.122.20:514
```

Don't forget to make sure that the rsyslog service is running and set to start in appropriate runlevels on this client system.

Lab 5

In this lab, you have the benefit of the /etc/named.conf configuration file. All you need to do is modify the following directives to include the IP address of the network adapter on the gamma.example.net system:

```
listen-on port 53 { 127.0.0.1; 192.168.122.20; };
```

Modify the **allow-query** directive to include the local IP network address:

```
allow-query { localhost; 192.168.122.0/24; };
```

Configure a special firewall rule for DNS communication to the caching-only nameserver on this system; to do so, enter the following options for the **iptables** command as a custom rule, added with a file in the Firewall Configuration tool:

```
-A INPUT -m state --state NEW -m tcp -p tcp -s 192.168.122.130 --dport
53 -j ACCEPT
-A INPUT -m state --state NEW -m udp -p udp -s 192.168.122.130 --dport
53 -j ACCEPT
```

Variations that accept communication from only the noted IP address are acceptable. You should be able to test the result from all three systems. A command like the following should work only from the gamma.example.net and whitehat.example.net systems:

```
$ dig @192.168.122.20 mheducation.com
```

Of course, you need to make sure the named service is running and is active on reboot. If desired, you could also set up that nameserver in the /etc/resolv.conf file for each noted system, but that's not a requirement for this lab.

Lab 6

This is a two-step lab. Despite the wording in the lab, you have to set up the gamma.example.net NTP server first. In the /etc/ntp.conf file, remove the **nopeer** and **noquery** options from the first **restrict** directive.

Then you need to specify the **restrict** option for the local network, as follows:

```
restrict 192.168.122.0 mask 255.255.255.0 nomodify notrap
```

You need to set up servers for synchronization. The commented server directives are sufficient for this purpose; if they're not yet active, as shown here, make them active by removing the pound sign (#):

```
# server 0.rhel.pool.ntp.org
# server 1.rhel.pool.ntp.org
# server 2.rhel.pool.ntp.org
```

Save the result, and restart the NTP service. Check the result with the **ntpq -p** command. If successful, you'll see output from three different NTP servers.

Now you can go to the NTP client on the whitehat.example.net system. Disable the NTP service with commands like **/etc/init.d/ntpd stop** and **chkconfig ntpd off**. Then add the following line to the step-tickers file in the /etc/ntp directory:

```
gamma.example.net
```

Now run the **/etc/init.d/ntpdate start** command. If successful, you see the following message:

```
ntpdate: Synchronizing with time server:    [ OK ]
```

You can confirm in the /var/log/messages file. If there are problems, you see a message like "can't find host server." If successful, you may see a message like:

```
step time server 192.168.122.20 offset - 0.000043 sec
```

A

Prepare a System for the Sample Exams

Randy Russell, Red Hat's Director of Certification, stated in a 2009 blog entry that the Red Hat exams no longer require "a bare-metal installation." In other words, when you sit down for a Red Hat exam today, preinstalled systems are provided for you.

As noted in Chapter 1, the DVD for this book includes compressed versions of three virtual machines (VMs) suited for this purpose. In fact, you can find all four sample exams on the gamma.example.net VM, in the /home/testuser/Desktop/ SampleExams directory. Yes, this forces you to use the Kernel-based Virtual Machine (KVM) system included with only the 64-bit version of RHEL 6.

As there are five RHCSA objectives directly related to VMs, it's important that you know how to use the Red Hat VM solution, KVM. This is an excellent time to start fresh with the VMs installed in Chapter 1. But to do so, you have to delete the existing versions of all three VMs on the example.net network (hosts gamma, whitehat, and blackhat).

To delete a system from the GUI Virtual Machine Manager, take the following steps:

1. Highlight the target VM.
2. Click Edit | Delete.
3. In the Delete Confirmation window that appears, activate the Delete Associated Storage Files option, and then click Delete.

Now you can repeat the steps described in Chapter 1 to unpack and reload the original three VMs from the DVD. (If space is tight, you may want to wait until the RHCE chapters, starting with Chapter 10, to reload the blackhat.example.net system.) If you just need some quick reminders on the reload process, you can unpack and install the VMs using the following guidelines:

- Use the **tar xzPvf** command to unpack the VMs. The **P** switch makes sure the disk files are unpacked to the original directory, in this case, /var/lib/ libvirt/images.

- Using the Virtual Machine Manager wizard, select Import Existing Disk Image and specify 768MB of RAM.

- Unless you're skipping the RHCSA exam, don't change the hardware address of the network card for any of the three systems. (Yes, it'll be one thing that you do during the RHCSA sample exams.)

FIGURE A-1

Deleting a VM
with the Virtual
Machine Manager

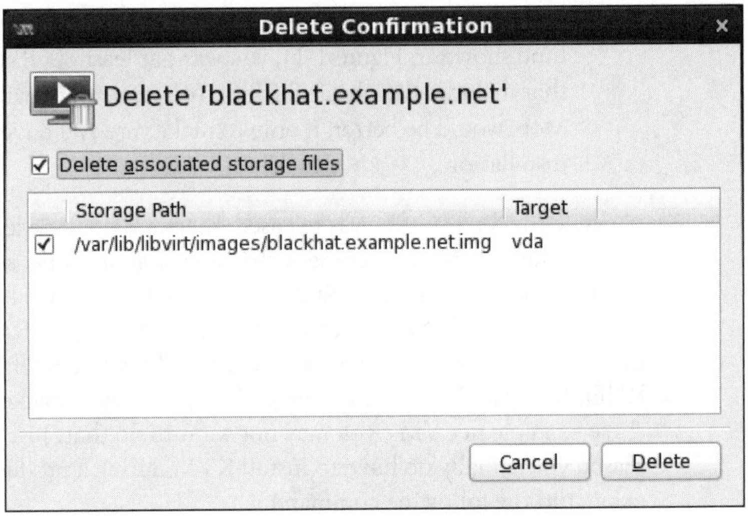

- For the gamma.example.net system, do import the gamma.example.net-1. img file as a second hard disk, configured as an old-style integrated drive electronics (IDE) disk (also known as a Serial Advanced Technology Attachment [SATA] disk).

Basic Sample Exam System Requirements

A test system for RHEL 6 requires more. There is no requirement for a *physical* "bare-metal" installation in the objectives for either the RHCSA or the RHCE exam. However, for the RHCSA, you do need to "configure a physical machine to host virtual guests." As the default RHEL 6 virtual machine solution (KVM) can only be installed from its 64-bit release, you should have 64-bit hardware.

You can expect to "install Red Hat Enterprise Linux systems as virtual guests." That's an implicit requirement for a "bare-metal" installation on a VM. With those objectives in mind, you can set up a test system based on the following requirements:

- Installation on physical 64-bit hardware.
- A dual-boot configuration with another operating system is acceptable.
- Red Hat does not support Intel Itanium CPUs.

■ Sufficient hard drive space. Based on the requirements listed in Chapter 1 (and shown in Figure 1-1), you want at least 80GB total space for the volume that includes the physical RHEL 6 system, along with the virtual guests. More would be better, if only to make sure you have room for that virtual installation.

Since the *Study Guide* was released, there are now moderately affordable options for installing a virtual machine within a virtual machine, such as VMWare Workstation 8.0. I did not test that configuration for this book.

One of the RHCSA objectives is to "configure a physical machine to host virtual guests." For that purpose, you need to know how to install KVM on an existing RHEL 6 system. But since you've probably already unpacked a fresh copy of the three example.net VMs, you may not want to do that. Just remember, if for some reason you actually do have to install KVM during a production situation such as an exam, run the following command:

```
# yum groupinstall Virtualization "Virtualization Client" \
"Virtualization Platform"
```

Once installation is complete, the system is ready for the RHCSA exam. Although Internet access is not allowed on any major certification exam, it's acceptable for the purpose of these sample exams. If you prefer a more "pure" exam environment, refer to Chapter 7, Lab 3, which includes instructions on how to create a local repository based on the contents of the installation DVD.

For the sample RHCSA exams, you'll do most of your work from the gamma. example.net system. You'll use the whitehat.example.net system to confirm network access to installed services as needed.

e x a m

ⓦatch

Although you could also use the physical host system as a client for the gamma.example.net VM, the whitehat. example.net system is better for this purpose. You may need to install client tools on the whitehat system, which can be a useful exercise.

Additional Sample Exam System Requirements for the RHCE

As the RHCSA and RHCE are separate exams, it may be helpful to reinstall the example.net systems once you finish the RHCSA. This time, you need all three VMs: gamma, whitehat, and blackhat. Although most of your work will be done on the gamma system, you'll frequently need to confirm accessibility from the whitehat system. To confirm proper security, you may also need to confirm protection from the blackhat system.

If you're already an RHCSA and are just studying for the RHCE, include the following hardware addresses for the three VMs. To review, in Chapter 1, Table 1-2, for gamma, whitehat, and blackhat, the addresses are 52:54:00:b8:a7:ea, 52:54:00:ec:81:11, and 52:54:00:9e:e2:28, respectively.

B

RHCSA:
Sample Exam 1

The following questions help measure your understanding of the material presented in this book. As discussed in the introduction, you should be prepared to complete the RHCSA exam in 2.5 hours.

The RHCSA exam is "closed book." However, you are allowed to use any documentation that can be found on the Red Hat Enterprise Linux computer. While test facilities allow you to make notes, you won't be allowed to take these notes from the testing room.

The RHCSA is entirely separate from the RHCE. Although both exams cover some of the same services, the objectives for those services are different.

In most cases, there is no one solution, no single method to solve a problem or install a service. There are a nearly infinite number of options with Linux, so I can't cover all possible scenarios.

Even for these exercises, *do not use a production computer*. In Appendix A, I suggest that you reload the VMs from the DVD for exam purposes. Not only will you work from a relatively clean system, but also you'll have VMs that should not affect any production files on other physical partitions or volumes.

Red Hat presents its exams electronically. For that reason, the exams in this book are available from the companion DVD, in the SampleExams/ subdirectory. This exam is in the file named RHCSA_practice_exam1 and is available in .txt format.

Don't proceed on to the next page until you're finished with the sample exam!

RHCSA Sample Exam I Discussion

In this discussion, I describe one way to check your work to meet the requirements listed for the RHCSA exam.

1. One way to see if SELinux is set in enforcing mode is to run the **sestatus** command.

2. Using the **find** command, you should be able to locate the gamma.hardware file in the /usr/share/doc/book-1.0.0 directory. If you've updated the file database with the /etc/cron.daily/mlocate.cron script, you could do the same with the **locate** command.

   To change the hardware address of a network card on a VM, you need to know how to manage it.

   One way to do so is from the Virtual Machine Manager. Double-click the gamma.example.net system. In the GUI window that opens, click View | Details. You should be able to remove the existing Network Interface Card (shown by its acronym, NIC). Then click Add Hardware; when the Add New Virtual Hardware window appears, click Network.

   You should then be able to specify the address from the gamma.hardware file. If successful, you'll see the eth0 device with the static 192.168.122.20 IP address in the output to the **ifconfig** command.

3. The one FTP server native to RHEL 6 is the vsFTP service. If it's installed and set to start in appropriate runlevels, you should be able to see it in the output to the **chkconfig --list vsftpd** command.

4. At minimum, you should be able to at least verify the operation of the Kickstart file that you create. The following command is one example that assumes the vsFTP server has a Kickstart file named ks.cfg configured on the gamma system, and an installation server is configured on the physical host at 192.168.122.1:

```
# virt-install -n testsystem.example.net -r 768 --disk \
path=/var/lib/libvirt/images/testsystem.example.net.img,size=6 \
-l ftp://192.168.122.1/pub/os \
-x "ks=ftp://192.168.122.20/pub/ks.cfg"
```

This command won't work unless SELinux contexts on /var/ftp/pub and the ks.cfg file match the standards for that directory (with the public_content_t file type) and read permissions are active for all users.

For detailed information on Kickstart, see Chapter 2 of the *Study Guide*.

5. If you've installed the lftp client on the whitehat system, you should be able to access the FTP server on gamma with a command like **lftp ftp://192.168.122.20**, in the pub/ subdirectory that should be available based on item 4.

6. One way to set the noted system to start automatically the next time the host is booted is with the **virsh autostart gamma.example.net** command. One way to confirm is to check the /etc/libvirt/qemu/autostart directory, which should have a soft link to the gamma.example.net.xml file in the /etc/libvirt/qemu directory.

7. The process associated with changing the hardware address for the network adapter on the whitehat system is similar to that for the gamma system described in item 2.

8. Bootloaders are configured in the grub.conf file in the /boot/grub directory. You can create a second option identical to the first by copying the associated stanza. The second stanza that I created looks like the following (yours may vary):

```
title Scientific Linux (2.6.32-220.el6.x86_64) Single User Mode
        password --md5 $1$neGOe0$LG8tObe7VE4grOhL0uKFR1
        root (hd0,0)
        kernel /vmlinuz-2.6.32-220.el6.x86_64 ro
root=UUID=028b5de5-5727-48e8-b8de-d083bc1cc17a rd_NO_LUKS rd_NO_
LVM LANG=en_US.UTF-8 rd_NO_MD quiet SYSFONT=latarcyrheb-sun16
rhgb crashkernel=auto  KEYBOARDTYPE=pc KEYTABLE=us rd_NO_DM 1
        initrd /initramfs-2.6.32-220.el6.x86_64.img
```

The next time you boot the gamma system and press a key to call up the menu, you'll see the following option in the list:

```
Scientific Linux (2.6.32-220.el6.x86_64) Single User Mode
```

If you try to select the option, the following prompt should appear:

```
Password:
```

When you enter **redhat** as the password, you should be taken to runlevel 1.

9. To set up a second partition as swap space, you need to make sure the partition is set to a Linux swap type. You then format it with the **mkswap** command, activate it with the **swapon** command, and make sure it runs the next time the system boots by adding it to the /etc/fstab file. If successful, you'll see both the existing and new swap partition active in the /proc/swaps file.

10. One way to set the noted parameters on user **testuser2** is with the **chage -E 2017-03-15 -M 21 testuser2** command; confirm with the **chage -l testuser2** command.

11. You can set up access to a specific directory of another user with the help of ACLs. The following two commands provide minimal ACLs required to give user testuser2 access to files in the noted directory.

```
# setfacl -R -m u:testuser2:x /home/testuser
# setfacl -R -m u:testuser2:r /home/testuser/Desktop/ChapterLabs/*
```

The testuser2 user must know the full path to the given files for this to work.

12. There are a number of ways to set up a cron job; given the specific timing, you'll want to set it up with appropriate time settings in a file in the /etc/cron.d directory. (You could also set it up as a cron job by a regular user.) In either case, the **delete** command would be associated using a command like this:

```
0 1 * * 0 /bin/rm /encrypt/*
```

13. The /home/super directory should be owned by the group supervisors. You should set 2770 permissions on that directory. Use a command like **chgrp supervisors /home/super** to set appropriate group ownership. Make sure users super1, super2, and super3 are members of the supervisors group.

14. Assuming you have a network connection, the simplest way to install the amanda RPM is with the **yum install amanda** command.

15. Finally, instead of just powering down the system as directed, you should reboot, and make sure the changes that you've made are active. You can't expect full credit, for example, if the FTP server isn't running upon reboot.

C

RHCSA:
Sample Exam 2

I n this sample exam, I've set up problems different from those in RHCSA Sample Exam 1. Therefore, you don't need to start fresh with new versions of the gamma and whitehat. example.net systems. If you do, make sure to set the hardware addresses of the network adapters on the gamma and whitehat systems to **52:54:00:b8:a7:ea** and **52:54:00:ec:81:11**, respectively (as you should have done in Sample Exam 1). Now on to the boilerplate description of the sample exam.

The following questions help measure your understanding of the material presented in this book. As discussed in the introduction, you should be prepared to complete the RHCSA exam in 2.5 hours.

The RHCSA exam is "closed book." However, you are allowed to use any documentation that can be found on the Red Hat Enterprise Linux computer. While test facilities allow you to make notes, you won't be allowed to take these notes from the testing room.

The RHCSA is entirely separate from the RHCE. Although both exams cover some of the same services, the objectives for those services are different.

In most cases, there is no one solution, no single method to solve a problem or install a service. There are a nearly infinite number of options with Linux, so I can't cover all possible scenarios.

Even for these exercises, *do not use a production computer*. In Appendix A, I suggest that you reload the VMs from the DVD for exam purposes. Not only will you work from a relatively clean system, but also you'll have VMs that should not affect any production files on other physical partitions or volumes.

Red Hat presents its exams electronically. For that reason, the exams in this book are available from the companion DVD in the SampleExams/ subdirectory. This exam is in the file named RHCSA_practice_exam2 and is available in .txt format.

Don't proceed on to the next page until you're finished with the sample exam!

RHCSA Sample Exam 2 Discussion

In this discussion, I'll describe one way to check your work to meet the requirements listed for the RHCSA Sample Exam 2.

1. One way to see if SELinux is set in permissive mode is to run the **sestatus** command. Enforcing mode is the default, as set in the /etc/sysconfig/selinux file. To make sure permissive mode is set, you have to change that default.

2. When encrypting a new partition, remember the following basic steps:

   a) Create a partition; call it /dev/sda2.

   b) Randomize the content of the partition with a command like **dd if=/dev/urandom of=/dev/sda2**.

   c) Set up the new filesystem with the **cryptsetup luksFormat /dev/sda2** command, in this case, with the **I will pass!** passphrase.

   d) Give that new file system a name using the **cryptsetup luksOpen /dev/sda2 *test1*** command (you may substitute a different name for *test1* as desired).

   e) Format the new encrypted volume device, /dev/mapper/*test1*, to the ext3 file system with a command like **mkfs.ext3**.

   f) Test a mount of the new encrypted volume on the /encrypt directory. When satisfied, configure it in /etc/fstab.

3. As discussed in Chapter 9 of the *Study Guide*, one way to set up VNC services with VMs is by installing the Tiger VNC server on the VM. Once installed, you need to configure the /etc/sysconfig/vncservers file. The following entries set up access to the GUI desktop for user testuser:

```
VNCSERVERS="2:testuser"
VNCSERVERARGS[2]="-geometry 800x600"
```

Then open up ports 5900 and 5901 in the firewall, and log into the testuser account. As that user, you can run the **vncserver :1** command to enable access over the noted pair of ports using TCP. You'll be prompted for a password. (If you followed the instructions in the sample exam, the password is **mcgraw**.) Once complete, you can install a VNC client on the physical host, and verify access to the gamma.example.net system.

4. Even though the SysVInit system has been deprecated for RHEL 6, the default runlevel is still controlled in the /etc/inittab file; you only need to change the one active line to read as follows:

```
id:3:initdefault
```

5. To install the Apache web server, install the **httpd** RPM package. One way to set it to start in only runlevel 3 is with the **chkconfig httpd --level 3 on** command. Of course, you should check the result with the **chkconfig --list httpd** command. If successful, you'll see the "I will pass this exam" statement when using a browser to navigate to this system.

6. The standard method for granting access to one user on a permission-limited directory is with ACLs. You can configure ACLs in this case with a command like **setfacl -m u:testuser:rw /var/www/html/index.html**.

7. If you created a swap partition in Exam 1, this question is trickier than it looks, as you'll also need to make sure that partition is not included in /etc/ fstab. The rest of the process should be straightforward, as you can create physical volumes with the **pvcreate** command, set up a volume group from that space with the **vgcreate** command, and specify a logical volume of 200MB with the **lvcreate -L 200M** command. Only then can you format the logical volume device. To identify the UUID, run the **dumpe2fs** command on the device file for the logical volume. You can then use the UUID to make sure the volume is mounted on the /vol directory during the boot process. (You did remember to create the /vol directory, didn't you?)

8. If you've looked at the file_contexts file in the /etc/selinux/targeted/contexts/ files directory, you'll note the /srv/ftp directory is already configured with appropriate contexts. To meet the requirements of this lab, after creating that /srv/ftp directory, all you need to do is run the **restorecon -F /srv/ftp** command.

9. The /etc/skel directory includes all files to be copied to the home directory of all new users. Thus, the simplest way to meet the requirements of item 9 is to copy the ChapterLabs/ subdirectory, in its entirety, to that /etc/skel directory. If you run a command as the root user, like **cp -ar /home/testuser/Desktop/ChapterLabs /etc/skel**, the ChapterLabs/ subdirectory, including all files therein, will be included in their entirety in the home directories of new users.

10. The process for setting up a new network card with the given hardware address, with help from the Virtual Machine Manager, has been documented in

Chapter 3. To make sure that network card actually activates the next time you boot the blackhat.example.net system, you need to look at the ifcfg-eth0 file in the /etc/sysconfig/network-scripts directory and set **ONBOOT=yes**. (You should make sure this setting is in effect on all three VMs.)

11. The installation process for a new kernel, either with the **yum** or **rpm** commands, should be elementary for anyone who is attempting the RHCSA exam. However, standard methods lead to the configuration of the newly installed kernel as the default in the GRUB menu. To make sure the original kernel is the default option in the GRUB menu, you probably have to change the value of **default** in the GRUB configuration file, grub.conf in the /boot/grub directory. If **default=0**, the default option is the first stanza in the noted file, which should be the newly installed kernel. You most likely need to change this to **default=1** to point to the original kernel.

12. The relevant services that require access through the firewall are SSH, the Apache web server service, and the VNC server. Although the SSH port of 22 is open by default, port 80 for the web server services, as well as 5900/5901 for VNC connections are normally closed by default.

13. As the /var/log/messages file is readable only by the root user, it's best to set this up as a job by that user, or in the /etc/cron.d directory. In either case, include the following line:

```
8 23 * * * root /bin/cp /var/log/messages /home/testuser
```

14. Perhaps the quickest way to meet the requirement of this lab is with the Authentication Configuration tool. Once complete, you can open the /etc/nsswitch.conf file, and verify **files sss** as the search path for the **passwd**, **group**, and **shadow** entries, which represent the authentication database. You'll also see **BASE dc=example,dc=net** and **URI ldaps://192.168.122.20** in the /etc/openldap/ldap.conf file. Pay attention to the **s** in ldaps; that points to the secure port for LDAP communications. (Unless you have an LDAP server on gamma.example.net, you should reverse these changes, once verified.)

15. Finally, instead of just powering down the system as directed, you should reboot, and make sure the changes that you've made are active. You can't expect full credit, for example, if the Apache web server isn't running on reboot.

D

RHCE:
Sample Exam 1

Before starting this exam, you may want to reinstall the VMs as described in Appendix A and as detailed in Chapter 1. This sample exam may include problems that overlap RHCSA objectives; however, a "clean" system best simulates what you may encounter. In any case, make sure to set the hardware addresses of the network adapters on the gamma, whitehat, and blackhat systems to **52:54:00:b8:a7:ea**, **52:54:00:ec:81:11**, and **52:54:00:9e:e2:28**, respectively (per Chapter 1, Table 1-2). Now on to the boilerplate description of the sample exam.

The following questions help measure your understanding of the material presented in this book. As discussed in the introduction, you should be prepared to complete the RHCE exam in 2.0 hours (120 minutes).

Like the RHCSA, the RHCE exam is "closed book." However, you are allowed to use any documentation that can be found on the Red Hat Enterprise Linux computer. While test facilities allow you to make notes, you won't be allowed to take these notes from the testing room.

While the RHCE exam is entirely separate from the RHCSA, you need to pass both exams to receive the RHCE certificate. Nevertheless, you can take the RHCE exam first. Although both exams cover some of the same services, the objectives for those services are different.

Even for these exercises, *do not use a production computer*. A small error in some or all of these exercises may make Linux unbootable. If you're unable to recover from the steps documented in these exercises, you may need to reinstall Red Hat Enterprise Linux. Saving any data that you have on the local system may then not be possible.

Red Hat presents its exams electronically. For that reason, the exams in this book are available from the companion DVD in the SampleExams/ subdirectory. This exam is in the file named RHCE_practice_exam1 and is available in .txt format.

In most cases, there is no one solution, no single method to solve a problem or install a service. There are a nearly infinite number of options with Linux, so I can't cover all possible scenarios.

Don't proceed on to the next page until you're finished with the sample exam!

RHCE Sample Exam I Discussion

In this discussion, I describe one way to check your work to meet the requirements listed for this sample exam. Because there is no *one* way to set up a Red Hat Enterprise Linux configuration, there is no *one* right answer for the listed requirements. But there are some general things to remember. You need to make sure your changes work after a reboot. For the RHCE, you need to make sure the services that you set up are active at the appropriate runlevels. For example, if you're configuring Samba, it should be active for at least runlevels 3 and 5.

1. The first task is essentially the default for both SELinux and iptables-based firewalls. SELinux should be set in enforcing mode, and the iptables-based firewall is enabled by default. You can check this with the **sestatus** and **iptables -L** commands.

2. This is a two-step process, run on gamma as a logging server and whitehat as a logging client. Both can be configured in their respective /etc/rsyslog.conf files. Make sure to open port 514 on the gamma iptables-based firewall, with the protocol that you configure for that purpose (TCP or UDP).

   The changes made to the rsyslog.conf file on gamma are simple. Pick TCP or UDP, and activate the appropriate directive related to "syslog reception."

   The changes made to the rsyslog.conf file on whitehat are slightly more complex in the remote logging section at the bottom of the file. You can activate all the commented directives in this section. Just remember to substitute the host name or IP address for the remote-host directive. If you've set up TCP communication, the double @@ is okay; if you're using UDP, make it a single @.

3. If you've set up this route with the Network Connections tool, you should see a route-eth0 file in the /etc/sysconfig/network-scripts directory, with three lines similar to this:

   ```
   ADDRESS0=10.20.30.0
   NETMASK0=255.255.255.0
   GATEWAY0=192.168.122.1
   ```

4. You should be able to use the Virtual Host stanza template at the end of the httpd.conf file in the /etc/httpd/conf directory as a model. You need to match the SELinux contexts in the /www/oahu and /www/maui to /var/www/html. Don't forget to update the file_contexts file with the help of the **semanage**

fcontext command. Include index.html files in both the /www/oahu and /www/maui directories, that give the noted message. Text format is acceptable; no HTML formatting is required. You also have to include oahu.example.net and maui.example.net in the /etc/hosts file for the noted systems. Of course, you need to open port 80 in the firewall of the gamma system as well.

5. If you don't know a scripting language, you can look up the Perl-based hello.pl script in the Apache manual. Because you installed Apache to address item 4, you should be able to install the httpd-manual RPM and then navigate to http://gamma.example.net/manual to start it. Once open, you can set up your own oahu.pl and maui.pl scripts, give them 755 permissions, set them up in corresponding cgi-bin/ subdirectories with appropriate SELinux file types, and configure appropriate options in the Apache configuration file. You should then be able to run the scripts via browser by navigating to the noted URLs.

6. To set up the /pub/ftp directory as the default for anonymous-only downloads, you need to create the directory, copy the noted files to that directory, set it as the home directory for the ftp user, and give it (along with the files therein) the same SELinux contexts as /var/ftp/pub.

7. The Samba server will be configured with a /home/masters directory, set with the samba_share_t type label. You can limit users with the **allow users** directive in the smb.conf configuration file stanza associated with the /home/masters directory. To prevent access from blackhat, you can set up a **hosts deny** directive, or modify the firewall to block the associated IP address (192.168.122.240).

8. To enable home directories on Samba, you need to activate the samba_enable_home_dirs boolean. You can then edit the **[homes]** stanza in the smb.conf file to add a **valid users = testuser** directive.

9. The simplest way to implement the given limits on SSH is in the sshd_config file in the /etc/ssh directory. Just add **PermitRootLogin no** and **AllowUsers testuser** directives to that file.

10. You have two options for SMTP servers: Postfix and sendmail. If you stay with the default, Postfix, make several changes to the main.cf file in the /etc/postfix directory:

```
myhostname = gamma.example.net
mydomain = example.net
```

```
inet_interfaces = all
mynetworks = 192.168.122.0/24, 127.0.0.0/8
```

Don't forget to open TCP port 25 in the firewall.

11. The NTP server should be installed by default. But it's set up to support access only from the localhost system. To allow access to other systems, set up the following directive:

```
restrict 192.168.122.0 mask 255.255.255.0 notrap nomodify
```

Don't forget to open UDP port 123 in the firewall.

12. To meet the requirement of this objective, you need to withdraw the mlocate .cron file from the /etc/cron.daily directory, since those jobs aren't necessarily run at the required times. But you'll want to save that file in some directory, perhaps in the /etc/cron.d directory. You then create a job, perhaps also in the /etc/cron.d directory, to execute it at the noted times, with lines such as:

```
2 5 * * * root /etc/mlocate.cron
3 19 * * * root /etc/mlocate.cron
```

13. This task should be easy, as the default installation of bind already includes a default caching-only nameserver, limited to the localhost system. However, you need to change the resolv.conf file to point to the IP address of the system (127.0.0.1) to use that nameserver.

14. You may want to reboot the system once, to make sure that all of the noted changes have been properly implemented. You can't expect full credit, for example, if the Postfix e-mail service isn't running on reboot.

E

RHCE:
Sample Exam 2

Before starting this exam, you may want to reinstall the VMs as described in Appendix A and as detailed in Chapter 1. This sample exam may include problems that overlap RHCSA objectives. Therefore, a "clean" system best simulates what you may encounter. In any case, make sure to set the hardware addresses of the network adapters on the gamma, whitehat, and blackhat systems to **52:54:00:b8:a7:ea**, **52:54:00:ec:81:11**, and **52:54:00:9e:e2:28**, respectively. Now on to the boilerplate description of the sample exam.

The following questions help measure your understanding of the material presented in this book. As discussed in the introduction, you should be prepared to complete the RHCE exam in 2.0 hours (120 minutes).

Like the RHCSA, the RHCE exam is "closed book." However, you are allowed to use any documentation that can be found on the Red Hat Enterprise Linux computer. While test facilities allow you to make notes, you won't be allowed to take these notes from the testing room.

Although the RHCE exam is entirely separate from the RHCSA, you need to pass both exams to receive the RHCE certificate. Nevertheless, you can take the RHCE exam first. While both exams cover some of the same services, the objectives for those services are different.

Even for these exercises, *do not use a production computer*. A small error in some or all of these exercises may make Linux unbootable. If you're unable to recover from the steps documented in these exercises, you may need to reinstall Red Hat Enterprise Linux. Saving any data that you have on the local system may not be possible.

Red Hat presents its exams electronically. For that reason, the exams in this book are available from the companion DVD, in the SampleExams/ subdirectory. This exam is in the file named RHCE_practice_exam2 and is available in .txt format.

In most cases, there is no one solution, no single method to solve a problem or install a service. There are a nearly infinite number of options with Linux, so I can't cover all possible scenarios.

Don't proceed on to the next page until you're finished with the sample exam!

RHCE Sample Exam 2 Discussion

In this discussion, I describe one way to check your work to meet the requirements listed for this particular sample exam. Because there is no one way to set up a Red Hat Enterprise Linux configuration, there is no one right answer for the listed requirements. But there are some general things to remember. You need to make sure your changes work after a reboot. For the RHCE, you need to make sure the services that you set up are active at the appropriate runlevels. For example, if you're configuring Apache, it should be active for at least runlevels 3 and 5.

1. To avoid responding to the **ping -b** command, which broadcasts echo requests over IPv4, the icmp_echo_ignore_broadcasts option must be active. You can set that up permanently in the /etc/sysctl.conf file with the **net.ipv4.icmp_ echo_ignore_broadcasts = 1** directive.

2. As you should already know, the process required to create an RPM is some-what complex. Although Chapter 12 in this book summarizes the required steps, you may need to refer to Chapter 12 of the *Study Guide* for detailed information. Success in this step is most straightforward; copy the RPM that you've created to a second system. Install it. If successful, you'll see the RHCE_practice_exam1.txt file in the /opt/rhce directory.

3. This particular system activity report requires just a slight change from the example shown in the **sadf** man page. As the report required is from the fifth of the month (yes, that report was preloaded onto the gamma system), the command is

```
# sadf -d /var/log/sa/sa05 -- -n DEV > /home/testuser/stat_net_05
```

As noted in the man page for the **sadf** command, the double-dash prefaces options to the **sar** command.

4. If you are successful, users terry and heinz, and no others, will have access to the /home/steelers subdirectory. In the Apache httpd.conf file, there is a tem-plate for single home directories. It can be modified to accommodate a group of users.

5. To expand the scope of the default caching-only DNS server, you need to revise the /etc/named.conf file. The **listen-on port** directive should include the IP address of the local network card, and the **allow-query** directive

should include the network. Don't forget to include the IP address of gamma (192.168.122.20) in the resolv.conf file for both gamma and whitehat.

6. When the share of the /home directory is mounted on whitehat, user testuser on the remote system should be able to read the mounted share of the /home/testuser directory. Of course, to set up read-only access, you need the **ro** in the /etc/exports file on the gamma.example.net system in the entry for the shared /home directory. The **root_squash** option is the default, so you should not have to add the option to /etc/exports. It's not harmful, however.

7. Since the /download directory will be shared with all users, in guest mode, you need to make sure it's set up with 777 permissions. You also need to set up the samba_share_t file type on the directory and in the file_contexts file. That's over and above the standard directives that you need to include in the /etc/samba/smb.conf file. To test guest access, mount the share with the **mount.cifs -o guest** command.

8. What you do to configure a relay to a smart host depends on whether you use Postfix or sendmail. For Postfix, set it up with the **relayhost** directive in the main.cf file. For sendmail, set it up with the preconfigured commented **SMART_HOST** directive defined in sendmail.mc.

9. The process for setting up a private/public keypair for SSH authentication is straightforward, as long as there are two matching accounts. The **ssh-keygen** command creates a private/public keypair. The **ssh-copy-id** command copies the given public key to a target remote system. You should then be able to log into the remote system with the help of the passphrase. The only thing that gets transmitted, if the passphrase is satisfied, is the public key.

10. The process of creating a secure virtual web site is almost as straightforward as creating a regular virtual web site. The template in the ssl.conf file may be a bit more confusing; just be sure to include the **NameVirtualHost *:443** directive, as well as separate **<VirtualHost *:443>** containers for each virtual host. Don't forget to change SELinux contexts now and on a permanent basis in the file_context file in the /etc/selinux/targeted/contexts/files directory.

    Bonus: If successful, you should have appropriate and unique listings for the **SSLCertificateFile** and **SSLCertificateKeyFile** directives.

11. On the gamma system, set up the ntp.conf file with a **restrict** directive that allows access from other systems on the network. On the whitehat system,

set up the ntp.conf file to use the peer directive to point the gamma system. Don't forget: communication is over UDP port 123.

12. One way to set up access from the whitehat system, and only that system, is with appropriate special firewall rules. You need to open up UDP port 53 for DNS, TCP port 2049 for NFSv4, UDP ports 137 and 138 along with TCP ports 139 and 445 for Samba, TCP port 25 for Postfix or sendmail, TCP port 22 for SSH, TCP port 443 for HTTPS, and UDP port 123 for NTP. In several cases, you can limit access to the whitehat system using other methods.

13. You may want to reboot the system once to make sure all of the noted changes have been properly implemented. You can't expect full credit, for example, if the DNS server isn't running upon reboot.

F

About the DVD

The DVD included with this book comes complete with three compressed virtual machines. We suggest you have at least 80GB available on a physical 64-bit system for these VMs. While the VMs themselves require only 37GB, the remaining space allows you to set up RHEL 6 (or an equivalent operating system such as CentOS 6 or Scientific Linux 6), on the physical system. Detailed instructions are available in Chapter 1. These VMs were built for the Kernel-based Virtual Machine (KVM) system included with RHEL 6.

This book assumes you need a 64-bit system with hardware virtualization enabled. (Nested virtualization solutions such as VMWare Workstation 8 and VMWare ESX were not tested for this book.) This book also assumes that you use RHEL 6 or equivalent. For the purposes of this book, do not use Fedora, Ubuntu, or any other Linux distribution unless it is built from the same source code as that used for RHEL 6.

You'll find almost all of the labs on the first VM on the DVD. To access these labs, you have to uncompress the VMs and import them into KVM. Chapter 1 includes detailed instructions for this purpose. Once imported, you'll be able to start that first VM, known as gamma.example.net, and find the labs (and sample exams) in the Desktop folder.

To access the compressed files with the VMs, insert the DVD. Unless you're running a GUI where automounting has been enabled, you'll have to mount the DVD with a command such as the following:

```
# mount /dev/cdrom /mnt
```

You'll find the three VMs available on the DVD, in compressed format, in three files:

```
gamma.tar.gz
whitehat.tar.gz
blackhat.tar.gz
```

When decompressed per the instructions given in Chapter 1, you'll find the associated files in the /var/lib/libvirt/images and /etc/libvirt/qemu directories. (Yes, the XML file in the /etc/libvirt/qemu directory is overwritten when you set up the VM via KVM as discussed in Chapter 1, but that record of how the VM was configured is still available in the compressed archive.)

The VMs are built on Scientific Linux, which is based on the source code for RHEL 6. Each of the VMs includes an mh.repo file, which points to a McGraw-Hill copy of a Scientific Linux 6.2 repository at www.mhprofessional.com/downloads/products/007180160X/VM/os.

System Requirements

As discussed in Chapter 1, the RHCSA exam includes KVM, which Red Hat supports on RHEL 6, only on 64-bit systems configured with hardware virtualization. As the rebuild distributions, Scientific Linux and CentOS are based on RHEL 6 source code; they also require installation on a physical 64-bit system to support KVM.

Technical Support

For technical problems or questions, please visit www.mhprofessional.com or e-mail customer.service@mcgraw-hill.com. For customers outside the 50 United States, e-mail international_cs@mcgraw-hill.com.

INDEX

Symbols

! (bang), 190

\ (backslash), 166

A

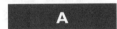

X

Y